D0597153

SUSTAINABLE INVESTING AND ENVIRONMENTAL MARKETS

Opportunities in a New Asset Class

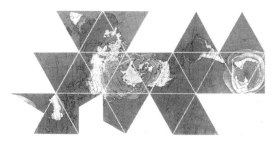

SUSTAINABLE INVESTING AND ENVIRONMENTAL MARKETS

Opportunities in a New Asset Class

Richard Sandor, Murali Kanakasabai,
Rafael Marques & Nathan Clark

Environmental Financial Products, LLC, USA

Foreword by
Amory B. Lovins

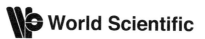 **World Scientific**

NEW JERSEY · LONDON · SINGAPORE · BEIJING · SHANGHAI · HONG KONG · TAIPEI · CHENNAI

Published by

World Scientific Publishing Co. Pte. Ltd.

5 Toh Tuck Link, Singapore 596224

USA office: 27 Warren Street, Suite 401-402, Hackensack, NJ 07601

UK office: 57 Shelton Street, Covent Garden, London WC2H 9HE

Library of Congress Cataloging-in-Publication Data
Sandor, Richard L.
   Sustainable investing and environmental markets : opportunities in a new asset class / Richard Sandor, Nathan Clark, Murali Kanakasabai, Rafael Marques.
     pages cm
   ISBN 978-9814612432 (hardcover : alk. paper)
   1. Investments--Environmental aspects. 2. Investments--Moral and ethical aspects.
3. Clean energy investment. 4. Sustainable development--Economic aspects.
5. Environmentalism--Economic aspects. I. Title.
   HG4521.S3324 2014
   332.6--dc23
                                                              2014014878

British Library Cataloguing-in-Publication Data
A catalogue record for this book is available from the British Library.

Cover image:
Buckminster Fuller and Chuck Bryne, *Dymaxion Air-Ocean World Map* (1981). This print belongs to Dr. Richard L. Sandor. The use of an image of the Dymaxion Map is courtesy of the Buckminster Fuller Institute (BFI). The word Dymaxion, Spaceship Earth and the Fuller Projection Map are trademarks of the BFI. All rights reserved.

In-house Editors: Chye Shu Wen/Rajni Gamage

Typeset by Stallion Press
Email: enquiries@stallionpress.com

Printed in Singapore by Mainland Press Pte Ltd.

FOREWORD

World Scientific is to be commended for publishing — and environmental market pioneer Richard Sandor and his three colleagues for writing — this masterly and path-finding overview of an asset class that is already important, rapidly gaining further scale and scope, and yet surprisingly and systematically underused.

My 1999 book *Natural Capitalism*, co-authored with Paul Hawken and L. Hunter Lovins, asked the question: If capitalism is the productive use of and reinvestment of capital, what is capital?[1] Industrial capitalism deals seriously with only two kinds of capital — financial capital and physical capital (i.e., money and goods). It ignores and even liquidates two even more valuable kinds of capital — natural capital and human capital (i.e., nature and people). Without people, there is no economy, and without nature, there are no people, so this omission is material. But if you play with a full deck, productively using and investing in *all four* forms of capital, then you make more money, do more good, have more fun, and gain stunning competitive advantage. The authors of this book provide here a vital toolkit for people to start capturing these opportunities by valuing and investing in the salient missing parts.

Familiar environmental markets already monetize and trade in the abatement of negative environmental externalities — unpriced costs to health, wealth, and security imposed by one party on

---

[1]Paul Hawken, Amory B. Lovins and L. Hunter Lovins, *Natural Capitalism: Creating the Next Industrial Revolution* (Boston: Little Brown, 1999): free download (with a summary of the article from the *Harvard Business Review*) at www.natcap.org.

another.[2] Avoiding these costs can be valuable: Air pollution has already cost a half-billion northern Chinese people an estimated 2.5 billion person-years of life expectancy — five years per person.[3]

Less familiar and less mature than improving air quality, but even more promising, are ways to make markets in *saved resources*.[4] Resource efficiency is typically profitable simply because (1) saving resources costs less than buying them; and (2) with new integrative design techniques, efficiency often produces expanding rather than diminishing returns.[5] The savings can be dramatic: A detailed 2011 book showed how the United States, for example, could run a 2.6-fold bigger 2050 economy with no oil, coal, or nuclear energy and one-third as much natural gas — $5 trillion cheaper in net present value than "business as usual" (with all externalities valued at zero).[6] This tripling of end-use energy-efficiency and shifting of energy supplies from one-tenth to three-fourths renewable would strengthen national security, require no new inventions or Acts of Congress, and could be led by business for profit.

Yet, that study's astonishing financial returns (e.g., tripling or quadrupling U.S. buildings' energy productivity with a 33% internal rate of return (IRR) and doubling that of industry with a 21% IRR)

---

[2]Hank Patton has devised a transactional framework for intergenerational commerce so that people not yet born can invest today in providing the goods and services — and avoiding the "bads" and nuisances — that will advance their interests and our own; see hank@worldste ward.org.

[3]Yuyu Chen, Avraham Ebenstein, Michael Greenstone and Hongbin Li, "Evidence on the Impact of Sustained Exposure to Air Pollution on Life Expectancy from China's Huai River Policy." *Proceedings of the National Academy of Sciences* (8 July 2013); available online at www.pnas.org/content/early/2013/07/03/1300018110.

[4]Amory B. Lovins, "Making Markets in Saved Resources." In *Festschrift for E.U. von Weizsäcker*, RMI Publication #E89-2725 (June 1989); available online at www.rmi.org/ Knowledge-Center/Library/2013-19_MakingMarketsinResourceEfficiency.

[5]Amory B. Lovins, "Integrative Design: A Disruptive Source of Expanding Returns to Investments in Energy Efficiency." RMI Publication #X10-09 (2010); available online at www. rmi.org/rmi/Library/2010-09_IntegrativeDesign; Amory B. Lovins, Michael Bendewald, Michael Kinsley, Lionel Bony, Hutch Hutchinson, Alok Pradhan, Imran Sheikh and Zoe Acher, "Factor Ten Engineering Design Principles." RMI Publication #X10-10 (2010); available online at www.rmi.org/rmi/Library/2010-10_10xEPrinciples.

[6]Amory B. Lovins and Rocky Mountain Institute, *Reinventing Fire: Bold Business Solutions for the New Energy Era* (White River Junction, VT: Chelsea Green, 2011); available online at www.rmi.org/reinventingfire.

reflect only private internal costs and benefits. Those results leave out all avoided environmental, security, and other negative external-ities (including the avoidance of 82–86% fossil carbon emissions). They also omit major positive externalities, such as side benefits that have been well documented to transform real estate by adding value often worth one, sometimes two, *orders of magnitude* more than the energy savings themselves.[7]

The markets already being made in saved resources — so that all ways to provide or save resources can compete fairly — are impressive and valuable. But they barely scratch the surface of the asset- and wealth-creating opportunities. For example, Chapter 13 of *Natural Capitalism* outlines some of the roughly 20 new ways my team devised in the 1980s for making markets in saved energy, water, and materials.[8] Many of these methods are gradually entering use. For example, electric grids in about three-fifths of the United States now let "negawatts" (saved electricity) and demand response (changing the timing of electrical demand) compete in formerly supply-side-only auctions. In the giant PJM power pool, 94% of the winning bids in a recent auction came from the demand side, because negawatts cost less than megawatts.

In transport, some jurisdictions are starting to make markets in "negatrips" and "negamiles," encouraging competition between different ways of getting around or of not needing to. Such markets can even reward real estate developers. "Smart-growth" or "new-urbanist" models create or restore compact, walkable, mixed-use cities and towns that help people be already where they want to be so they need not go somewhere else. Since such layouts are more desirable and valuable, they generally boost developers' profits. In water, efficient use is starting to bid against increased supply, and the same is true for some other resources.

---

[7] Scott Muldavin, "Value Beyond Energy Cost Savings." (2010); available online at www.greenbuildingfc.com.

[8] This discussion is also provided in Chapter 5.3 of the predecessor to Hawken *et al.*, *Natural Capitalism, op. cit.* — namely, Amory B. Lovins, Ernst U. von Weizsäcker and L. Hunter Lovins, *Factor Four: Doubling Wealth, Halving Resource Use* (London: Earthscan, 1987), pp. 164–176.

These markets can spur "solutions economy business models," which typically lease the desired service rather than sell a product whose use produces the service. Solutions-economy business models align providers' interests with customers' interests — that is, rewarding both for doing more and better with less for longer.[9]

Underlying environmental markets are the vital principles of financial economics — sound but often dangerously overlooked. For example, the lower financial risk of the small, fast, modular investments now taking over the electricity market is one of the reasons these projects are often worth an order of magnitude more than is normally assumed.[10] Some traditional suppliers of capital continue to chase big, slow, lumpy projects. For example, huge investments are still being made on the basis of apparently low spot prices for fracked natural gas that reflect neither the attendant risks and uncertainties nor the value of the gas's price volatility. (The volatility is discoverable from the straddle in the options market and is likely to rise if the apparent cheapness of wellhead gas causes expanded exports of liquefied natural gas, petrochemical producers' pivots to cheaper gas, and downstream bottlenecking.) Counting price volatility alone approximately doubles the price of gas that is relevant for fair comparison with its constant-price carbon-free physical hedges — energy-efficiency and renewables — that are increasingly outpacing and outcompeting it. Financial analysts have a duty to warn investors who ignore volatility — which is akin to constructing a bond portfolio of all junk bonds and no U.S. Treasury bonds by considering yield but not risk. Analysts could also advise investors to short the portfolios of those who persist in such foolishness.

In addition to such tactical openings, the strategic horizon for applying financial economics and making environmental markets

---

[9] See *Natural Capitalism, op. cit.*, Chapter 7.

[10] Amory B. Lovins, E. Kyle Datta, Thomas Feiler, Karl R. Rabago, Joel N. Swisher, Andre Lehmann and Ken Wicker, *Small Is Profitable: The Hidden Economic Benefits of Making Electrical Resources the Right Size* (Snowmass, CO: Rocky Mountain Institute, 2002); for more information, visit www.smallisprofitable.org.

stretches boundlessly. Herman Daly, ecological economist and professor at the School of Public Policy of University of Maryland, neatly summarizes how the first Industrial Revolution made people about 100 times more productive because the relative scarcity of people limited the exploitation of seemingly boundless nature. Today, we have the opposite pattern: abundant people but scarce nature. So, it is no longer people that we must strive to use far more productively, but nature. The four interlinked principles of natural capitalism — (1) radical resource productivity; (2) producing in the same way nature does (closed loops, no waste, no toxicity); (3) rewarding these shifts through solutions-economy business models; and (4) investing some of the resulting profits back into the kinds of capital in shortest supply (natural and human capital) — can, together, create an extraordinarily less risky, more durable, and more rewarding economy for all — forever.

In today's dirty, depleted, and dangerous world, environmental markets are the key both to short-term tactical opportunities and to longer-term transformational ones. I applaud Richard Sandor, Nathan Clark, Murali Kanakasabai, and Rafael Marques for crisply describing where to find the key and how to insert and turn it — and for giving us a glimpse of the treasures behind that golden door.

Amory B. Lovins
Cofounder and Chief Scientist,
Rocky Mountain Institute
Old Snowmass, Colorado
October 2014

PREFACE

Forty percent of deaths worldwide are the result of environmental factors, including the secondary effects environmental degradation has in promoting disease.[1] No corporation, government, or population is untouched by this issue. The role of markets, however, in reducing pollution and environmental degradation is not widely understood. Markets, when designed properly, can be a powerful agent for social and environmental transformation. In the United States alone, environmental markets have saved hundreds of thousands of lives and generated hundreds of billions of dollars in human health benefits.[2] In addition to saving lives, these markets also act as economic drivers, generating jobs and improving the overall quality of life while acting as catalysts for innovation.

Population growth, industrialization, and urbanization in the past 200 years have resulted in local, national, and global pollution of our environment. Fossil fuel combustion has resulted in over-accumulation of pollutants that cause smog, acid rain, and climate changes. Entire populations — including China, India, Africa, and large areas elsewhere — face inadequate access to clean air and water.

The lack of ownership of these precious commodities is the cause of the problem. The profit maximization model for a firm takes

---

[1]"Pollution Causes 40% of Deaths Worldwide, Study Finds." *ScienceDaily* (14 August 2007); available online at http:www.sciencedaily.com/releases/2007/08/070813162438.htm.

[2]Douglas A. Burns, Jason A. Lynch, Bernard J. Cosby, Mark E. Fenn and Jill S. Baron, "An Integrated Assessment." National Acid Precipitation Assessment Program Report to Congress, U.S. EPA Clean Air Markets Division (2011).

into account only the direct costs incurred by the firm, such as the negative repercussions associated with the pollution of air and water and not the spillover costs. Therefore, more goods and services are being produced than necessary if pollution was either controlled by fiat or internally priced (a condition in which the social or external cost of the pollution is figured into the decision about how much of the good or service to produce).[3]

These spillover costs, called "negative externalities," can be dealt with by mandating limits on emissions or requiring specific modifications in the production of goods and services. Spillover costs or benefits can also be mitigated by taxes and/or subsidies. In addition, externalities can be mitigated when public or private entities create a limited number of emission or use rights — that is, by a cap. These property rights, called "allowances," can be purchased by companies for the purpose of compliance with environmental laws if they exceed the cap. Similarly, companies that reduce emissions in excess of their targeted reductions can sell their allowances, thereby motivating compliance at the least cost.

The creation of a limited number (cap) of property rights and their transferability (trade) has come to be known as "cap-and-trade." The transferability of allowances results in the market putting a price on the right to pollute. If that price is higher than the technology required to reduce or eliminate the pollution, companies will install the technology. If the opposite is the case, they will buy allowances. The price signals and flexibility enabled by a cap-and-trade program result in a least-cost solution to environmental problems and promote innovation.

Early program outcomes, such as the phasing out of leaded gasoline and the virtual elimination of acid rain, have led to widespread adoption of cap-and-trade throughout the world. The result has

---

[3]An easy way to understand this statement is as follows: The external (e.g., pollution) cost of a good is added to the internal, or ordinary, cost to arrive at the total, or social, cost. If the external cost is a positive number, this process makes the good more expensive. All other things being equal, if a good becomes more expensive, then the quantity demanded is lower, so the "right" amount to produce is also lower.

been creation of a new asset class — the environment — to join the traditional asset classes of stocks, bonds, real estate, foreign exchange, and tangible commodities.

Markets in emissions and rights exist for a variety of pollutants and natural resources. They range from sulfur and carbon allowances, which were created to combat acid rain and global warming, to water and fishing rights, which fight drought and depletion of the ocean's resources. The commoditization of air and water has also been extended to catastrophe and weather risk. Finally, the commoditization of "sustainable stocks" — the equities of companies believed to be conducting environmentally sound or sustainable operations — into new indices has provided investors new ways to participate in these markets.

The purpose of this book is to introduce this new asset class to financial analysts, investors, and corporations. It is of interest to these readers because it allows them to profit or reduce costs while promoting environmental and social benefits. Here is a new way "to do well while doing good."

This book reflects economic theory and practical experience. The chapters will cover three broad asset classes: air and water, catastrophe and weather risk, and sustainability. It will demonstrate how these environmental asset classes are being incorporated into commodities and into fixed-income and equity instruments. The book concludes with some insights into the current state of this emerging asset class, some food for thought, and predictions about the class's future. We hope that the reader will walk away with a solid preliminary understanding of the promising and transformational investment category of environmental assets after reading this book.

ACKNOWLEDGMENTS

We would like to thank the following individuals who provided valuable comments, suggestions, and criticisms for this book: Alexander Barkawi, Don Blackmore, Bruce Braine, John Briscoe, Sylvie Bouriaux, Henry Derwent, Brad Georges, John Langford, Tauni Lanier, Tom Libassi, Mike MacGregor, Stephen McComb, Brian McLean, Jeff O'Hara, Brian Richter, Dan Scarbrough, Eric Taub, and William Welch. In addition to being world-class experts in their respective fields, they were incredibly generous with their time, and they worked with tight deadlines but always gave us high-level feedback and insights. Any improvements to this book should be credited to them, and any errors or omissions are certainly ours.

A special thank-you goes to our colleague Fang-Yu Liang. She diligently and tirelessly performed the tasks of researching, editing, and organizing the many versions of the manuscript while providing a fresh and critical read of the chapters. Important research assistance was also given by Joseph Tabet, Yanjie Liu, Defne Ozaltun, and Karen Peterson. Our gratitude goes to all of them.

This book is an expanded version of a book we wrote for Research Foundation of CFA Institute as an introduction to the emerging field of environmental finance. We are very grateful to Laurence Siegel and to Bud Haslett for their original support to this project.

Finally we would like to thank our editors and the team at World Scientific Publishing, with a special mention to Max Phua, Shu Wen Chye, and Rajni Nayanthara Gamage. They have been great supporters and also provided great suggestions and editorial work.

Richard Sandor is grateful to his wife, Ellen, and his daughters, Julie and Penya, for their suggestions and unwavering support.

Murali Kanakasabai is grateful to his wife, Mathula Thangarajh, and his parents, Mr. Kanakasabai and Mrs. Nalini Kanakasabai, for their patience, support, and guidance.

TABLE OF CONTENTS

Chapter 1

A BRIEF SURVEY OF
ENVIRONMENTAL ASSET CLASSES

Environmental asset classes are not a hope for tomorrow but a reality today. This new asset category promises to grow dramatically as the world focuses on sustainable development.[1] Examples of environmental assets are rights to emit local and regional pollutants, such as sulfur dioxide and nitrogen oxide; rights to emit global pollutants, such as carbon dioxide; renewable energy credits; water quality and quantity rights; and indices of sustainable corporate equities. This new asset class is the manifestation in securities markets of an emerging field of endeavor called "environmental finance." Environmental finance is the art and science of using economic incentives, financial tools, and market mechanisms to achieve desired environmental outcomes.[2]

The purpose of this chapter is to introduce financial analysts, investors, and corporate executives to this new asset class, which should interest readers for many reasons. From a corporate

---

[1] The most commonly used definition of "sustainable development" appeared in the 1987 Brundtland Report: "Development that meets the needs of the present without compromising the ability of future generations to meet their own needs." See United Nations, "Report of the World Commission on Environment and Development: Our Common Future." United Nations (1987). The Brundtland Commission (the World Commission on Environment and Development) was established by the United Nations in 1983.

[2] The term "environmental finance" was first adopted in an eponymous course offered by Richard L. Sandor at Columbia University in 1992. It helped ratify the academic underpinning of this growing new field. It has become widely used by other academic courses, industry publications, and conferences.

standpoint, businesses today have to be cognizant of, and prepare for, new kinds of corporate risks, including those arising from environmental problems and resource scarcity. These environmental risks include, among others, those related to production inputs (e.g., clean water for a beverage company), by-products of production (e.g., wastewater from chemical processing), and corporate social responsibility.

In addition, for companies to be competitive, their executives have to be aware of opportunities that environmental markets have to offer. Environmental asset classes allow businesses to pursue major new opportunities while simultaneously achieving their energy and environmental goals.

Similarly, to evaluate companies on the basis of their environmental performance, exposure to environmental risks, and response to environmental opportunities, financial analysts need to understand emerging environmental asset classes. Portfolio managers may also want to incorporate these new asset classes in their portfolios.

This chapter provides an overview of environment use rights, fixed-income securities, and equity instruments. It lays the framework for understanding the detailed discussion of the topics addressed in later chapters.

Emergence of the Environmental Asset Class

The first application of the innovative concept of cap-and-trade was the phasing out of lead-based gasoline in 1982. Although relatively small, this program was immensely successful and was important as a "proof of concept." The success of the lead phase-out program enabled the first large-scale environmental market in the United States — namely, the Environmental Protection Agency (EPA) Acid Rain Program. Implemented in the early 1990s, this program used the cap-and-trade market model to reduce sulfur and nitrous oxide emissions from fossil fuel combustion in electricity power plants. The environmental objectives of the Acid Rain

Program were achieved with minimal costs relative to benefits. The implementation of the program was accompanied by the evolution of over-the-counter (OTC) spot and forward markets in emission allowances. A host of financial derivatives followed, including futures, options, and swaps.

Note that, in addition to providing a transparent price for the rights to pollute and flexibility in meeting environmental mandates for regulated entities, the Acid Rain Program promoted entrepreneurship, job creation, and market incentives for new technology. These intangibles clearly demonstrated the huge social benefits that can be accrued through well-designed environmental markets.

The acid rain markets led economists and policymakers to use cap-and-trade to combat a much larger problem: global warming. The passage of international and regional mandates to reduce greenhouse gases implicated in causing global warming served as an early catalyst for environmental financial markets. The global markets in trading carbon allowances are the largest and most successful application of the cap-and-trade model.

Parallel to the growth of emissions markets, there has been a push for more environmental disclosure from investors and public interest groups. Indeed, concerns about climate change liability have captured the attention of equity and debt analysts and corporate executives. This trend has produced growth in all aspects of environmental finance. In addition to emissions markets, we now have renewable energy certificates, energy-efficiency credits, and a developed market in sustainable stock indices. Corporations are also paying greater attention to satisfying their energy needs by using cleaner and more sustainable energy sources, leading to investment interest in that activity. Other emerging environmental markets — in water, biofuels, and ecosystems — are similarly promising.

The following section gives an overview of environmental asset classes discussed in detail later.

Environmental Asset Classes

Environmental asset classes include the securities or instruments created through the commoditization of environmental and natural resource assets, such as emissions rights and water; instruments arising from the monetization of specific environmental attributes, such as renewable energy or energy-efficiency; and equity indices, called "sustainable indices," to reflect the overall environmental performance of their constituent companies.

Sulfur Dioxide and Nitrous Oxide Allowances

When coal is burned, four main pollutants are released into the atmosphere — oxides of sulfur, nitrogen, mercury, and carbon. The first two pollutants are associated with acid rain and smog. The prevalence of acid rain in the 1980s motivated the widespread application of cap-and-trade as a mechanism to solve that particular environmental problem. Emissions products in this category include sulfur dioxide (SO_2 or SO_x) emissions futures and options contracts and nitrous oxide (NO_2 or NO_x) emissions futures and options contracts.[3]

The primary markets for trading these commodities are the IntercontinentalExchange and the Chicago Mercantile Exchange (CME). Variants of these kinds of contracts include products that are specific to a certain year's SO_2 or NO_x emissions, referred to as vintages. These markets have long histories as the earliest emissions markets in existence. Market participants are utilities, industrial corporations, brokers, investment banks, and investment managers.

Carbon Dioxide Allowances

The widespread intellectual and political support of emissions trading was reflected in the Kyoto Protocol of 1997, which

---

[3]The first symbol shown is the chemical formula, and the second is the symbol usually used to refer to these substances in a financial context.

established several emissions trading mechanisms. Industrialized countries that accepted the treaty agreed to legally binding commitments to reduce greenhouse gas (GHG) emissions. The European Union implemented the largest of the existing cap-and-trade markets for GHGs, with a volume of emissions in excess of 2.2 billion metric tons of carbon dioxide (CO_2) per year. In addition, two regional programs currently operate in the United States: the Regional Greenhouse Gas Initiative and the California cap-and-trade program, also known as AB 32 (i.e., Assembly Bill 32). China has set up seven pilot markets to reduce its carbon intensity, and India is about to establish markets to address energy efficiency.

GHG emissions products are a direct result of mandatory and voluntary programs to reduce GHG emissions. These markets are the largest category in environmental finance and are discussed in Chapter 4. At present, 10 regulated futures exchanges around the world offer derivative products in GHGs. Of these, the most popular marketplace is the IntercontinentalExchange (ICE), which accounts for more than 85% of regulated exchange-traded volumes. ICE currently offers futures and options products for the European Union Allowances (EUA), Certified Emission Reduction, and emission reduction units. ICE and EUA futures began in 2012 with an open interest of 560,520 and peaked at 1,226,797 (around 94% of ICE Brent futures) in December 2012 before declining.[4] Other prominent exchanges offering climate products are the CME, the Germany-based European Energy Exchange, and Norway-based Nord Pool. In addition to derivatives based on emissions products, a small set of financial products have emerged, including climate-based exchange-traded funds, carbon and clean energy indices, and structured financial instruments.

---

[4]"Brent" is a reference to Brent crude oil, a major trading classification of sweet light crude oil. In 2012, ICE Brent became the world's largest crude oil futures contract in terms of volume.

Renewable Energy and Energy-Efficiency Assets

This category of environmental finance, discussed in detail in Chapter 5, involves trading in environmental attributes. The renewable energy and energy-efficiency markets represent innovation in electricity wherein a specific "clean" attribute of power has been monetized.

The first set involves an interesting innovation in the power markets — renewable energy certificates (RECs). Also known as green certificates, green tags, or tradable renewable certificates, RECs represent the environmental attributes of the power produced from renewable energy projects and are sold separately from the electricity itself. RECs may be traded among regulated entities that have a mandate to include renewable power in a portion of their generation mix or may be traded by retail and corporate customers that wish to include renewable power in their consumption mix.

Already, national and regional REC markets are operating in many countries, including the United States, the United Kingdom, and Australia. Currently in the United States, about 29 states and the District of Columbia require utilities to include a certain percentage of renewable energy in their power generation mix. In addition, a voluntary market for RECs is growing as is individual retail demand for green power.

The second set involves the development of energy-efficiency markets through energy-efficiency credits. Energy-efficiency credits are tradable instruments guaranteeing a certain amount of energy savings. These credits are most commonly generated in response to policy directives requiring improvements in energy-efficiency standards. Energy-efficiency credits are increasingly being used as a policy tool to attain certain levels of energy-efficiency in various economic sectors.

An example is India's Perform, Achieve and Trade program, which covers 478 plants in various sectors. Each plant has been assigned a specific reduction target in energy consumption compared with its baseline consumption (which is the average amount consumed between April 2007 and March 2010). The assigned target is to be attained by 2015. Plants that can achieve energy-efficiency gains beyond their reduction targets will receive energy saving certificates (ESCerts). Those that fail to meet their targets can buy ESCerts from other plants or pay a fine. This program is expected to have a significant impact on GHG emissions and energy-efficiency.

Water Assets

The idea of treating water as an asset class is being driven by the fundamental need for water for human survival and the fact that the world is running out of usable clean water. Freshwater, which accounts for less than 1% of available water, is needed for food production, energy production, and most manufacturing processes. Chapter 6 discusses water as an environmental asset class. The chapter delves into both water quality and quantity issues and the associated financial risks and opportunities in this asset class. The various categories of water markets include the following:

- *Water quantity assets.* These markets involve trading in water permits that deliver a certain quantity of water at a certain time. Such permits are the most common in the existing water markets.
- *Water quality assets.* These markets involve trading in various nutrients and other water pollutants that are responsible for causing water quality problems. Most common are those in agricultural runoff, such as nitrogen and phosphorus, which can contaminate a local water resource. Water quality trading aims to reduce nutrient levels through trading of permits that limit the total amount of nutrients in the watershed.
- *Water temperature assets.* The development of creative regional markets regulating riparian water temperature in the western United States to protect local fishery resources serves as a

reminder that many environmental outcomes can be achieved through properly designed markets.[5]

Catastrophic and Weather Event Assets

This category involves environmental markets designed to manage risks from weather conditions and such catastrophic events as hurricanes and earthquakes. The products include index-based futures and options contracts on weather outcomes and insurance products. The weather derivatives markets were valued at $11.8 billion in 2010 and were growing at a 20% annual rate.[6] Active weather contracts for several international cities are currently hosted by the CME. These markets are discussed in detail in Chapter 7.

Sustainability-Focused Portfolios

The traditional business model contains a tradeoff between a company's economic performance and its environmental performance. In other words, corporate profits are increased at the expense of the environment. A growing body of research suggests, however, that a company's environmental performance can enhance its long-term shareholder value and, therefore, be a good predictor of future economic performance.

This idea led to the emergence of sustainability-focused portfolios, mutual funds, and equity indices (detailed in Chapter 8). Ratings of corporate performance with respect to their carbon footprint, water use, and energy-efficiency have emerged to enable portfolio managers to effectively screen for the environmental performances of companies. Such ratings are provided by CERES (developed by the California Resources Agency), the Carbon Disclosure Project (CDP), and the CDP Water Disclosure Project.

Sustainability approaches are also increasing inroads into the management of mutual funds. It is common for some funds to

---

[5] "Riparian" refers to the interface between land and water, such as on the banks of a river.
[6] Unless otherwise noted, in this book the $ sign refers to the U.S. dollar.

Table 1.1. Examples of Environmental Programs.

Category/Name	Region	Commodity	Start date	Value	Stage
Emissions					
SO_2 Trading Program	United States	SO_2	1990	$290M[a]	Mature (but with legal challenges)
Regional Clean Air Incentives Market (RECLAIM)	California	SO_2 and NO_2	1994	$1.02B[b]	Mature
Regional Greenhouse Gas Initiative	Northeastern U.S. states	CO_2	2003	$ 249M[c]	Mature
EU Emissions Trading Scheme (ETS)	European Union	GHG	Phase I: 2005–2007, Phase II: 2008–2012	$171.0B[d]	Mature
California Emissions Trading Program	California	CO_2	2013	$2.5B–$7.5B[e]	Nascent
South Korea Emissions Trading Scheme	South Korea	CO_2	2013–2015	NA	Proposal
China Emissions Trading Scheme	China	CO_2	2013	NA	Proposal

(*Continued*)

Table 1.1. (*Continued*)

Category/Name	Region	Commodity	Start date	Value	Stage
Emissions-related markets					
Reducing Emissions from Deforestation and Forest Degradation	Global	Offsets	2009	$85M[f]	Nascent
Certified Emission Reductions (Primary)	Global	Offsets	1997	$1B[g]	Mature
Verified Carbon Standard	Global	Offsets	2007	$1.7B	Developed
Energy-efficiency/renewable fuels					
Perform, Achieve and Trade	India	Energy-efficiency	2011	$144M[h]	Developed
CRC (Carbon Reduction Commitment) Energy-Efficiency Scheme	United Kingdom	Energy-efficiency	2007	$68B[i]	Mature
Renewable identification numbers (RINs)	United States	Biofuel	2005	$8.7B[j]	Mature

(Continued)

Table 1.1. (*Continued*)

Category/Name	Region	Commodity	Start date	Value	Stage
Water					
Water quantity trading	Australia	Water quantity allowances	1980–1990	$1.67B[k]	Mature
Water quality trading: Chesapeake Bay nutrient trading	Pennsylvania	Water quality credits	2010	$45M–$300M[l]	Nascent
Temperature credits (e.g., temperature TMDL [total maximum daily load])	Oregon	Water quality	2008	$3.2M[m]	In progress
Weather					
Weather derivatives	Global	Weather-related events (e.g., CME hurricane futures)	Late 1990s	$12B[n]	Mature
Catastrophe bonds	Global	Catastrophes	Mid-1990s	$15.6B[o]	Mature

NA = Not available.

[a]Total value of the allowance market is a snapshot based on the average nominal price as of December 2010 ($19/ton) and total allowance volume available for 2010 compliance. *Source:* EPA 2010 Progress Report. Emission, Compliance and Market Analyses; available online at http://www.epa.gov/airmarkets/progress/ARPCAIR_downloads/ARPCAIR10_analyses.pdf] (2011).

[b]This number reflects the amount traded since RECLAIM was adopted. *Source:* Annual RECLAIM Audit Report for 2011 Compliance Year (1 March 2013).

[c]This number indicates the value, in U.S. dollars, of transactions that occurred in 2011. *Source:* Molly Peters-Stanley and Katherine Hamilton, "Developing Dimension: State of the Voluntary Carbon Markets 2012." Ecosystem Marketplace and Bloomberg New Energy Finance (May 2012).

Table 1.1. (*Continued*)

[d]This figure reflects the total transaction value in the EU ETS allowances in 2011. *Source:* "State and Trends of the Carbon Market 2012." Carbon Finance at the World Bank (May 2012).

[e]Estimates for the first year of the program (2012). The market value is predicted to increase to $21.9 billion by 2020. *Source:* "Designing the Allocation Process for California's Greenhouse Gas Emissions Trading Program: The Multi-Billion Dollar Question." Next 10 (December 2010).

[f]David Diaz, Katherine Hamilton and Evan Johnson, "State of the Forest Carbon Markets 2011: From Canopy to Currency." Ecosystem Marketplace and Forest Trends (September 2011).

[g]"State and Trends of the Carbon Market 2011." Carbon Finance at the World Bank (June 2011).

[h]Estimated market value by 2015.

[i]The next compliance period (2013–2017) requires the United Kingdom to limit its carbon emissions to 2,782 million metric tons of carbon dioxide equivalent. The price floor is currently set at £16/ton. Multiplying the two provides the indicative market size. For more program details, visit www.gov.uk. *Source:* Edward Craft, "United Kingdom: In Counsel — The New CRC Energy Efficiency Scheme Order 2013." Mondaq (May 2013); available online at http://www.mondaq.com/x/238230/Energy+Law/In+Counsel+The+New+CRC+Energy+Efficiency+Scheme+Order+2013.

[j]According to a report by Goldman Sachs, approximately 15 billion RINs were issued in 2012. The RIN price today is around $0.58/RIN. Multiplying the two gives us the market size estimate. *Source:* "Americas: Energy: Oil — Refining." Goldman Sachs Group (25 March 2013).

[k]The figure reflects the total turnover of Australian water markets in 2011–2012. *Source:* "Australian Water Markets Report 2011–2012." Australian Government National Water Commission (March 2013); available online at http://nwc.gov.au/_data/assets/pdf_file/0008/29186/Introduction.pdf.

[l]This number is an estimate for how much the program can generate per year. *Source:* Cy Jones, Evan Branosky, Mindy Selman and Michelle Perez, "How Nutrient Trading Could Help Restore the Chesapeake Bay." World Resources Institute (February 2010).

[m]This number reflects the total value of transactions in 2008. *Source:* Tracy Stanton, Marta Echavarria, Katherine Hamilton and Caroline Ott, "The State of Watershed Payments: An Emerging Marketplace." Ecosystem Marketplace and Forest Trends (June 2010).

[n]PriceWaterhouseCoopers 2011 Weather Risk Derivative Survey. Prepared for the Weather Risk Management Association (May, 2011).

[o]This figure reflects the amount outstanding as of the end of 2012. *Source:* "Insurance-Linked Securities (ILS) Market Review 2012 and Outlook 2013." Munich Re (2013); available online at http://www.munichre.com/app-pages/www/@res/pdf/reinsurance/business/non-life/financial_risks/ils-market-review-2012-and-outlook-2013-en.pdf.

have sustainability-focused strategies. For example, the Neuberger Berman Socially Responsible Investment Fund screens for companies that demonstrate leadership in the environment, and the Firsthand Alternative Energy Fund invests primarily in equity securities of companies that are involved in developing alternative energy. Another strategy for sustainability-focused mutual funds is to avoid investing in companies that produce goods and services with negative social impacts, such as alcohol, tobacco, and weaponry companies. Finally, sustainability-related equity indices, such as the Dow Jones Sustainability Indices, have emerged to track the financial performance of selected companies identified as leaders in corporate sustainability. Such indices help financial analysts pick companies on the basis of their corporate sustainability performance and assess risks on the basis of the belief that long-term returns are correlated with the sustainability ratings of corporations.

Table 1.1 provides examples of environmental markets in existence today. The list indicates the vast array of financial innovations that have been created in a relatively new field in recent years.

Conclusion

Growth in environmental markets has helped integrate corporate climate and environmental risks and liabilities into the balance sheets of businesses. Climate risks and pollution are no longer under the exclusive purview of the environmental, health, and safety departments of companies but are also of interest to the finance and accounting departments. Environmental financial markets have helped corporations hedge and manage long-term business risks associated with environmental mandates. In addition, as the markets mature, the opportunity arises to use these financial tools as catalysts for achieving numerous environmental sustainability and social development goals. Just as corporations must adjust their business models in response to the climate challenge, those concerned with the health of the environment must inform and motivate societies around the world to adapt to an environmentally sound mode of living.

But why have these environmental markets flourished? They have flourished because of the existence of externalities and the efficacy of cap-and-trade in dealing with them. The next chapter will explain what externalities are and how cap-and-trade works.

Chapter 2

MARKET FAILURES
AND POLICY RESPONSES

Economic theories and concepts are needed to understand the role of markets in addressing pollution. This chapter analyzes environmental problems from the perspective of market failure, explores several solutions to environmental problems, and provides numerical examples to better illustrate the advantages of some of these solutions. A description on the evolution of markets in general and environmental markets in particular is also presented. While most people would agree that market-based solutions are superior to command-and-control measures, there is an ongoing debate regarding the desirability of market solutions versus taxes and subsidies.

Externalities, Property Rights, and Market Imperfections

Externalities are defined as spillover costs (negative) or benefits (positive) from the production of a good or service that accrue to individuals or entities not involved in the production process. Environmental pollution is widely used in microeconomics as an example of a negative externality. Economists have long debated the proper societal responses for preventing and remedying them.

Externalities are most likely to occur where property rights are not clearly defined. Private and public entities that own resources outright are incentivized to manage the resource properly, as any gain or loss in the resource's value affects them directly. A resource owner will require that a polluter compensate them for any diminution in the resource's value; if the polluter does not compensate them, the resource owner will not allow the resource to be used. By this process, resources are conserved in a pure property system. (Of course, it is not possible or desirable for all resources, such as air, to be owned outright; we will get to that later.) It is important to note that property rights need not be private in order to achieve desirable outcomes. As long as property rights are enforced and there are private reasons, either legal or economic, to maintain the resource, a socially desirable outcome can be achieved.

Thus, well-defined property rights are central to our approach of managing externalities. When polluters do not have to compensate society for the pollution caused by their production processes, they do not have an incentive to reduce pollution and will produce at levels that maximize their individual profits. The level of production in the absence of fair pricing of externalities (fair compensation of resource owners) is usually above the socially optimal level. By polluting, producers impose costs on society in the form of health hazards and environmental degradation.

Some illustrative examples may be helpful. Consider air and water pollution caused by a factory. The *private* profit-maximizing actions of the factory may result in negative impacts on individuals in the vicinity of the plant. Local water and air quality can deteriorate from pollutants released into local lakes and rivers and the atmosphere. Similarly, a beekeeper who is located next to a farm can produce positive externalities. The bees help pollinate and, therefore, increase the crop productivity of the nearby farm.

All externalities are a form of market failure. Market failures occur when the pricing mechanism does not take into account all of the actual costs and benefits of producing or consuming a good. A rational private actor, such as a firm, with a goal to maximize profit, is only interested in his or her private benefits and costs. However, the result of those private actions can result in positive (benefits) or negative (costs) externalities for the society as a whole, which are not accounted for by the private actor. The result is a level of private production and consumption that is different from the socially optimal level of production and consumption. Let us use a simple numerical example to illustrate the point.

Suppose there is a factory located next to a town and lake. Assume that it makes a product from the power it generates by burning fossil fuels. Assume the burning of the fossil fuel releases sulfur dioxide into the atmosphere locally, thereby causing respiratory problems for the local population. Further suppose the factory uses fresh water in the manufacturing process and this water is returned to the lake filled with toxic chemicals. Table 2.1 presents the output of widgets, the price of widgets, the total revenue, total costs of producing the widgets, and the social costs of damage from the pollution of air and water.

In this example, the profit maximizing production for the firm is 50 widgets, which gives the firm a profit of $90. For the surrounding town, the value of these widgets is –$10 (profit – cost of pollution [i.e., $90–$100]). Thus, 50 widgets is not the socially optimal level of production. If the firm had to pay for its pollution, the optimum output for the firm would be 40 widgets, as this amount yields the highest profit after paying for pollution. In this example, the market imperfection of not pricing the emissions results in an undesirable social outcome.

Table 2.1. How Private Optima Diverge from Social Optima.

Widget output (units)	Widget price ($)	Total revenues (units × price) ($)	Total cost of production ($)	Profit (revenues – cost) ($)	Emissions (tons)	Cost of pollution ($)	Profit after paying for pollution ($)
10	10	100	60	40	20	30	10
20	10	200	150	50	40	40	10
30	10	300	240	60	60	45	15
40[a]	10	400	320	80	80	60	20
50[b]	10	500	410	90	100	100	−10
60	10	600	660	−60	120	180	−240

[a] Social optimum.
[b] Private optimum.

Solutions to Externalities

This simple example provides insight into the policy tools available to reach the optimal societal production of 40 widgets. Three policy tools that can be used to achieve this target are: (1) command-and-control; (2) subsidies and/or taxes; and (3) cap-and-trade.

Command-and-control in its most basic form would involve a law that limits the firm's production to no more than 40 widgets. In a more complex form the local environmental regulator could require the firm to install technology that reduces its emissions. The choice of these alternatives would depend on the transaction costs. In this case, the regulator would weigh the cost of enforcing and administering these command-and-control measures against the benefit to the firm and society.

Another alternative is to impose a tax on the output of widgets or on the amount of pollution emitted. In this particular example, a tax of $1.08 per widget would result in a profit maximizing production of 40 widgets. Table 2.2 extends the example in Table 2.1 by showing the possible outcome of imposing a tax on production units.

If each widget produced resulted in two tons of pollutants then a tax of $0.60 per ton would achieve the same result. Table 2.3 demonstrates the outcomes of levying a tax on the externality itself.

Table 2.2. Taxing the Production.

Widget output (units)	Price per widget $	Total revenues (units × price) $	Tax ($1.08 per widget) $	Total cost of production $	Profit (revenues − tax − cost) $
10	10	100	11	60	29
20	10	200	22	150	28
30	10	300	32	240	28
40	10	400	43	320	37
50	10	500	54	410	36
60	10	600	65	660	−125

Table 2.3. Taxing the Externality.

Widget output (units)	Widget price $	Total revenues (units × price) $	Total cost of production $	Profit (revenues – cost) $	Emissions (tons)	Pollution Tax ($0.6 per ton) $	Profit after paying for pollution $
10	10	100	60	40	20	12	28
20	10	200	150	50	40	24	26
30	10	300	240	60	60	36	24
40	10	400	320	80	80	48	32
50	10	500	410	90	100	60	30
60	10	600	660	−60	120	72	−132

Lastly, there is cap-and-trade, a mechanism that was briefly discussed in the Foreword. There has been growing consensus among the scientific and environmental communities that market mechanisms, such as cap-and-trade, are one set of viable tools to manage environmental challenges. Environmental and emission markets represent new opportunities for both sellers and buyers of environmental assets.

A cap-and-trade program establishes limits on overall emissions, specifying limits at the firm level. Firms with low-abatement costs can reduce emissions below their required limit and sell the excess reductions. Firms with high-abatement costs may buy these excess reductions in order to comply with their own regulatory limits. The market allows for efficient use of the limited resource (environmental goods) and yields a price that signals the value society places on the use of the environment. The following example can also be applied to the widget factory case if one assumes that the widget factory and the town are two separate entities with different marginal costs of pollution abatement. Appendix A provides an illustration of the essence of a cap-and-trade emissions trading system.

The concept of emissions trading stems from Ronald Coase's theory of social cost[1] and is articulated by John H. Dales.[2] The

---

[1] Ronald H. Coase, "The Problem of Social Cost." *Journal of Law & Economics*, Vol. 3 (1960): 1–44.

[2] John H. Dales, *Pollution, Property and Prices* (Toronto: University of Toronto Press, 1968).

argument is that, by assigning clear property rights, the market can play a valuable role in ensuring that these rights will go towards their most efficient use. The initial allocation of allowances is irrelevant from the point of economic efficiency, if there are no transaction costs.[3] However, it may have income distribution implications. Such market-based solutions are less costly than command-and-control measures, which usually do not cause the property rights to flow into their highest valued use. Refer to Appendix A for a numerical illustration of the superiority of market-based solutions to traditional command-and-control measures.

This section illustrates the superiority of cap-and-trade to command-and-control. Although cap-and-trade and taxes can achieve the same results under very narrow assumptions, the authors of this book regard cap-and-trade to be the preferred alternative. These alternatives are being debated in the United States and internationally. It should be emphasized that the purpose of this book is to inform financial professionals of the role of markets in addressing pollution and concomitantly educate the readers about the opportunities they provide. The next section describes the evolution of environmental markets. In doing so, it explains through examples from other mature markets the process of market development and its requirements.

Evolution of Environmental Markets

So far, this chapter has discussed the economic underpinning of environmental financial markets. The concepts of externalities, property rights, and resulting market imperfections have been explained in great detail. The environmental consequences of resources being treated as having a "zero" price, led to over consumption and contributed to the problem referred to as "the Tragedy of the Commons." On the other hand, market-based approaches treat the environment as a truly scarce resource

---

[3]This principle is known as the Coase theorem.

by establishing limits on its use. The use of a property-like instrument — such as emissions allowances and offsets — provides a mechanism that can assure efficient use of the resource and yields a price in a market that was previously not available. Financial innovation that led to "commoditization" of natural resources resulted in the creation of a new asset class based on environmental attributes. Market-based mechanisms such as emissions trading have become widely accepted as a cost-effective method for achieving environmental improvements.

In order to better understand the current state of environmental markets, it is useful to examine the historical development of other "mature" markets. The evolution of environmental markets is undergoing a process similar to that experienced by other established or "mature" markets. This will help guide us in the development of these new environmental markets and the fundamental rationale for value creation in these markets. Examples can be drawn from the equity, commodity, and fixed-income markets.

Historical precedent seems to indicate that the evolutionary nature of markets follows a concise seven-stage process. Successful market development typically follows a seven-stage process, spanning from the recognition of a new challenge, the launch of pilot trading schemes and the formalization of the trading process to the organization of futures and over-the-counter (OTC) markets. Like their commodity, equity, and fixed-income predecessors, environmental markets did not start by spontaneous combustion. On the contrary, like any other good or service, these were responses to latent or overt demand. Their successful evolution required the development of specific legal and institutional infrastructures. Minimization of price mechanism use costs was the objective. Once we understood the evolutionary process, the specific steps necessary to implement an environmental market became more obvious. The seven-stage process can be observed in the emergence of sulfur dioxide trading under the Acid Rain Program in the United States as well as the greenhouse gas (GHG) emissions trading in the global context.

The Seven-Stage Market Development Process

To understand how markets can evolve, we present a seven-stage process that helps describe the many forces which accrue over time and sometimes develop into more sophisticated and efficient markets. The steps can be characterized as:

(1) A structural economic change occurs and creates the demand for capital.
(2) The creation of uniform standards for a commodity or security.
(3) The development of a legal instrument which provides evidence of ownership.
(4) The development of informal spot markets (markets for immediate delivery) and forward markets (non-standardized agreements or future delivery) where receipts of ownership are traded.
(5) The emergence of securities and commodities exchanges.
(6) The creation of organized futures markets (standardized contracts for future delivery on organized exchanges and options markets) with rights, but not guarantees for future delivery in commodities and securities.
(7) The proliferation of over-the-counter (OTC) markets/deconstruction.

Importantly, the seven-stage process is not an unalterable course that markets must pass through sequentially. Rather, it is an analytical construct that seems to describe fairly well the steps which occur over time and sometimes lead to standardized spot and futures contracts at organized exchanges. As such, it does not purport to be an unassailable theory but serves only to highlight a natural dialectic.

Examples of the Seven-Stage Process

This section will examine cases of market creation in established commodities such as agricultural commodities futures representing commodity markets, the emergence of the market for mortgage-backed securities representing fixed income market, and the launch of sulfur dioxide trading in the United States representing environmental markets. The analysis reveals that although the four cases are quite diverse, they followed a similar pattern of market evolution. Table 2.4 indicates for each of the four cases the evolutionary process according to the seven-stage framework.[4]

In the case of agricultural commodities, the structural change that stimulated grain production in the United States was from the removal of restrictions on grain imports into England and the Crimean War. This was the primary factor that enabled the U.S. to become a large exporter of agricultural goods. Growth in demand for grain continued as the U.S. population reached 35 million by the end of the Civil War. Capital was needed to finance the storage and shipment of grain from the Midwest to the major population centers in the East Coast. At that time, there was unorganized trading in physical sacks of grain, which had to be inspected on an individual basis. The creation of the Chicago Board of Trade (CBOT) in 1848 ushered in grain standards and grading procedures, an innovation that preceded the creation of government standards by 50 years. Ultimately, a tradable legal instrument called the "warehouse receipt" emerged, which provided evidence of ownership and facilitated both capital raising and ownership transfer. The birth of futures trading in 1865 was followed by options trading at a later stage.

A similar pattern is recognized in the evolution of the fixed income market for mortgage-backed bonds. The post-World War II economic boom in the United States created a great demand for housing in California, which had to be financed by institutions in

---

[4]For a more detailed discussion of the four cases presented in the following, see Richard L. Sandor, Eric C. Bettelheim and Ian R. Swingland, "Overview of a Free-Market Approach to Climate Change and Conservation." *Phil Trans Roy Soc Land*, Vol. 360, No. 1797 (August 2002): 1607–1620.

Table 2.4. The Seven Stages of Market Development.

	Market		
Stage	Agricultural Commodities Futures Trading at the Chicago Board of Trade (1848)	Trading of Mortgage-Backed Securities (1970)	Sulfur Dioxide Trading under the Acid Rain Program of the United States (1990)
(1) Structural change	• Removal of restrictions on grain imports into the United Kingdom (1846) and • Crimean War (1854–1856) leading to rising demand for imports from America • Population increase in America adds further demand — encouraging new investments and expanding trade	• Widening gap between demand for, and supply of, housing finance in the late 1960s/early 1970s	• Rising concerns about the effects of SO_2 emissions on human health and the environment • A tripling of U.S. pollution-control costs between 1972 and 1990 • Keen interest in least-cost solution to SO_2 problem

(Continued)

Table 2.4. (*Continued*)

Stage	Market		
	Agricultural Commodities Futures Trading at the Chicago Board of Trade (1848)	Trading of Mortgage-Backed Securities (1970)	Sulfur Dioxide Trading under the Acid Rain Program of the United States (1990)
(2) Emergence of uniform standards	Standards for measuring and grading grains set by the Chicago Board of Trade (CBOT)	Mortgage-backed pass-through security issued by Ginnie Mae (1970)	SO_2 allowance as defined by the Clean Air Act Amendments (CAAA) of 1990
(3) Development of legal instrument	"Warehouse receipts" issued as proof of ownership and made legally enforceable as of 1859	Mortgage-backed securities (pass-throughs and bonds) find growing acceptance as financial products	• SO_2 allowance • Registry of U.S. Environmental Protection Agency (EPA)
(4) Development of informal spot markets	Trading based on "warehouse receipts" begins	Informal trading between the government-sponsored agencies and Wall Street dealers, mortgage originators and investors	• Various trading pilots during 1970s/1980s and private sales of allowances in early 1990s • Test auctions in 1993 and 1994

(*Continued*)

Table 2.4. (*Continued*)

Stage	Market		
	Agricultural Commodities Futures Trading at the Chicago Board of Trade (1848)	Trading of Mortgage-Backed Securities (1970)	Sulfur Dioxide Trading under the Acid Rain Program of the United States (1990)
(5) Emergence of formalized exchanges	CBOT Charter (1859)	Secondary Mortgage Market Enhancement Act of 1984 and Tax Reform Act of 1986	Annual auctions conducted by CBOT (on behalf of EPA)
(6) Creation of organized futures or options markets	Futures contracts being formalized (1865)	• Ginnie Mae futures introduced at CBOT (1975) • Collateralized Mortgage Obligations (CMOs) issued by Freddie Mac (1983)	Futures being used but not yet within an official framework
(7) Proliferation of over-the-counter markets	Options ("privileges") and over-the-counter ("bucket shop") trading begins to take off (1879)	Increasing number of private retailers in mortgage-backed securities markets	Informal over-the-counter trades

the Eastern part of the country. Although standardized mortgages guaranteed by the Federal Housing Authority (FHA) and the Veterans Administration (VA) assured capital flows into the sector, it was a highly inefficient market. Mortgages were sold on an individual basis or in small packages and the buyer had to have individual documentation for each loan. The "credit crunch" of 1966 and 1969 and the uncertainty surrounding the timely payment of the principal and interest during foreclosures gave rise to the formation of the Government National Mortgage Association (GNMA). This enabled the "bundling" of small loans into securities to be collateralized by the FHA/VA and backed by the U.S. government. It provided an efficient and homogeneous evidence of ownership and conveyance vehicle, which ultimately evolved into spot and forward markets, primarily among Wall Street dealers and mortgage bankers. This informal arrangement served the function of an exchange until the world's first interest rate futures contract — based on the GNMA Mortgage-Backed instrument — was launched at the Chicago Board of Trade in 1975. From that date, financial futures secured acceptance and ultimately, in the 1980s, so did collateralized mortgages.

This is the same pattern that was noticed in the evolution of the equities market. It is important to note that these markets were formed in a wide time period between 16th to 20th centuries but still followed the same evolutionary pattern. We now extend this model to the evolution of environmental contracts and derivatives.

Here, the example from the sulfur dioxide (SO_2) market in the United States is particularly informative. The burning of high-sulfur coal by electric utilities in the United States led to an increase in sulfur dioxide (SO_2) emissions. Increased pollution in the form of sulfuric emissions accompanied the increased output of electricity. Generated in more densely populated sections of the U.S., this pollution resulted in large increases in respiratory problems for affected populations. In addition, acidification damaged rivers, streams, and forests. Recognizing their adverse effects on human health and on the environment, legislators passed the Clean Air Act in 1970, which was followed by the Clean Air Act Amendments (CAAA) in 1990. It introduces an overall limit on these emissions, pronounces how within this limit, emission allowances should be distributed across individual actors (mainly the utilities), and requires the creation of a trading scheme for these allowances. This represented the structural change, i.e., Stage 1, that enabled the development of a market for acid rain credits. The CAAA further performed three functions that enabled market development:

(1) It standardized an environmental commodity (a legally-authorized allowance to emit one ton of sulfur dioxide);
(2) it produced the "evidence of ownership" necessary for financial instruments; and
(3) it established the infrastructure to efficiently transfer title.

In doing the above, the CAAA established the requirement for uniform standardized commodity for sulfur dioxide. This represents stage 2 of the market process. In addition, the U.S. Environmental Protection Agency (EPA) set up an electronic tracking system that recorded information on each party's allowances and actual emission levels. Thus, it was possible for companies to know precisely what their quota was and how they fared in meeting the reduction targets, whether they had surplus allowances or whether they needed to buy additional ones (stage 3). Private sales and purchases of allowances occurred even before the CAAA entered into force in 1995 (stage 4). Organized exchanges began when the EPA chose the CBOT to conduct annual auctions of allowances on its behalf. These auctions, which started in 1993, established price signals to the market (stage 5).[5]

Later in December 2004, organized trading in SO_2 futures commenced with establishment of the Chicago Climate Futures

---

[5] In fact, the auctions are designed to be revenue-neutral. The proceeds are returned to the participating utilities.

Exchange (stage 6). Similarly, OTC trades are happening, mainly on the sidelines of the official exchanges (stage 7).[6]

History shows that market evolution involving the seven-stage process has been consistent across equities, fixed income securities, physical commodities, and the SO_2 allowance trading program. While the SO_2 cap-and-trade emission reduction program has been enormously successful, there was great skepticism at the start, much like the skepticism now being expressed with other markets. The sulfur trading model can be successfully extended to greenhouse gases. To illustrate the growing importance of market-based mechanisms, the next section will look at some of the historical uses of these mechanisms to achieve environmental objectives.

Early Applications of Market-Based Mechanisms to Environmental Problems

For most of the 1960s and early 1970s, command-and-control was the preferred measure among federal regulators, as shown by the Clean Air Act of 1970. Regulators not only set environmental goals, but imposed industry-wide standards that applied to all firms, regardless of their cost of compliance. Since the introduction of federal pollution-control regulation, however, economists have advocated the allocation of property rights to environmental wastes as a cheaper alternative to traditional command-and-control measures.

The Environmental Protection Agency (EPA) began experimenting with emissions trading in 1974, when it adopted "netting" — a policy that allows a firm to net the increased emissions from one source against reductions in another source at the same

---

[6]For accounts of how the SO_2 market evolved, see, among others, Paul L. Joscow, Richard Schmalensee and Elizabeth M. Bailey, "The Market for Sulfur Dioxide Emissions." *The American Economic Review*, Vol. 88, No. 4 (September 1998): 669–685; Sandor, Bettelheim and Swingland (2002); and Robert N. Stavins, "Experience with Market-Based Environmental Policy Instruments." In *The Handbook of Environmental Economics*, edited by Karl-Goran Maler and Jeffrey Vincent (Amsterdam: Elsevier, 2003), pp. 355–435.

facility. Before netting was introduced, companies had to register all new plants as a "new" source under the Clean Air Act, which could be costly. After netting was introduced, multiple sources were treated as one large source. Netting resulted in an aggregated cost savings between \$525 million and \$12 billion from 1974 to 1984, according to Hahn and Hester.[7] Similarly, "offsets" were introduced by the EPA in 1976 when it became clear that many of the nation's Air Quality Control Regions could not attain the National Ambient Air Quality Standards by the deadline. The introduction of offsets allows for the construction of new stationary sources of emissions in non-attainment areas, provided that their new emissions were offset by reductions at existing sources. By 1988, 2,000 offset transactions had already taken place. The savings are difficult to quantify but the fact that these transactions occurred at all illustrates the intrinsic economic need that they fulfill.

In 1979, the EPA encouraged companies to use "bubbles" to cut the cost of regulations. For example, a single plant may contain many sources of pollution. A bubble policy can include facilities owned by different firms and treat their emissions as if they are from a single source. By doing this, a bubble policy is essentially allowing for the implicit transfer of emission from smokestack to smokestack within the bubble. This policy tool has resulted in \$435 million in savings.[8] Notably in 1979, EPA introduced "banking" — a policy measure whereby companies can save or "bank" their emission credits for future use.

Although none of the measures introduced above constitute a trading program, together they paved the way to the first ever application of cap-and-trade in 1982: The phasing out of lead-based gasoline. The EPA launched a trading scheme for lead use across refineries in 1982. The "cap" was set at 1.1 grams of lead per gallon. This trading scheme also included the banking feature

---

[7] Robert W. Hahn and Gordon L. Hester, "Where Did All the Markets Go? An Analysis of EPA's Emissions Trading Program." *Yale Journal in Regulations*, Vol. 6, No. 1 (Winter, 1989): 374.

[8] *Ibid.*

so that refineries that reduced more than they needed could store the lead rights for later use. EPA analysis shows that the program resulted in an estimated savings of about $250 million per year.

These early programs paved the way for SO_2 and NO_x trading, as demonstrated in the next chapter.

Appendix A. Cap-and-Trade

Suppose that two emissions sources each emit 100 tons during a baseline period (a reference situation used to define emission reductions). If the policy mandate is to reduce overall emissions by 20%, one means of achieving that goal would be to assign each of the two emitters 80 tons of tradable emission allowances (for a total of 160 tons). Each emitter would then be required to monitor and report (using prescribed methods) its emissions and to annually achieve compliance by surrendering to the program authority emission allowances in an amount equal to its year-long emissions. Figure A.1 illustrates the essence of such a cap-and-trade emissions trading system.

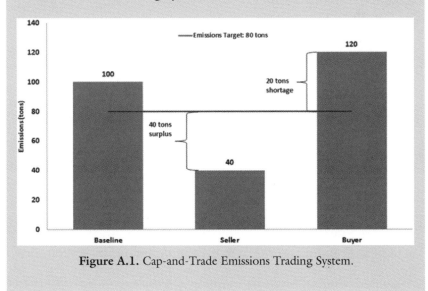

Figure A.1. Cap-and-Trade Emissions Trading System.

Although each emitter has a nominal reduction target of 80 tons (20 tons below its baseline), the emitter represented by the middle bar in Figure A.1 was able to cut its emission to 40 tons, giving it a surplus of 40 emission allowances that it could sell to the other emissions source (or, in many programs, could bank for possible use or sale in later periods). The emitter represented by the bar on the right did not reduce its emissions; in fact, its emissions rose to 120 tons. Because it must surrender to the program authority emission allowances representing 120 tons of emissions, it must acquire 40 tons of emission allowances from other emitters who have made extra emission reductions. In this simple case, one emitter has just enough surplus allowances to sell to the emitter that experienced rising emissions. Together, the two emitters reduced total emissions to the desired amount, which is 160 tons (40 + 120).

Suppose an emitter projects that its emissions will increase during the year as a result of increased demand for its product or service, lack or low-cost emission reduction opportunities, or perhaps the need to meet other regulatory mandates — and it finds it cannot easily purchase surplus emission allowances from others. In that case, it may bid up the price of emission allowances to induce others to sell to it. If this emitter fails to acquire allowances, it will have to weigh the choice among curtailing production, taking high-cost measures to reduce emissions while maintaining production, or in many programs, paying a fine (and possibly still be required to acquire and retire emission allowances at a later date).

Cap-and-trade is a cheaper alternative to a command-and-control system. Suppose there are two plants, Plant A and Plant B, which contribute to air pollution. An engineering analysis finds that Plant A has options to upgrade its equipment, install emission control devices, switch fuels, or take other managerial actions that could allow it to reduce air emissions by several tons at a cost of $0.50 per ton reduced. A similar analysis for Plant B

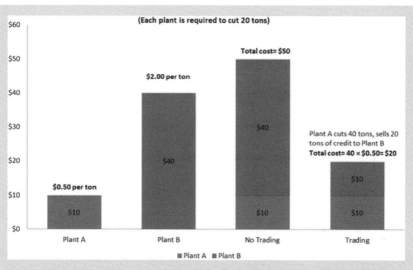

Figure A.2. Cost of Emission Reductions.

finds that its cheapest option will cost $2.00 per ton of reduced emissions.

Figure A.2 illustrates the costs of emission. Suppose a new environmental regulation requires the owners of Plant A and Plant B to take actions that reduce *overall* air emissions by a total of 40 tons. The third and fourth vertical bars illustrate the total cost society would face to achieve the 40 tons of emission reductions with and without the flexibility allowed through emissions trading. If emissions trading were not allowed, Plant A would have to reduce its emissions by 20 tons (at a cost of $10) and Plant B would have to reduce its emissions by 20 tons (at a cost of $40). The total mitigation cost faced by society would be $50. If emissions trading were allowed, Plant A and Plant B could both find an economically superior outcome by negotiating to have the low-cost Plant A reduce emissions by 40 tons and allow Plant B to meet its obligations of cutting its emissions by 20 tons by hiring — through an emissions trade — Plant A to make the extra cut on its behalf. Plant A could sell its environmental protection service — in the form of a tradable emissions credit — to Plant B, which could then present the credit to the environmental regulator as evidence that Plant B met its commitment to make sure one ton of acceptable emission reductions was realized.

As long as Plant A is willing to sell emission reduction credits to Plant B at less than $2.00 per ton, then (in the absence of transaction costs), Plant B spends less money complying with the regulation by buying credits instead of cutting its own emissions. (Naturally, the environmental regulator would have to enforce all rules that might affect local air quality in the vicinity of Plant B. For this example, we assume the pollutant has no particular health impact on those close to the source, in the way that nitrogen oxide emissions from transport do.)

The total cost to society is $20 in the trading scenario (Plant A spent a total of $40 \times \$0.50 = \$20$ to cut its emissions by 40 tons). The amount paid by Plant B to Plant A is a cost to one side but a revenue to the other, resulting in no extra net cost to society.

Chapter 3

ACID RAIN POLLUTANTS AS AN ASSET CLASS

"Acid rain" is a broad term referring to a mixture of wet and dry deposition from the atmosphere containing higher-than-normal amounts of nitric and sulfuric acids. It has been virtually eradicated in the United States. Emissions of sulfur dioxide (SO_2) and nitrogen oxides (NO_x), the main precursors of acid rain, have declined more than 75% from their 1980 levels.[1] In addition, the reductions in SO_2 and NO_x have dramatically reduced health costs associated with lung disease — the main impact of SO_2 and NO_x emissions on humans — at a minimal cost to the economy. The eradication of acid rain helped reduce smog, prevented damage to forests, and reduced acidification of lakes and rivers.

How did this happen? A cap-and-trade model, the Acid Rain Program, enabled by the Clean Air Act Amendments of 1990 put a price on SO_2 emissions for the first time. In doing so, it lowered the transaction costs associated with reducing emissions that cause acid rain. The success of the program demonstrated that the cap-and-trade mechanism is not only theoretically sound but also practical. It provided empirical evidence that was useful in extending cap-and-trade to other pollutants, such as NO_x — a significant contributor

---

[1] EPA, "Clean Air Interstate Rule, Acid Rain Program and Former NO_x Budget Trading Program 2011 Progress Report." U.S. Environmental Protection Agency (November 2012); available online at http://www.epa.gov/airmarkets/progress/ARPCAIR11_01.html.

to both acid rain and ground-level ozone (smog) — and carbon dioxide (CO_2) — the principal cause of global warming.

Pricing pollution provided benefits to both the private and public sectors. The price signal of SO_2 allowances gave utilities and industrial corporations a way of achieving the mandated reductions in the most cost-effective way. Financial analysts, with the aid of these price signals, were able to evaluate investment opportunities in the technologies used for reducing SO_2 emissions and in related companies, such as investor-owned utilities, coal companies that could benefit from increased use of low-sulfur coal, and manufacturers of pollution-control technologies. Financial institutions also saw an opportunity to benefit from the marketing, financing, and brokering of SO_2 allowances.

This chapter provides an overview of the Acid Rain Program. Of the two acid rain pollutants, this chapter will focus on the main pollutant, SO_2. The main drivers of the SO_2 allowance market and lessons learned from dealing with it are also applicable to the NO_x market.[2]

Causes of Acid Rain and Public Policy Responses

Combustion of coal for power generation leads to release of sulfur dioxide and nitrogen oxides into the atmosphere. Because these gases are the principal precursors of acid rain and its damage to lakes and forests, as well as fine particulates that pose human health risks, emissions from coal power generation constitutes a negative externality. As indicated in Chapter 2, this negative externality was not priced or significantly constrained by law during most of the 20th century; indeed, electrical power was generated with little or no regard for its externalities. Thus, a large volume of pollutants resulted.

---

[2]For a complete description of the N_2O program, visit http://www.epa.gov/airmarkets/progsregs/nox/index.html.

Increased electricity demand from the mid-20th century onwards caused utilities to build new coal-fired power plants (then, the cheapest source of electricity) and burn more coal in general to meet the new demand. In some regions, such as in the midwestern United States, utilities burned unusually large amounts of coal because power plants were located near coal deposits. As a result, atmospheric emissions of SO_2 and NO_x increased substantially.

The level of SO_2 emissions also became geographically more widespread because of local laws. These laws, in an attempt to alleviate local air quality problems in the 1970s, required utilities to construct tall smokestacks. Utilities in the United States constructed more than 429 smokestacks — many of them higher than 500 feet — on coal-fired boilers, causing winds to carry the emissions to other states.[3] As a consequence, the vast majority of urban areas in the 1980s attained the local ambient air quality standards for SO_2. The smokestack remedy for local problems, however, contributed to the deterioration of air quality at a regional level. Released high in the atmosphere, SO_2 emissions from coal plants traveled hundreds of miles and increased acid rain.[4] This circumstance caused large increases in acidification, particularly in the eastern half of the United States.

Public concern over these environmental issues motivated legislators to pass the Clean Air Act Amendments (CAAA) of 1990. The U.S. program for trading SO_2 emission allowances was enabled by Title IV of the CAAA. The Acid Rain Program required electric utilities to reduce their SO_2 emissions by about 50% from 1980 levels. For the total electricity sector, SO_2 emissions were approximately 17.5 million tons in 1980, and the reduction target was approximately 3.5 million tons over a five-year period with a further 5 million tons mandated in the second phase of the program.

---

[3] James L. Regens and Robert W. Rycroft, *The Acid Rain Controversy* (Pittsburgh: University of Pittsburgh Press, 1988).

[4] Dallas Burtraw and Sarah Jo Fueyo Szambelan, "U.S. Emissions Trading Markets for SO_2 and NO_x." Resources for the Future Discussion Paper No. 09-40 (October 2009); available online at http://papers.ssrn.com/sol3/papers.cfm?abstract_id=1490037.

The law directed the U.S. Environmental Protection Agency to implement a phased-in program.

Results of the Public Policy Responses

Title IV successfully reduced emissions of SO_2 and NO_x from power generation (i.e., the sources covered by the Acid Rain Program). It was complemented by subsequent cap-and-trade programs, specifically the NO_x Budget Trading Program and the Clean Air Interstate Rule (CAIR). The result of these efforts was a reduction in SO_2 emissions to 5.2 million tons in 2010, an amount 67% lower than 1990 emissions and below the original 2010 statutory cap of 8.95 million tons. Another result was a reduction in NO_x emissions to 2.1 million tons in 2010, an amount 67% lower than 1990 emissions and substantially better than the Title IV goal.[5] Figure 3.1 illustrates the reductions made relative to the targeted cap.

The emission reductions achieved under the Acid Rain Program and its offshoots have contributed to measurable improvements in air quality, decreases in acid deposition, the beginning of recovery in some acid-sensitive lakes and streams, and improvements in visibility (air clarity). A report of the National Acid Precipitation Assessment Program to Congress estimated that the human health benefits of improved air quality were in the range of $170 billion to $430 billion in 2010 alone.[6] The EPA estimated in 2010 that 20,000–50,000 lives are saved annually by reductions in the number of diseases associated with acid rain.[7] Because the cost of the program was estimated at about $3 billion, its net benefit has been in the range of $167 billion to $427 billion and thus a significant contribution

---

[5] U.S. EPA, "Clean Air Interstate Rule." *op. cit.*

[6] Douglas A. Burns, Jason A. Lynch, Bernard J. Cosby, Mark E. Fenn and Jill S. Baron, "National Acid Precipitation Assessment Program Report to Congress 2011: An Integrated Assessment." U.S. EPA Clean Air Markets Division (January 2012).

[7] U.S. EPA, "Highlights from the Clean Air Act 40th Anniversary Celebration." U.S. Environmental Protection Agency (2010); available online at http://www.epa.gov/air/caa/40th_highlights.html.

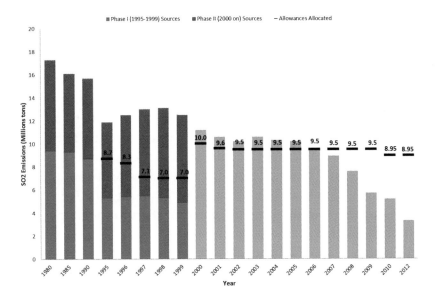

Figure 3.1. Acid Rain Program Results.

Source: U.S. EPA, "Clean Air Interstate Rule." *op. cit.*

to GDP and job creation. Moreover, this benefit number does not capture the number of lives that were saved by the program or other, more intangible benefits, such as improved visibility and ecological conditions.

Enabling and Implementing the Acid Rain Program

The sulfur dioxide reduction legislation in the CAAA simultaneously performed three functions: (1) It standardized an environmental commodity by creating a legally authorized property right (an allowance to emit one ton of sulfur dioxide); (2) it produced the "evidence of ownership"; and (3) it established the infrastructure for the efficient transfer of titles of ownership. These enabling functions created the infrastructure for a market.

The vast majority of entities covered by the Acid Rain Program were power plants (mostly, investor-owned utilities). To a lesser degree, entities included large industrial producers that were major users of coal, such as BP Amoco and International Paper.

The law directed the EPA to implement a phased-in program that first targeted 110 large emitting plants (which comprised more than 400 fuel-consuming power plant units) for the years 1995–1999. Starting in 2000, Phase II extended the limits to all fossil fueled power plants larger than 25 megawatt capacity. Eventually, more than 3,200 units were regulated.

Power plants were allocated a 30-year stream of tradable allowances, each worth one ton of SO_2. In passing the CAAA, the U.S. Congress codified into law much of the economic theory of environmental finance described in the previous chapter. In just 15 short pages, it specified the emissions baseline, reduction targets, and entities covered by the program. The salient features are as follows:[8]

- *Phases and reductions.* Title IV of the CAAA set a goal of reducing annual SO_2 emissions to a level 10 million tons below 1980 levels from all sources (8.4 million tons below 1980 levels from power plants). To achieve these reductions, the law required a two-phase reduction program. Phase I began in 1995, and Phase II began in 2000.

- *Allowance allocation.* Phase I required 100 power plants to reduce their emissions to a level equivalent to the product of an emissions rate of 2.5 pounds of SO_2/mmBTU × an average of their 1985–1987 fuel use.[9] Phase II required approximately 2,000 utilities to reduce their emissions to a level equivalent to the product of an emissions rate of 1.2 pounds of SO_2/mmBTU × the average of their 1985–1987 fuel use. Each allowance permitted a power plant to emit one ton of SO_2 per year.

---

[8]U.S. EPA, "Acid Rain Program." U.S. EPA Clean Air Markets Division (25 July 2012); available online at http://www.epa.gov/airmarkets/progsregs/arp/basic.html.

[9]mmBTU = millions of British thermal units.

- *Allowance registry.* Regulated entities held their allowances in the EPA-administered electronic allowance-tracking registry. The allowance registry facilitated transfer of the allowances from one account to another. Allowances were serialized and designated by vintage year, which denoted the first year they could be used for compliance.

- *Annual reconciliation (compliance).* For each ton of SO_2 emitted in a given year, one allowance was retired; that is, it could no longer be used. Allowances could be bought, sold, or banked for use in subsequent years. At the end of each year, sources were granted a 60-day grace period to ensure that they had sufficient allowances to match their SO_2 emissions during the previous year. If they needed to, they could buy allowances during the grace period. Sources could sell allowances that exceeded their emissions or bank them for use in future years.

- *Allowance trading.* SO_2 allowance trading minimized compliance costs, and because unused allowances could be sold to other program participants, the system encouraged emitters to reduce emissions *beyond* required levels.

- *Flexible compliance.* Each source could choose the most efficient way to reduce its SO_2 emissions. Options were installing new control technology, switching to lower-sulfur fuel, or optimizing existing controls.

- *Stringent monitoring.* Each source had to continuously measure and record its emissions of SO_2, NO_x, and CO_2, as well as heat input, volumetric flow, and opacity. Most emissions were measured by a continuous emissions-monitoring system.

- *Automatic penalties and enforcement.* Any source that failed to hold enough allowances to match its SO_2 emissions for the previous year had to pay the EPA an automatic penalty of $2,000 per ton of emissions in excess of allowances held. The source also had to immediately surrender to the EPA an amount of allowances, issued for the year the payment was due, equaling the tons of excess emissions.

The program required the EPA to conduct an annual allowance auction of current vintage (spot) and seven-year forward allowances. This auction was intended to facilitate market transactions of allowances and achieve price discovery. The mechanism involved auctioning 2.8% of the allowances allocated to the utilities in a competitive market and returning the proceeds to the individual utilities.

The clear and transparent guidelines set by the Acid Rain Program enabled the development of an active market for SO_2 allowances. In fact, over-the-counter trades in forwards and options occurred before the EPA registry was operational and the program went into effect. Organized exchanges entered when the Chicago Board of Trade (CBOT), on behalf of the EPA, competitively won the right to conduct the annual auctions of the spot and forward allowances. Figure 3.2 details the clearing price of the spot and forward allowances at these annual auctions.

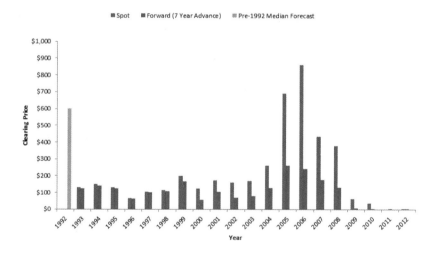

Figure 3.2. Spot and Forward SO_2 Auction Results (1993–2012).
Source: U.S. EPA, "Annual Auction." U.S. EPA Clean Air Markets Division (26 March 2013); available online at http://www.epa.gov/airmarkets/trading/auction.html.

Price History of Acid Rain Program and Its Determinants

Liquid markets and transparent prices contributed to allowing power plants to choose the best option to comply with the Acid Rain Program regulations. In other words, plant operators could compare the risks and costs of the technological solutions with the allowance price. The pricing of SO_2 pollution also led to enormous opportunities for financial institutions and market makers to earn a profit. Given the importance of price in this program, we provide an overview of the program's price history and how price was determined.

Initial Price Forecasts

Experts estimated that these emissions rights would command a high premium. (Some initial estimates ran as high as $1,500 per ton.[10]) Pre-1992 estimates of forecasted prices for sulfur emission allowances ranged from $309 (Resource Data International) to $981 (United Mine Workers of America).[11] Table 3.1 provides a summary of these early estimates.

Because of the uncertainty of a new program, the initial price forecasts were vastly different for various studies, as indicated by Table 3.1. Although the average cost of achieving SO_2 reductions through a scrubber installation was approximately $600 per ton, analysts' forecasts of this price spanned an unexpectedly wide range. A scrubber is a chemical factory built near the smokestack. The flue gas is passed through a limestone mix that removes the sulfur. Uncertainty about scrubber costs for retrofits was another reason

---

[10]On 10 March 1997, EPA Administrator Carol Browner argued, "During the 1990 debate on the Acid Rain Program, industry initially projected the cost of an emission allowance to be $1,500 per ton of sulfur dioxide ... Today, those allowances are selling for less than $100"; see Commonwealth Club of California, "New Initiatives in Environmental Protection." *The Commonwealth* (newsletter) (31 March 1997).

[11]Robert W. Hahn and Carol A. May, "The Behavior of the Allowance Market: Theory and Evidence." *Electricity Journal*, Vol. 7 (March 1994): 2, 28–37.

Table 3.1. Pre-1992 Forecasts of Phase I SO_2 Allowance Prices.

Source	Price forecast ($/ton)
United Mine Workers of America	981
Ohio Coal Development Office	785
Electric Power Research Institute	688
Sierra Club	446
American Electric Power	392
Resource Data International	309

Source: Hahn and May, "Behavior of the Allowance Market." *op. cit.*

the cost estimates were so high, and few believed that low-sulfur coal would become prevalent and relatively cheap.[12]

If the price of the allowances is less than the cost of the scrubber technology, then compliance should be reached using purchasing allowances. Conversely, if the price of the allowances is higher than the cost of the technology, then a user should install the scrubber. Therefore, it would have been reasonable to purchase allowances at prices significantly below the $600 forecast. Early OTC trades occurred between $180 and $300.[13] Those prices suggest that purchasing allowances was the correct investment decision. It was correct in the long-term but wrong in the short-term. The first auction in 1993 had a spot market clearing price of $131. Prices continued to fall, reaching a low of $65 in 1996. Thereafter, prices rose until 2003.

By the end of 2004, prices had risen to $700, primarily because of the impending promulgation of the CAIR, which would significantly lower the SO_2 cap by requiring surrender of additional

---

[12]Based on the authors' conversation with Bruce Braine, Vice President of strategic policy analysis at American Electric Power.

[13]The first publicized trade was of 10,000 allowances at $265 per allowance from Wisconsin Power and Light Company to the Tennessee Valley Authority; see Frank Edward Allen, "Tennessee Valley Authority is Buying Pollution Rights from Wisconsin Power." *Wall Street Journal* (11 May 1992): A12. The second was a trade of 25,000 allowances from ALCOA to Ohio Edison for $300 per allowance; see Joan E. Rigdon, "Alcoa Unit Arranges $7.5 Million Sale of Pollution Allowances to Ohio Edison." *Wall Street Journal* (1 July 1992): A6.

allowances for each ton of emissions. This price rise was exacerbated by an increase in demand for coal-fired generation in response to an increase in natural gas prices and electricity demand. The buyers of this asset class at the outset of the program would have been handsomely rewarded.

Price Determinants in the Long-Term

Over the long-term, the drivers of price in this asset class have been railroad deregulation and the emergence of Powder River Basin coal, scrubber technology and fuel mix, improvements in the mining of low-sulfur eastern U.S. coal, the banking provisions in the Acid Rain Program, and the impact of regulatory changes and legislative uncertainty.

Railroad deregulation and Powder River Basin coal

The deregulation of the railroad industry was a contributing factor to the persistence of low allowance prices. The resultant competition among the major railroads for long-haul traffic from the Powder River Basin (PRB) in Wyoming and Montana to the midwestern United States was particularly fierce. The ability to ship low-sulfur coal from the PRB to places east of the Mississippi at low rates prompted utilities to modify their boilers and switch from high-sulfur and medium-sulfur coals to coals containing much lower sulfur from the West. The choice was not always binary: Blending of eastern bituminous and western subbituminous types of coal was also prevalent. The burning of subbituminous coal emits less SO_2 and NO_x than the burning of bituminous coal.

The effort to find cheaper emission reduction options also led to experimentation that improved understanding and increased the use of fuel blending and the ability to use large amounts of PRB coal without incurring substantial capital costs and/or reducing combustion rates at power plants. This ability, in turn, reduced the cost of reducing emissions.

Scrubber technology and fuel mix

The cost and efficiency of new emissions-control equipment played an important role in keeping emissions allowance prices at low levels. Because SO_2 scrubbers typically reduce emissions by 90% or more, each installed scrubber can free up significant quantities of SO_2 allowances.[14]

Scrubbing technology has improved and installation costs have fallen over time, making scrubbing the economical choice for more plants. The cost of installing and operating scrubbers varies from plant to plant, with upfront costs reaching into the hundreds of millions of dollars. Installation time can range from one to three years.[15]

Note that the regulatory treatment of costs of installing scrubbers influences the extent to which this compliance option is elected. State utility regulatory treatment that allows full cost recovery and an adequate return on investment of the costs of building and operating scrubbers encourages scrubber adoption. Thus, such treatments reduce allowance consumption and possibly increase available supply.

Productivity improvements in low-sulfur eastern coal mining

During the 1990s, substantial improvements in coal mining productivity occurred in mines in both the eastern and western United States.[16] This change allowed substantial increases in the production — and reductions in the prices — of low-sulfur coal. Coupled with the increased technological ability to mix high- and low-sulfur fuels, the improvements also meant that utilities had access to cheaper fuel sources closer to home. The

---

[14] Chicago Climate Exchange, *The Sulfur Dioxide Emission Allowance Trading Program: Market Architecture, Market Dynamics and Pricing* (Chicago: Chicago Climate Exchange, 2004), p. 16.

[15] Chicago Climate Exchange, *Sulfur Dioxide Emission Allowance Trading Program*, *op. cit.*

[16] U.S. EIA, "Annual Energy Review 2011." U.S. Energy Information Administration (September 2012); available online at http://www.eia.gov/totalenergy/data/annual/pdf/aer.pdf.

allowance markets had a positive impact in forcing low-sulfur coal producers in the eastern states to compete with their western counterparts.

Banking

The Acid Rain Program provided emission sources with temporal flexibility through banking. It created an incentive for polluters to decrease emissions below allowable levels sooner than required, resulting in human health and environmental benefits occurring earlier than expected. Banking delivered liquidity, provided a cushion for price volatility, and created a safety mechanism for unforeseen market events. For example, over the five years of Phase I, regulated sources reduced emissions by 10.5 million metric tons more than required and were able use those banked allowances to cushion the effect of the declining cap in Phase II.[17]

Regulatory changes and legislative uncertainty

Regulatory changes (such as tightened SO_2 emissions limits) and legislative uncertainty (such as inaction by the legislative body, which forced action by executive mandate that was eventually challenged in courts) can and did have an impact on the SO_2 emission allowance market in both the long- and the short-term.[18]

As demonstrated throughout this book, emissions markets are extremely dependent on policy developments. Even though enabling legislation in the CAAA gave birth to the Acid Rain Program, regulatory uncertainty and court battles have, for the time

---

[17]Jeremy Schreifels and Sam Napolitano, "Efficient, Effective, and Credible Cap and Trade: Lessons Learned from the U.S. Acid Rain Program." (2007); available online at http://www.caep.org.cn/english/paper/Lesson-from-U.S.-Emission-Trading-Program-Edited-by-Jeremy.pdf.

[18]Another type of regulatory impact arises from regulatory changes related to other pollutants. Because burning coal releases carbon dioxide, sulfur dioxide, nitrogen oxides, and mercury, regulation of any of these pollutants may have an impact on the others.

being, greatly damaged the functioning of a cap-and-trade system in the Acid Rain Program.

As the Acid Rain Program entered its first decade, various proposals to tighten the cap were made. For example, in 1997, Senator Daniel P. Moynihan (D, New York) proposed legislation that would have reduced the SO_2 cap by 50%. Then, in 2002, the George W. Bush Administration proposed the Clear Skies Act, which would have tightened the SO_2 cap by 65%. Finally, in 2005, in the absence of Congressional action, the Bush Administration promulgated the CAIR, which proposed a stringent cap on SO_2 emissions of 70% below their 2003 level. These actions caused a run-up in prices.

In 2006, however, North Carolina, a few other states, and a few utilities sued the EPA, arguing that the interstate trading allowed under CAIR was inconsistent with a provision of the Clean Air Act of 2003. In July 2008, the Circuit Court of Appeals for the District of Columbia ruled on this lawsuit by vacating CAIR completely. This ruling basically invalidated the core principle of the cap-and-trade system that had been enabled by the CAAA. In one day, SO_2 prices plummeted from $315 to $115. Neither the outgoing Bush Administration nor the incoming Barak Obama Administration challenged the ruling, and Congress was unable to provide a simple legislative fix. Given the unlikely scenario that more stringent caps would be put into place, along with mounting regulatory uncertainty, SO_2 prices collapsed. This uncertainty depressed allowance prices to $65 by March 2009. In the EPA auction, future vintage allowances sold for $6.65.

In 2010, the Obama Administration proposed a replacement of CAIR. The objective was to limit annual SO_2 and NO_x emissions in 28 states. The proposed rule established state-specific emissions caps for power plant emissions but limited interstate trading. The rule was finalized as the Cross-State Air Pollution Rule (CSAPR, or "Caspar," as it is commonly called) which allowed for intrastate trading but only limited trading between two groups of states. This rule was also challenged in court, and in August 2012, the DC

Circuit Court vacated CSAPR and ordered the EPA to keep CAIR in force pending a review of CSAPR. In March 2013, the Obama Administration appealed the decision to the Supreme Court.

The courts struck down CSAPR and as of 2014, are forcing the EPA to develop a replacement rule, which will take several years at least. In the interim, CAIR will remain in place.

What is driving further SO_2 reductions, in actuality, is the Mercury and Air Toxics Standards rule that sets limits for new power plants.[19] As a result, CAIR is no longer binding.[20]

The importance of the impact of sovereign risk on the prices of environmental assets cannot be *overestimated*. This recurring theme will be further discussed in Chapter 4.

Price Determinants in the Short-Term

Factors that affect electricity demand and the composition of electricity supply affect allowance consumption and have the potential to significantly influence SO_2 allowance prices. Utilities may burn more coal in a short period for three main reasons: weather, demand for power from the various sectors, and the price of competing fuels.

Seasonal weather patterns and natural disasters

Short-term fluctuations in total electricity production arise from variations in weather conditions (hot summer days, cold winter days) and economic activity, particularly industrial production. SO_2 emissions tend to be highest during the summer quarter, reflecting the system-wide peak load associated with the operation of air conditioners. The second-highest quarter for SO_2 emissions is the winter quarter. These patterns make clear that SO_2 allowance consumption is driven by the degree of weather extremity during summer and winter. Market analysts may consider heating-degree days and

---

[19] U.S. EPA, "Fact Sheet: Updates of the Limits for New Power Plants Under the Mercury and Air Toxics Standards (MATS)." U.S. Environmental Protection Agency (28 March 2013); available online at http://www.epa.gov/mats/pdfs/20130328fs.pdf.

[20] Authors' conversation with Bruce Braine.

cooling-degree days in major coal-based regions to be a factor in assessing SO_2 allowance prices. Another factor is lack of rainfall, which can decrease power output from hydroelectric dams.

Natural disasters, such as hurricanes, may damage facilities that produce gas, thereby driving gas prices higher. Utilities then change from gas to coal, thereby increasing emissions and the demand for allowances.

Competing energy sources and fuel switching

In the case of SO_2, nearly all allowance consumption is related to coal-based electricity production. With generation from natural gas-fired plants increasing, natural gas has become an easy alternative for utilities with fuel-switching ability. The decline in natural gas prices since 2011 has motivated power generators to switch to gas-fired plants instead of other electricity-generation resources. The flexibility to switch between coal- and gas-fired power generation is generally a factor reflected in SO_2 emission allowance prices.

Figure 3.3 highlights the impact of some of the short-term and long-term price drivers on the price of allowances. Early low prices for allowances were a result of switching from high- to low-sulfur coal and installation of scrubbers. The subsequent price increase is the result of the increase in industrial activity and the Clear Skies announcement. Also, exogenous effects, such as Hurricanes Katrina and Rita and train derailments, caused prices to peak. The downward trend from the peak is primarily a result of regulatory uncertainty.

Use of this Asset Class as a Financing Mechanism

In addition to the relationship between price and technology decisions in the SO_2 allowance spot prices, this market has a long-term price structure. On any given day, prices are available for a stream of future compliance years. This relationship is known as the forward curve. The first registered trade in the EPA was for a 30-year stream of allowances.

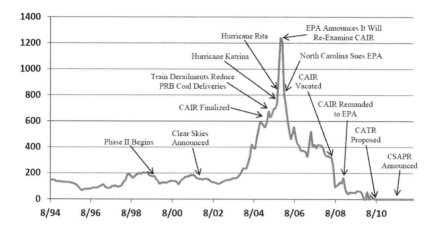

Figure 3.3. Impact of Weather, Substitutes, and Regulations on SO_2 Allowance Prices, 1994–2012.

Note: PRB refers to Powder River Basin; CATR is the Clean Air Transport Rule.

Source: Data on spot prices compiled by Power & Energy Analytic Resources from Cantor Fitzgerald until 11 September 2001 and from ICAP United thereafter.

Because scrubbers are expensive (costing up to $50 million or more), utilities borrow the money to install a scrubber and pay for it from future sales of emission allowances. The following example illustrates a financing approach that took price and technology factors into consideration. It also highlights the initial participation of financial players in the SO_2 market in earlier years.

In 1993, Henderson Municipal Power & Light in Kentucky sold 150,000 tons of sulfur dioxide pollution allowances to Centre Financial Products (CFP), a boutique investment bank, for $26.8 million.[21] The sale of allowances represented the third-largest SO_2 trade since 1992 (as of 1995). This was a unique sale because the revenue from the sale was used to finance and install scrubbers in the Station Two plant of Henderson Municipal, planned in April 1993. The scrubbers were estimated to cost $41 million. By installing these

---

[21] Clean Air Act Implementation: Hearings before the Subcommittee on Energy and Power of the Committee on Energy and Commerce, House of Representatives (29 September and 5 October 1994).

scrubbers, however, Henderson Municipal was able to decrease its sulfur emissions by 95%.[22] At the market price, the proceeds from the sale of allowances would be enough to finance the scrubbers.

In September 1993, CFP, in turn, sold the original 150,000 allowances to Carolina Power & Light (CP&L). CP&L used very low-sulfur coal in its generators. Thus, for it, the marginal cost of removing the remaining sulfur by a scrubber was higher than the industry average. In 1993, CP&L estimated this cost to be approximately $500 per ton of SO_2. Comparatively, in March 1993, the EPA auctioned 150,010 allowances at the CBOT at an average price of $143. Furthermore, CP&L had little interest in installing scrubbing equipment at the time because scrubbing technology was still evolving.[23]

CP&L planned to introduce fuel switching and demand-side management to reduce emissions but, nonetheless, expected to exceed its EPA emission allotment. For the years from 2000 to 2009, the EPA allocated 143,968 allowances to CP&L per year. By CP&L estimates, if it failed to make any changes in the way it operated its system, it would emit approximately 230,000 tons of sulfur dioxide in the year 2000, creating a deficit of 86,000 tons. As a result, CP&L would have to reduce its SO_2 emissions or purchase additional allowances.

CP&L first purchased 85,103 allowance credits at the 1993 EPA auction for $11,490,000 for an average price of $135 per credit. Requiring additional credits, the company entered into a formal agreement with CFP in 2000 for the purchase of 150,000 emission allowances for $47,250,000.[24] Using an 8% market interest rate over eight years, the discounted present value of that payment in

---

[22] Richard Sandor, *Good Derivatives: A Story of Financial and Environmental Innovation* (New York: John Wiley & Sons, 2012).

[23] State of North Carolina Utilities Commission–Raleigh, Docket No. E-2, Sub 642.

[24] "Execution of Proprietary Title IV Sulfur Dioxide Emission Allowances Purchase Agreement, Together with Note and Security Agreement." Signed by Robert M. Williams.

1993 was $27,560,000. CP&L needed to raise additional capital or borrow money to pay for the SO_2 allowances, which posed a problem for CFP. Not only did CFP have to guarantee the interest rate for CP&L's capital increase, but it also had to guarantee the price and quantity of the allowances. To solve the first problem, CFP agreed to lend money to CP&L. Solving the second problem was more challenging. Because the EPA registry was not operational at the time the deal was consummated, CFP wrote the contract so that it would close when the registry was inaugurated.

Although the price and quantity of allowances were fixed through a forward purchase agreement with another utility, CFP still had to hedge against the interest rate risk. Because no futures market in corporate bonds existed, CFP had to use the U.S. Treasury bond futures contract offered by the CBOT, which created basis risk. To mitigate this risk, CFP decided to also buy puts on the T-bond futures contract.

This last step was critical because CFP bought and sold the allowances at the same price. The profit came from the price at which CFP bought the debt from CP&L and then sold it to an insurance company. Interest rates fell between the time the contract was signed and the time the deal was closed. The structured transaction turned out to be very profitable in spite of the fact that CFP made little money on the purchase and sale of the allowances.

In the end, CP&L secured its future allowances at favorable prices and financed the transaction at attractive interest rates. The seller of the allowances (Henderson) also fared well. The sale and purchase were completed at a higher price than the OTC bid and a lower price than the OTC offer. This transaction seems simple, but a close examination reveals that the allowance market enabled not only a low-cost compliance tool but also a financing vehicle.

Investment Opportunities in this Asset Class

The constraints imposed by the SO_2 cap-and-trade program also created opportunities. So far, we have focused on prices and allowances as an asset class, but other, related assets might be considered as investments.

Air Pollution Control

As previously mentioned, a major application for scrubbers is flue gas desulfurization (FGD), which constitutes a major share of the scrubbing business. Traditionally, FGD referred to wet scrubbers that remove SO_2 emissions from large electric utility boilers used for coal combustion. FGD systems are being increasingly used, however, to remove SO_2 emissions from process plants, including smelters, acid plants, refineries, and pulp and paper mills.

FGD scrubbing systems may be wet or dry. Wet scrubbers use liquid to remove particles or gases from exhaust systems. In contrast, dry scrubbers operate by spraying chemicals that neutralize flue gas and do not use a lot of water. Thus, dry scrubbing systems generally do not require wastewater management/treatment. Dry scrubbers are most commonly used to control SO_2 and other acid gases from utility and industrial boilers and incinerators.[25]

For NO_x at coal plants, selective catalytic reduction systems (SCRs) are installed at the plants. In an SCR, ammonia is injected, with the power plant flue gas, into a device that contains a catalyst to improve NO_x removal efficiencies. According to the EPA, SCR can achieve up to 90% NO_x removal. SCR in combination with SO_2 scrubbers can also achieve up to 80% mercury removal.[26]

Today, with a significant number of units in the United States already having installed scrubbers and an increase in the use of natural gas, domestic opportunities in air pollution-control equipment

---

[25]U.S. EPA, "Lesson 9: Flue Gas Desulfurization (Acid Gas Removal) Systems." U.S. Environmental Protection Agency (2013); available online at http://yosemite.epa.gov/oaqps/eogtrain.nsf/b81bacb527b016d785256e4a004c0393/d4ec501f07c0e03a85256b6c006caf64/$FILE/si412c_lesson9.pdf.

[26]"IPM Analysis of the Final Mercury and Air Toxics Standards (MATS). Documentation: Updates to EPA Base Case v4.10_MATS." (December 2011); available online at http://www.epa.gov/airmarket/progsregs/epa-ipm/toxics.html.

are limited.[27] The next promising opportunities for pollution-control equipment are in Asia's emerging economies. Such countries as China and India are not only highly coal dependent in their generation of electricity but are also expecting further emissions-control policy mandates.

China has become the world's largest emitter of SO_2. In 2010, absolute SO_2 emissions in China approached 31 million tons, with approximately 66% coming from industry. For comparison, the United States had 5.17 million tons in 2010 in SO_2 emissions (from electric power generation), which had been reduced from 17.5 million tons in 1980. China's government set a goal in the 11th Five-Year Plan (2006–2010) of a 10% reduction below 2005 levels of SO_2 emissions by 2010. In the 12th Five-Year Plan, that goal became an 8% reduction for SO_2 and a 10% reduction for NO_x. Several pilot cap-and-trade programs for emissions reductions have built some knowledge of the markets but have been less than distinguished in achieving reductions. China needs significantly greater rigor in its emissions monitoring and reporting as well as improved enforcement of emissions limits and allowance-holding requirements if the benefits of emissions markets are to be realized.

The social consequences of these emissions are devastating for China. The country currently has 16 of the 20 most polluted cities in the world. Some 500,000 people die prematurely from respiratory illnesses annually. Healthcare costs associated with air pollution amount to approximately 4% of China's gross domestic product (GDP). Furthermore, the environmental problems are not confined to China's borders. Japan and South Korea, in particular, have been adversely affected by acid rain. This pollution also travels across the

---

[27] Between 2007 and 2011, U.S. coal-fired power plants invested more than $30 billion in FGD systems. Scrubbers were installed in about 110 coal-fired plants in 34 states during this time (around 60% of U.S. coal-fired, steam electric generation capacity); see "U.S. Coal-Fired Power Plants Invested More than $30bn on Scrubbers in Four Years." *Power Engineering* (25 March 2013); available online at http://www.power-eng.com/articles/2013/03/us-coal-fired-power-plants-invested-more-than-30bn-on-scrubbers-.html.

Pacific Ocean and may be responsible for as much as 25% of particulate matter pollution in California on certain days.

A simple comparison might provide a sense of the magnitude of the challenge China faces in addressing the issue of acid rain. In the United States, the reduction of nine million tons of SO_2 was worth approximately $125 billion annually in reduced medical costs. Because China's current SO_2 emissions are approximately 31 million tons (or six times the size of the U.S. electric power industry's emissions) and China has approximately the same landmass as the United States but four times the population, a nine million ton SO_2 reduction could be four times more valuable in China, generating approximately $500 billion annually in reduced medical costs. Therefore, a SO_2 emissions reduction of 18 million tons could avoid more than $1 trillion in contingent liability that hinders economic growth.

Even without mandates, power plants in East Asia will spend $4.8 billion on FGD this year, which represents 63% of the total worldwide expenditure. Including repair parts, upgrades, and such inputs as lime and limestone, total expenditures by the power sector for FGD in the worldwill exceed $15 billion in 2013.[28] The majority of the FGD sales in East Asia will be to power plants in China. Most of the sales in China will be to new power plants, but some retrofits to old power plants without FGD will take place. China has more scrubbers than any other country but also more power plants without scrubbers. China continues to spend more for new FGD systems than the rest of the world combined.[29]

---

[28]"East Asia Will Spend $4.8 Billion on FGD This Year." *Power Air Quality Insights*, No. 92 (31 January 2013); available online at http://www.mcilvainecompany.com/Decision_Tree/subscriber/Tree/DescriptionTextLinks/Power%20Air%20Quality%20January%2031%20 2013.htm. The figure does not include repairs, or inputs such as as lime and limestone.

[29]China is the largest consumer of limestone and a leading producer of lime and limestone. It has a large lime reserve — 190,000 metric tons as of 2010, according to the 2010 U.S. Geological Survey, which is available at http://minerals.usgs.gov/minerals/pubs/country/2010/myb3-2010-ch.pdf.

The Financial Sector

As emissions markets mature, the growth of organized futures and options exchanges presents several opportunities for investors. Investors could gain exposure to the emissions marketplace by purchasing equity in specialized listed exchanges. Emitters/users can similarly gain access to this market by buying or selling SO_2 spot and derivatives contracts and using the market for hedging purposes.

Exchanges offer enormous opportunities. Exchanges add value because they reduce the transaction costs of buying and selling allowances and make efficient risk transfer possible.[30] Opportunities also exist for financial players, such as investment banks, commercial banks, and brokers. Regulatory uncertainty in the United States suggests, however, that large financial institutions will play a diminished role in emissions markets. Evidence is the recent closing of trading desks by major investment banks.[31]

The preceding discussion of the role of financial players and exchanges in the U.S. Acid Rain Program could be informative for emerging economies that are contemplating establishing emissions markets. China and India, for example, have the potential to be large emissions markets. There could also be a role for commercial and investment banks and other market makers in jurisdictions where certain regulatory requirements on commercial and investment banks' trading activities are not in place. As was true in the United States, financial institutions play an important role in providing liquidity and efficiency to nascent markets.

Conclusion

Although the SO_2 program is nominally still in place, the legal battles, regulatory uncertainty, and limitations on trading have virtually stalled market activity as of this writing. With regard to

---

[30] Estimates suggest that transaction costs for compliance in the Acid Rain Program were reduced from $500 million to $20 million because of the existence of exchanges.

[31] "London Banks Quit Carbon Trading." *Financial Times* (18 November 2003).

this particular pollutant, the United States has, in an ironic turn of events, turned its back on one of the most successful environmental programs ever put into place. Because of lack of congressional action and the DC Circuit Court's interpretation of the law, the United States has reverted to administrative solutions to climate change mitigation. This turn of events has resulted in largely bifurcated emissions markets and, therefore, limited options for utilities to reduce emissions.

The Acid Rain Program in the United States — specifically, its allowance-trading component — is a policy tool that proved to be successful from an economic and environmental standpoint. Despite regulatory setbacks, the Acid Rain Program built a track record that proves the system worked. Moreover, it helped build an institutional infrastructure in terms of compliance tools, monitoring, financial expertise, and technical expertise that are now about to be emulated in other parts of the world. It opened financial possibilities for entrepreneurs and investors in exchanges, and pollution-control companies in the United States have been expanded to carbon markets in other jurisdictions (see Chapter 4). Opportunities for market participants in the SO_2 and NO_x space will probably be present as emerging economies with serious pollution problems institute environmental regulations. That future will create further demand for these market participants' products, services, and ingenuity.

The Acid Rain Program also inspired the expansion of the cap-and-trade concept to deal with the perceived threat of climate change. In addition, it has been applied to Europe in the form of the European Union Emissions Trading Scheme.

Chapter 4

GREENHOUSE GAS POLLUTANTS
AS AN ASSET CLASS

Global warming has continued unabated since 1896 when Nobel Prize-winning Swedish scientist Svante Arrhenius first predicted it on the basis of increases in atmospheric CO_2. The pace of warming, measured through the concentration of CO_2 in the atmosphere rather than actual temperature, has increased from roughly 316 parts per million (ppm) in 1958 to about 400 ppm today.[1,2]

Global warming can be the result of natural causes, such as the global water cycle, volcanic eruptions, or natural aerosols and biogenic emissions. But the evidence is strong that combustion of fossil fuels, commercial agriculture, deforestation, and other man-made causes related to industrialization have led to a rapid increase in CO_2, methane, and other greenhouse gas (GHG) emissions in the Earth's atmosphere — and thus to higher temperatures.[3] The effects are evident in the fact that the top 10 warmest years have all occurred since 1998; 2010 was the warmest year since the data began in 1880.

Our view is that the current debate about what causes global warming and political attitudes toward the subject are irrelevant

---

[1] The reference year 1958 is important because it denotes the first comprehensive measure of CO_2 levels in the atmosphere by Charles Keeling from the Scripps Institution of Oceanography.

[2] Measuring the temperature of a whole planet is difficult, but sound theoretical reasons exist why the temperature of the Earth's surface should be related to atmospheric CO_2 concentration; see the Intergovernmental Panel on Climate Change; available online at www.ipcc.ch.

[3] According to the Glossary of the UN Framework Convention on Climate Change, a GHG is any gas that absorbs infrared radiation in the atmosphere; see http://unfccc.int/resource/cd_roms/na1/ghg_ inventories/english/8_glossary/Glossary.htm.

and do not provide sufficient reason for inaction. From a purely risk management view, when opportunities exist to reduce the dangers of global warming that are cheaper than the catastrophic losses global warming may create, any and all options must be considered to combat it.[4]

Acid rain, our focus in Chapter 3, is primarily caused by SO_2 and NO_x, but the phenomenon of global warming on which we focus in this chapter is caused by many pollutants.[5] Moreover, acid rain pollutants are regional pollutants; that is, their impact is generally restricted to the areas in which they are emitted (for example, the East Coast of the United States). Global warming is a much larger problem than acid rain because it is believed to be caused by an *overall* increase in the atmosphere's CO_2 concentration. The effects of global warming are multifold, and all countries are affected in one way or another. Global warming can cause climatic shocks, including variability in precipitation, flooding, changes in trade wind flows, and an increase in the intensity of extreme climate events, such as hurricanes. These events can have an economy-wide impact by affecting crop productivity, desertification (the degradation of arable land to desert), animal and human health, and sea levels. In addition, unlike acid rain, the effects of global warming are long-term, so it truly is an intergenerational problem.

The policy responses to global warming include incentive schemes that shift demand away from fossil fuels and toward renewable energy and enhance fossil fuel efficiencies. Examples of policy measures are direct subsidies to promote renewable energy, policy mandates requiring increased energy-efficiency or that a certain percentage of power be generated from renewable sources, and preferential electricity tariffs for renewable energy generation.[6]

---

[4]This view is similar to those expressed by Richard A. Posner in *Catastrophe: Risk and Response* (Oxford, UK: Oxford University Press, 2004).

[5]GHGs include but are not limited to water vapor, carbon dioxide, methane, nitrous oxide, hydrochlorofluorocarbons, ozone, hydrofluorocarbons, perfluorocarbons, and sulfur hexafluoride.

[6]Preferential electricity tariffs are special (higher) rates provided as incentives to promote electricity generation from a certain source.

In accordance with the previous discussion of acid rain, we will focus on the use of market-based mechanisms to reduce global warming — specifically, cap-and-trade.

The European Union Emissions Trading Scheme (EU ETS) is the largest and most successful implementation of the cap-and-trade model for GHGs. The EU ETS is a market for carbon permits among affected European companies within the 27 member states of the EU (the EU-27). Its goal is to achieve the GHG emissions-reduction goals agreed upon in the Kyoto Protocol, which will be discussed later, and reductions expected from future international agreements. So far, the EU ETS has enabled the EU-27 to successfully reduce its GHG emissions by 13% below its 1990 emissions levels. Currently, the EU ETS commands a market size in excess of $170 billion and accounts for nearly 75% of all international carbon trading.[7] The dynamics of the EU ETS are the principal drivers behind global carbon emissions markets today, and its success has led nations outside the EU to adopt a similar approach.

The purpose of this chapter is to use the EU ETS to demonstrate the role of cap-and-trade in reducing GHG emissions, a discussion that should be of interest to corporations, investors, and financial analysts. Under a cap-and-trade system limiting GHG emissions, corporations face new challenges and have to understand how to manage new risks and opportunities. Financial analysts need to understand the specific nature of carbon risk that corporations and their sectors are exposed to. In addition, analysts need to understand the new business challenges, commodity risks and opportunities, and most importantly, trading opportunities that emerge as a result of emissions trading. Firms and entrepreneurs in finance, agribusiness, and industry have important investment opportunities in the sector. Climate change can affect the insurance industry, the health

---

[7]The source for the market size data is Carbon Finance at the World Bank, "State and Trends of the Carbon Market 2012." Washington, DC (May 2012); available online at http://siteresources.worldbank.org/INTCARBONFINANCE/Resources/State_and_Trends_2012_Web_Optimized_19035_Cvr&Txt_LR.pdf.

care industry, agricultural production, and resource scarcity. Quantifying and understanding the specific nature of climate change risk is crucial in asset management and portfolio allocation.

Several financial products have emerged because of the EU ETS. Moreover, emissions trading has provided new opportunities for financial institutions to create over-the-counter markets and new exchanges. New methods of financing, similar to those for SO_2 allowances, have been created. This chapter provides the fundamentals to help the reader understand the drivers in asset classes related to global warming.

Global Warming: Causes and Public Policy Responses

Largely as a result of rapid industrialization, the concentration of GHGs in the Earth's atmosphere has been steadily increasing since the Industrial Revolution. Figure 4.1 shows that the rise in GHG concentrations closely correlates with the start of industrialization in the 19th century. In 1958, Charles Keeling from the Scripps Institution of Oceanography used scientific techniques to measure

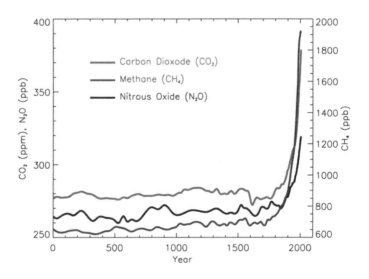

Figure 4.1. Historical GHG Concentrations.

Note: ppb = parts per billion.

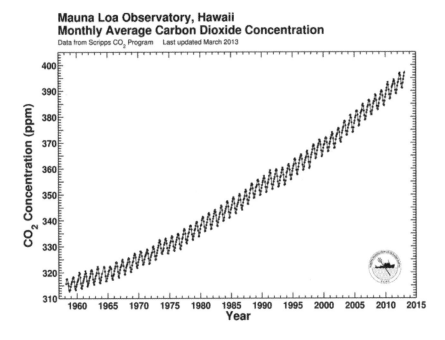

Figure 4.2. Keeling Curve Measuring Atmospheric CO_2 Levels, 1958–2013.

Note: Data measured in Mauna Loa, Hawaii; last updated March 2013.

CO_2 levels in the Earth's atmosphere. The Keeling curve, presented in Figure 4.2, roughly matches the year-on-year increase in fossil fuel combustion and helped to draw the world's attention to global warming. The Keeling curve in May 2013 showed that atmospheric concentration of CO_2 had reached 400 ppm, the highest level in at least three million years.[8] A large majority of scientists believe that the principal cause of this steady and alarming increase in atmospheric CO_2 levels is human activity (that is, the increase is "anthropogenic"). This is the focus of our discussion.

Historically, the developed nations in Europe, North America, and Australia have been the primary contributors to GHG emissions. The United States was, until recently, the single largest

---

[8] See the Intergovernmental Panel on Climate Change publications; available online http://www.ipcc.ch/publications_and_data/publications_and_data_reports.shtml#.UZUeZUqfVKI.

contributor to GHG emissions, followed by the EU. Rapid industrialization in the developing world, however — the combustion
of fossil fuels — is causing many developing countries to have
high growth rates in emissions. In 2008, China emerged as the
largest GHG emitter, with 6.5 billion metric tons of CO_2 per year.[9]
India, the second most populous country, is also experiencing rapid
increases in GHG emissions.

The sources for GHG emissions include electric utilities, manufacturing, and industrial entities producing these pollutants from
either fossil fuel combustion or as by-products of chemical processing. The primary pollutant believed to cause global warming is carbon dioxide, which is largely emitted from the combustion of fossil
fuels in electricity production, transportation, and manufacturing.
Other contributors are methane released from landfills and agriculture (especially from the digestive systems of livestock), nitrous
oxide from fertilizers, gases used for refrigeration and industrial processes, and the loss of forests that would otherwise store CO_2. The
primary GHGs and their designations are as follows:[10]

- carbon dioxide (CO_2),
- methane (CH_4),
- nitrous oxide (N_2O),
- sulfur hexafluoride (SF_6),
- hydrofluorocarbons (HCFCs), and
- perfluorocarbons (PFCs).

Each of the six GHGs has a different ability to trap heat, which
is called its "global warming potential." For example, one ton of
methane is roughly 26 times as potent as the equivalent amount of
carbon dioxide. For the purposes of measurement relative to their
global warming potential and the presentation of GHG emissions
in standardized terms, emissions from all six gases are expressed in

---

[9] UN ESCAP, *Statistical Yearbook for Asia and the Pacific 2011*. UN Economic and
Social Commission for Asia and the Pacific; available online at http://www.unescap.org/
stat/data/syb2011/II-Environment/Air-pollution-and-climate-change.asp.

[10] Some of the designations are not precise chemical formulae but are in common use in the
discussion of environmental finance and policy.

CO_2-equivalent terms. Appendix B provides an illustration of this mechanism and how it relates to emissions trading. The mechanics are shown to illustrate how the potential value of GHG reductions from various sources can have different impacts on supply and market price.

The policy response to climate change has largely been through the Kyoto Protocol of 1997, which had its genesis at the Earth Summit in Rio de Janeiro in 1992. The Earth Summit established the UN Framework Convention on Climate Change, which was the basis for the negotiation and agreement of the Kyoto Protocol. The Kyoto Protocol, ratified in 2004 (but not by the United States), limited GHG emissions to 5.2% below 1990 levels as an initial goal to be achieved between 2008 and 2012. The protocol included all six greenhouse gases and emissions from the industrial, electricity, and manufacturing sectors from 37 countries (most of which were developed) and set binding emissions targets. The signatory countries agreed to various national reduction targets based on historical emissions levels and stages of economic development. The Kyoto Protocol action to set the emissions baseline on the basis of historical emissions levels was similar to the process followed in the Acid Rain Program.

Importantly, the Kyoto Protocol provided several market-based avenues to meet the mandated national targets. The idea behind the Kyoto market mechanisms was to have flexibility in achieving each national target at the lowest costs with a goal of collectively achieving the overall GHG targets. These market mechanisms include (1) emissions trading; (2) a "clean development" mechanism, whereby developed countries can buy carbon allowances, called "Certified Emission Reductions" (CERs), that result from carbon-friendly investment in developing countries that lack GHG commitments; and (3) "joint implementation," whereby developed countries with binding emissions targets can earn emission-reduction units (ERUs) for investments among themselves in projects that reduce carbon emissions.

Under the Kyoto Protocol, the EU as a whole had a reduction target of 8% below 1990 levels. The EU shared this burden: Its members reallocated their Kyoto emission reduction commitments among themselves and launched their own initially CO_2-focused program, the EU Emissions Trading Scheme (EU ETS), as the centerpiece of the climate policy. Therefore, some countries had steep targets whereas others had much more gradual emission reduction slopes. Still others were allowed to increase their emissions. For example, Germany and Austria agreed to reduce their emissions to levels 21% and 13% below 1990 levels, respectively, whereas Ireland and Greece were allowed to increase their emissions by 13% above 1990 levels.[11] Finland and France were required to keep their emissions stable at 1990 levels. The purpose of this "bubble" within the Kyoto Protocol was to assist the EU in reaching its overall Kyoto target of 8% "with the least possible diminution of economic development and employment."[12] The core elements of the EU ETS were set out in a directive issued by the European Commission on 23 October 2003. Policymakers from other nations with large emissions, such as China and India, can learn from the EU model on the applicability of achieving national GHG targets by using "bubbles" among their states and provinces.

The EU ETS was implemented in three phases:

   (I) An initial pilot, often referred to as EU ETS Phase I, operated from 2005 to 2007.

  (II) EU ETS Phase II operated from 2008 to 2012 to achieve the agreed Kyoto reductions over that period.

(III) EU ETS Phase III operates currently — that is, from 2013 through 2020.

These phases are discussed in detail later in this chapter.

---

[11]Average 2008–2011 emissions in Ireland were 11.5% higher than the base-year level but below the burden-sharing target of 13% for the period 2008–2012; see http://www.eea.europa.eu/publications/ghg-trends-and-projections-2012.

[12]European Council, "Greenhouse Gas Emission Allowance Trading Scheme." Directive 2003/87/EC of the European Parliament and of the Council (13 October 2003); available online at http://europa.eu/legislation_summaries/energy/european_energy_policy/l28012_en.htm.

With this background on the Kyoto mechanisms provided, we turn to the results of the EU ETS in the next section.

Results of the Public Policy Responses

The EU ETS more than achieved its established environmental goal, and there are strong reasons existing to believe it was accomplished with the least cost to society. This outcome was facilitated by the cap-and-trade market mechanism, which allowed flexibility in achieving emissions targets by establishing a price on emissions. Like the Acid Rain Program, the EU ETS — by setting a price on pollution, establishing a reduction target, and allowing flexibility in achieving the goal — proved that the cap-and-trade model can work even in the case of a multinational effort to manage a multi-source global pollutant.

From an environmental standpoint, the program has delivered significant emission reductions between its inception in 2005 and its third phase. The European Environment Agency states not only that the mandated EU-15 (the 15 countries that were EU members as of the 2004 enlargement) are on track to meet their 8% reduction target but also that they have overachieved the target by 4.9%, or 211 million metric tons per year. A Center for European Policy Studies (CEPS) study confirms that the EU ETS drove down emissions in Phase II beyond levels that could have been caused by the economic recession that struck in late 2008.[13] These studies use EU-wide emissions and EU ETS sectoral emissions data, together with economic data, to point out that the reductions were achieved at the same time as significant improvements in *emission intensity* (which refers to the amount of emissions per unit of production or GDP). Other estimates of the specific role the EU ETS played in EU emission reductions indicate that it accounted for about 40% of the

---

[13] Anton Georgiev, Monica Alessi, Christian Egenhofer and Noriko Fujiwara, "The EU Emissions Trading System and Climate Policy towards 2050: Real Incentives to Reduce Emissions and Drive Innovation?" *CEPS Special Reports and Climate Change* (January 2011).

3% EU emission reduction achieved in 2008 alone.[14] In addition, these observed reduction trends are continuing well beyond 2008.

Note that EU emission reductions have been achieved even as GDP has increased, which suggests that low-carbon economic growth is feasible. The EU economic numbers suggest that, although the output of the EU economy has recovered to about the 2007 level, emissions are significantly lower than in 2007. Compared with 1990 levels, EU-27 emissions are 17% lower, even though GDP grew by more than 40% and manufacturing by more than 12%. With regard to the impact on competitiveness, a 2011 study summarizing published literature and data from more than 2,000 European firms covered by the ETS[15] concluded that the program did not significantly affect profits, employment, or added value, despite concerns expressed by some affected firms and sectors.

The EU Emissions Trading Scheme

The fundamental structure and operational mechanism for the EU ETS mirror the Acid Rain Program. The EU ETS operates through the allocation and trading of GHG allowances, the EU Allowances (EUAs). Each EUA represents one ton of carbon dioxide or its equivalent and is the EU emissions trading unit.

The EUAs are held as serialized electronic records within an electronic registry operated *and* overseen by the European Commission. These web-accessible registry systems contain and track transfers of the issued EUAs, including those held by non-emitting entities (and individuals) that wish to participate in trading. The registry system can also be used for tracking and monitoring the binding compliance targets for mandated entities and installations

[14]"Emissions from EU ETS down 3% in 2008." [Press release] New Carbon Finance (16 February 2009).
[15]C. Egenhofer *et al.*, "The EU Emissions Trading System and Climate Policy towards 2050." CEPS Special Report (2011).

within the EU. At the end of each year, the European Commission matches the actual emissions of regulated entities with their surrendered EUAs. Non-compliance leads to a penalty of €100 per ton in addition to making available to surrendering the required allowances to meet compliance. Recall that the same model was applied for SO_2. In fact, even the term "allowance" was borrowed from the Acid Rain Program.

However, some points of divergence between the operational setup of the Acid Rain Program and that of the EU ETS are worth noting. Specifically, individual EU member states developed their own national EUA registries. These registries were then interlinked in an EU-wide network to facilitate transfer among the various registries. This model differs from the Acid Rain model, where a single centralized registry managed allowance transfers.

The creation of multiple registries was a complex undertaking and created some operational inefficiencies and delays in early days of the EU ETS. In the initial days, national registries also reflected some sovereign risks that do not exist for a single-nation centralized registry. In the later days of the EU ETS, some fraudulent transactions and allowance theft took place that perhaps could have been avoided with a single-registry system.

The EU ETS is a far more complex system than the Acid Rain Program. It involves many nations, multiple gases from diverse sectors versus two gases largely from electricity generators, and implementation through international agreements versus national environmental directives.

Implementation Schedule

This subsection begins with salient aspects of Phase I of the program and then focuses largely on Phase II and beyond.

Phase I

Phase I of the EU ETS began in 2005, three years ahead of the first Kyoto commitment period. Phase I was intended to be a "learning-by-doing" phase to initiate the process of capacity building and infrastructure establishment in preparation for the Kyoto commitments. Phase I was confined to carbon dioxide emissions, and the EU-wide total allocation of emission allowances was approximately 2.1 billion metric tons of CO_2 per year.

As intended, Phase I involved much learning by both regulators and market participants. Much of the institution building, including the hardware setup for allowance trading, was established in this phase. The price movement in this phase reflected several uncertainties in a developing marketplace. In the early periods of Phase I, regulatory uncertainties surrounding allowance allocations by participating EU nations and Russia's ratification were the primary sources of price risk. Two design flaws in Phase I stand out, however, and deserve further description.

First, verified EU emission reductions in early 2006 revealed that the EU had over-allocated emission allowances. When developing Phase I, the EU lacked reliable emissions data for specific industries and corporations for prior years. The EU allowed member countries to allocate allowances on the basis of polluters' own estimates of emissions rather than verified data of historical emissions. This oversight resulted in member countries applying their own rules for national allowance allocations and issuing allowances on the basis of optimistic (low) forecasts of emissions growth.

This practice represents a major departure from the Acid Rain Program, in which facilities were allocated allowances on the basis of historical emissions from individual electricity-generating units. The Acid Rain Program teaches us that sound measurement and emissions monitoring are critical in building a viable emissions market.

Another controversial issue related to the allowance allocation was that allowances were issued free of cost. Some critics pointed out that such allowance allocation led to windfall profits, particularly in the partially deregulated power sector.[16] One such analysis

---

[16]The allegation was that windfall profits occurred when the deregulated power sector was able to pass on the cost of allowances to consumers, although it received the allowance for free.

estimated that windfall profits for the power sector were on the order of $16.6 billion for Phase I.[17] Note, however, that these problems were not EU-wide and varied from country to country. In all, the oversupply of allowances resulted in EU ETS Phase I allowance prices falling dramatically in early 2006.

In the later part of Phase I, the allowance price fell close to zero. This outcome reveals the second flaw, a structural fault in the design. In designing the market framework for the EU ETS, banking or borrowing of EUAs between Phase I (2005–2007) and Phase II (2007–2012) of the program was not allowed. In addition, uncertainty about whether this provision would be implemented affected market decisions and price volatility. By rule, EU ETS Phase I allowances remaining in registry accounts were to be cancelled at the end of the program. As expected, any unused Phase I allowances held by affected entities became worthless at that time.

Management of the release of price-sensitive information could also have been better. The price decline accelerated toward the end because Phase I entities with surplus allowances sold whatever inventory remained of the allowances. Combined with the fact that EU ETS Phase I was already over-allocated, the price of Phase I allowances fell drastically toward the end of the phase, as depicted in Figure 4.3.

The trading and market-making community responded to these expected price movements and profited from the arbitrage opportunities. One astute trading strategy involved shorting the 2007 allowance contract and "going long" the 2008 allowance contract. The trade worked because over-allocation and the absence of a banking provision caused the 2007 allowance price to fall to zero whereas those problems did not apply to the 2008 allowances.

Phase II

This phase ran from January 2008 through December 2012 and coincided with the first commitment period in the Kyoto Protocol,

---

[17]A. Denny Ellerman, Frank J. Convery and Christian de Perthuis, *Pricing Carbon: The European Union Emissions Trading Scheme* (Cambridge, UK: Cambridge University Press, 2010).

Figure 4.3. Historical EUA Price and Price Drivers, 2005–2013.
Source: European Environment Agency Data and Maps; available online at http://www.eea.europa.eu/data-and-maps.

which included all six of the greenhouse gases recognized under Kyoto (although the EU ETS still focused on CO_2) and intended to reduce their emissions to a level 8% below 1990 levels. In July 2003, the EU further adopted a proposal to link offsets from the clean development mechanism (CDM) and joint implementation (JI) with Phase II and subsequent phases of EU ETS. Under the directive, European emitters are allowed to supplement their carbon-mitigation measures with offsets earned from CDM and JI projects, up to specified limits. The directive stated that the purpose of the link was to achieve cost-effectiveness in reducing global GHG emissions and increased liquidity by introducing diverse low-cost compliance options.

Phase III

The EU ETS is now in its third phase, which will run from 2013 through 2020. Phase III covers roughly 45% of total EU CO_2

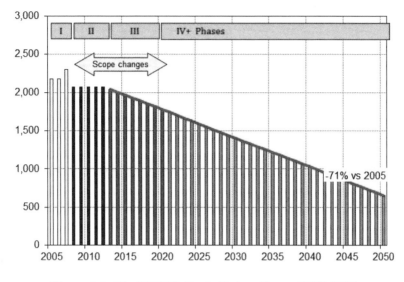

Figure 4.4. The EU ETS Cap in Various Phases, 2005–2050.

emissions and more than 11,000 power stations and manufacturing plants in 31 nations in Europe.[18] Covered emissions include those from power stations and other combustion plants; oil refineries; coke ovens; iron and steel plants; and the cement, glass, lime, bricks, ceramics, pulp, paper, and board sectors. Furthermore, Phase III includes a separate emissions trading program intended to reduce CO_2 emissions from the aviation sector. The emissions-reduction in this phase is 1.74% per year, which means that by the end of Phase III in 2020, EU-wide GHG emissions should be 21% lower than in 2005.

The fourth trading period is expected to run from 2021 to 2028. Figure 4.4 shows the EU emissions caps for various phases of the program.

Market size

With an annual allowance allocation of approximately two billion EUAs and an assumed price of $6 per allowance, the total notional

---

[18] Countries of the EU ETS are the EU-27 plus Croatia, Iceland, Liechtenstein, and Norway.

value of the EUA market is about $12.8 billion. The traded volumes of the EUAs far exceed the annual allocations, however, which indicates a market size that is several times larger. Part of the reason is that trading includes forward transactions for compliance in future years as well as trading by portfolio investors, market makers, and speculators. Thus, the secondary market is maturing. In 2011, a total of 7.9 billion EUAs were traded, representing a value of $148.8 billion.

To put this amount in perspective, consider that the 2011 value of the "carbon crop" exceeded the production value of all U.S. corn, wheat, and soybeans for the same year.[19] Figure 4.5 presents

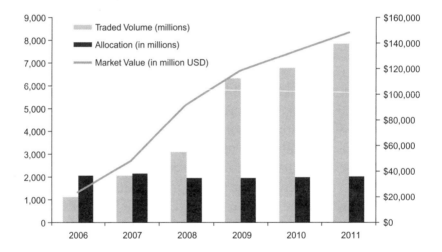

Figure 4.5. EU ETS Market Statistics, 2006–2011.
Notes: "Allocation" refers to the initial allocation of EUAs to entities in the EU mandated to reduce their emissions. "Traded Volume" refers to the quantity of EUAs traded in a year. "Market Value" refers to the product of market price and quantity traded in a given year.

---

[19]The U.S. Department of Agriculture crop value of production for corn was $76.9 billion; wheat, $14.3 billion; and soybeans, $38.5 billion (National Agricultural Statistics Service, U.S. Department of Agriculture).

the historical growth in the EU ETS market from 2006. Relative to the allocation, the traded volume of allowances has increased substantially. Since 2008, the markets have turned over more than the annual allocation of allowances each year. One of the signals for a maturing market used by the derivatives industry is an increasing "churn" rate. EU ETS churn rates in 2011 were close to four times the allowance allocation.

The EU ETS market is liquid, which is essential for reducing transaction costs and improving market efficiencies. Organized exchanges create economic value by narrowing the bid–ask spread and through price transparency. To illustrate, note that the initial bid–ask spread in the EU ETS was €0.20–€0.25. By the end of 2010, this spread had narrowed to €0.02, generating more than €1 billion in savings for the EU.

Trading in EUA allowances takes place through various avenues, including bilateral transactions, spot markets, and futures and options markets. About 10 regulated commodity futures exchanges provide hedging products for managing risks from EU ETS. The smallest segment is the spot market, with $2.8 billion in transaction value and representing about 2% of total EU transaction volume. EUA futures, with $130.8 billion in value and more than 88% of all EUA transactions, represent the largest segment. The options market, at about $14.2 billion, represents 10% of the EUA transaction volumes.

The CER and ERU markets are much smaller than the EUA market. In 2011, the combined value of CER and ERU transactions was only about $23 billion, representing a volume of about 1.8 billion allowances. Trading in CERs represented 97% of the transaction value. Following a trading pattern similar to that of the EUA, the vast majority (92%) of the traded volume in CERs and ERUs was done with futures and options instruments. The transaction volume and value of the various instruments are shown in Table 4.1.

Table 4.1. Composition of the Greenhouse Gas
Market in 2011.

	Transaction volume (MtCO$_2$e)	Transaction value ($ millions)
EUA	7,853	147,848
CER	1,734	22,333
ERU	76	780
Total	9,663	170,961

Note: MtCO$_2$e = million metric tons of carbon dioxide
equivalent.

Table 4.2. EUA Allowance Price Forecasts.

Source	Range
Industry survey by Point Carbon (June 2007)	$30–$35 per allowance
Industry survey by Point Carbon (October 2008)	$30–$45 per allowance
Deutsche Bank (2007)	$35 per allowance
Société Générale(2010)	$22–$60 per allowance
Trend of price forecast for European allowances[20]	$15.5–$33.6 per allowance

Price History

Early estimates for EU ETS Phase II allowance prices were not only optimistic but also predicated on an increase in the allowance price over time. The price expectations for EUAs and the actual market prices show a remarkable similarity with the SO$_2$ allowance market. Table 4.2 gives a range of price forecasts for Phase II allowances from various studies. In reality, the actual price for EUA allowances between 2008 and 2013 has largely been below the optimistic forecasts. From an investment standpoint in early 2009, comparing these predictions with actual EUA prices would suggest that buying allowances was a good investment opportunity. The history of EUA prices indicates, however, that a decision to hold a long position in

---

[20]J.J. Barberis, M. Prada and A. Tignol, *La regulationdes marches de CO$_2$*. Ministere de L'Ecologie 2010; Mongraphie 18730 (French).

allowances would have been incorrect. Figure 4.3 shows the major factors that triggered price movements.

Clearly, early predictions of EUA prices factored in some high-cost technological solutions. Technological solutions available to power plants included emerging carbon capture and storage, which becomes feasible in the range of \$30–\$55 per allowance.[21] Similarly, alternative fuel technologies, such as solar photovoltaic and concentrated solar power, are economically viable when allowance prices are higher than \$28 per ton. In Europe, a recent report states that allowance prices of \$35–\$40 are needed to switch from burning highly polluting coal to natural gas. Société Générale estimates that utilities will invest in clean technology at an EUA price on the order of €30 per ton.

As with the Acid Rain Program, a combination of factors determined EUA prices. In addition to the technological alternatives that allowed companies to achieve reductions, such as fuel switching and improvements in energy-efficiency, an important factor was the so-called banking provisions. These provisions allowed entities to manage their EUA requirements over time and thereby kept prices stable. (This method was also frequently used in the Acid Rain Program, as noted in Chapter 3.) Other price determinants in the EU ETS involved economic shocks and regulatory policy uncertainties. These developments are discussed here.

First, the worldwide 2008 financial crisis was a significant economic shock that reduced industrial production globally, thereby curbing emissions. The price of EUA allowances fell to less than €15 per ton. Following the economic crisis, the EUA price remained

---

[21] McKinsey & Company, "Pathways to a Low-Carbon Economy." McKinsey & Company (January 2009); available online at https://solutions.mckinsey.com/climatedesk/default.aspx; Luis M. Abadie and Jose M. Chamorro, "European CO_2 Prices and Carbon Capture Investments." *Energy Economics*, Vol. 30, No. 6 (November 2008): 2992–3015; Richard G. Newell, Adam B. Jaffe and Robert N. Stavin, "The Effects of Economic and Policy Incentives on Carbon Mitigation Technologies." *Energy Economics*, Vol. 28, Nos. 5–6 (November 2006): 563–578; Ram C. Sekar, John E. Parsons, Howard J. Herzog and Henry D. Jacoby, "Future Carbon Regulations and Current Investments in Alternative Coal-Fired Power Plant Technologies." *Economic Policy*, Vol. 35 (2007): 1064–1074; Dag Martinsen, Jochen Linssen, Peter Markewitz and Stefan Vögele, "CCS: A Future CO_2 Mitigation Option for Germany? A Bottom-Up Approach." *Energy Policy*, Vol. 35, No. 4 (April 2007): 2110–2120.

depressed because European economic growth was slower than expected. Second, and more recently, Europe was hit by a severe government debt crisis. EUA prices fell in 2011 to below €10 per ton and continued to fall in 2012.

Sadly, the biggest shock to the EUA emissions market turned out to be sovereign risk which proved true with the Acid Rain Program. Keep in mind that the emissions allowance market exists largely as a result of a mandated cap by a regulatory authority. The European carbon market is currently witnessing a substantial oversupply of credits because of various factors. Estimates of oversupply are in the range of 1.4 billion tons for the phase until 2020. The EU, reeling from low economic growth, the debt crisis, and government austerity measures, has so far not reached a consensus on dealing with the oversupply. Industry analysts suggest that EUA prices could remain depressed in the medium and perhaps long-term as a result of sovereign risk. In retrospect, EUA market prices indicate that, in light of such shocks, investors should have sold allowances short.

The EUA market became further depressed because of delays and/or the lack of a policy to tackle the over-allocation of EUAs in the market. Although more than the required emission reductions have been achieved in a cost-efficient manner, the EU is considering a determination, called "back loading," to restrict excess allowances in an effort to slow the price decline. Lack of consensus on this issue has led to EUA prices falling below €5 as of 2014. We believe that the best way to manage this problem is to focus on further emission-reduction goals.

Where changing the reduction target is not politically feasible, a price floor has been implemented. This mechanism is in place for California cap-and-trade and the Regional Greenhouse Gas Initiative program, which will be discussed in later sections of this chapter.

Price Determinants

In monitoring and analyzing market and price developments, financial analysts need to understand how these drivers interact, which drivers carry the most market weight, and last but not least, to what extent and in what circumstances various drivers affect allowance prices. Entities affected by EU ETS exposure have to be informed about their trading and risk management, investment decisions, and abatement options. These decisions span a wide range of expertise germane to the technical, managerial, financial, and legal issues arising from the EU ETS.

EU ETS emissions allowance prices can be subject to two sets of factors: (1) long-run, systemic factors, such as policy and regulatory developments, advances in emission reduction technology, and taxation and accounting issues; and (2) energy market developments, such as electricity transmission issues (i.e., new lines, and regulations mandating open access). Energy market developments can influence not only electricity production levels but also emissions prices. Long-term developments that affect access to coal use, such as coal transportation infrastructure and pricing, can change the economics of coal selection and thereby influence emissions levels. As in the case of most commodities, also important are long-term macroeconomic variables, such as population growth, demographics, and natural resource scarcity, all of which influence prices.

Short-term fluctuations in the consumption of GHG emission allowances are influenced by, among other things, factors that affect electricity production and the composition of electricity production. Electricity production is influenced by economic activity, particularly industrial production, and by weather conditions (often measured by heating- and cooling-degree days). The composition of electricity production — in particular, the share of total production coming from fossil fuel plants — is influenced by the availability of nuclear power, renewable energy, hydroelectric generation resources, and prices of substitute lower-emitting fuels, each of which may be affected by government support and other policies.

Many of the market drivers that affect the SO_2 allowance market also affect the GHG allowance market because the majority of GHG emissions arise from combustion of fossil fuels that are also implicated in SO_2 emissions. Rather than discuss those drivers again, we will focus on the drivers unique to GHGs in this section.

Technological Options

The primary options are fuel switching and energy-efficiency, although some other options are possible.

Fuel switching

Similar to the examples noted for acid rain, fuel switching was a major avenue used by emitters to meet EU ETS compliance targets. Studies suggest that 80% of the abatement occurred in the EU-15, with the bulk of it in the energy sector. Here, the abatements were driven primarily by converting from coal to natural gas (fuel switching) as a direct result of either the observed or the expected carbon price.[22] Fuel switching in the power sector alone in Phase I contributed between 53 million and 98 million tons of reductions.[23] The Spanish utility Iberdrola reported switching 63% of its coal-fired generation to natural gas and increasing its natural gas generation by 52% in the first three quarters of 2008.[24] Similarly, Unión Fenosa, another Spanish utility, reduced coal-fired generation by 42% and increased gas-fired generation by 38% in the first half of 2008.[25] Spanish electricity-sector emissions of CO_2 went down in 2008 in spite of increases in net generation. This development is a good signal that economic growth and the transition to low carbon can be done in parallel.

The trends observed in the power sector were true also for the industrial sector. In 2006, SABMiller, the multinational brewing and beverage company headquartered in London, used fuel switching in

---

[22] Ellerman *et al.*, *Pricing Carbon*, *op. cit.*

[23] Note, however, that even though Phase I was a warm-up phase, companies planned ahead for the tighter restrictions to come in Phase II. Thus, they invested in the best methods to comply with future regulations.

[24] "Spanish Utility Iberdrola Cuts Carbon Emissions." *Point Carbon* (23 October 2008).

[25] "Union Fenosa Switches from Coal to Gas." *Point Carbon* (16 July 2008).

its breweries and achieved a 12% improvement (decrease) in carbon intensity.[26]

Energy-efficiency

Another avenue in the power sector was to upgrade power plant efficiencies. Drax Group, a large coal-fired plant in the United Kingdom and one of the top five emitting sources in Europe, used this strategy. In response to the EU ETS, in 2007 the company invested about €100 million in upgrading its turbines and another €80 million to increase its renewable biomass co-firing facility fivefold. These measures combined resulted in a 15% reduction in emissions in the plant and, in addition, generated renewable energy certificates (RECs) that could be monetized. Financial analysts must note that the payback in this investment was from fuel savings as well as RECs.

Another utility, CEZ Group in the Czech Republic, implemented a range of efficiency measures, such as reconstructing feeding pumps, cooling pumps, and boilers and replacing turbines. These upgrades had been in the works but were implemented sooner than planned. They cost CEZ an additional €21 million in 2005,[27] but by selling the EUAs saved by the project, CEZ ended up recouping these costs and earning a profit of €7.7 million. RWE in Germany responded to the EU ETS by increasing its R&D investments in energy-efficiency and fossil fuel emission reduction technologies by almost 32%.[28] Other utilities did the same. Planned 800 megawatt coal-fired plants in Poland, to be constructed by 2015 by RWE and the Polish utility Kompania Weglowa, are expected to have an efficiency of about 46% as opposed to the reference level of 33% in Polish coal-fired plants.[29,30]

---

[26] "SAB Miller Cuts Carbon Intensity 12% in 2006." *Point Carbon* (4 July 2007).

[27] Ellerman *et al.*, *Pricing Carbon, op. cit.*

[28] "EUA Cost RWE €1 Billion in Jan–Sept 2008." *Point Carbon* (4 July 2007).

[29] "RWE to Build New Coal Plant in Poland." *Point Carbon* (4 July 2007).

[30] Efficiency in this context is defined as the ability to generate more electricity from the same quantity of coal combustion.

Other technological avenues

The EU ETS experience included industry-specific avenues for emissions abatement. For example, the manufacture of blended cement, which involves partial substitution of such additives as fly ash for CO_2-intensive clinker in the cement industry, resulted in significant reductions in emissions.[31] Although the choice of blended cement cannot be attributed only to the ETS, its manufacture did have an impact on ETS compliance. CEMEX UK's 1.2 million ton blended-cement facility in Essex will cut CO_2 emissions in half by using substitutes such as flyash for clinker. Studies have also suggested that the EU ETS triggered behavioral changes among managers by encouraging investment in energy-efficiency, with the biggest gains resulting from large investments.

At present, a method that is technologically and economically viable to remove GHGs — comparable to the SO_2 scrubbing technologies — does not exist. The closest alternative in the power sector is the use of carbon capture and storage (CCS) technologies, which can have a significant impact on emission reductions. CCS involves capturing the CO_2 produced by large combustion plants, compressing it for transportation, and then injecting it deep into a rock formation at a carefully selected and safe site, where it is permanently stored. CCS technologies are still in the early stages of development, however, and are not economically viable at current prices of carbon.

Regulatory Issues

The biggest factor affecting all cap-and-trade markets is the policy and regulatory framework because these markets are created either through political decisions framed in law or by means of caps imposed by some form of public or private contract. Hence, changes in laws, regulations, and operating guidelines can have a significant

---

[31] Clinker is small lumps or nodules, usually from limestone, that are ground to produce cement. It is a heavily CO_2-intensive input in cement manufacture.

impact on market and price developments. In addition, regulation of, or taxation guidance on, the treatment of allowance transactions (including issuance, sales, purchases, swaps, and so on) for value-added taxes and financial accounting may influence trading and, therefore, prices. Anyone aiming to analyze and forecast market and price developments thus needs to understand the role and potential impact of policy choices.

Banking and borrowing provisions

An important flexibility provision in emissions trading systems is the ability of companies to transfer or bank any surplus allowances from one compliance period to use in future compliance periods. This option helps companies with the intertemporal risk management of their carbon exposure. For example, companies that have surplus emission allowances and expect that the demand for allowances will increase (either externally in the market or internally for their own future compliance) can bank these allowances for future years. Conversely, because in many cases allowances for the entire commitment period are issued in advance, companies can borrow from future years for current compliance. The option of borrowing can be seen as a relief valve for companies, to the extent that extreme weather conditions may have a large impact on the allowance balance for a single year. Limited or no banking or borrowing provisions would leave allowance prices largely determined by the need to comply fully in each period, which could affect short-term fundamentals and increase market volatility without necessarily improving long-term environmental compliance.

As shown in Chapter 3, the Acid Rain Program allowed for banking of allowances for use in future years. This provision allowed power plants to manage their compliance needs over time and played a role in maintaining price stability in the initial phases of the SO_2 program. The EU ETS story demonstrates the adverse outcome that may result from not having this policy. As discussed, the lack of banking allowances between Phases I and II of the EU ETS (justified by an unwillingness of policymakers to create a bridge between the learning-by-doing phase and the period of Kyoto obligations) was a major reason for the decrease of Phase I prices to zero.

Regulatory Uncertainty

A lack of policy certainty regarding the rules governing an emissions trading program has had major effects on allowance prices. In the EU ETS, numerous regulatory shocks — including uncertainties about the overall reduction goals, intermediate emission targets, quantity and method of allocation, provisions for banking or use of past allowances in future years, rules governing linking of the market with other programs, and the future status of the program — affected allowance prices.

Examples of regulatory influences on EU ETS prices are numerous. In the early days of the program, considerable uncertainty surrounded the aggregate national allowance allocations and the share of allowances to be allocated to each industrial sector within individual EU members. Naturally, this uncertainty had a higher impact in large EU economies that depended on coal-generated power, such as Germany. Recently, the debate on an appropriate mechanism to manage low EUA prices, such as back loading EUAs, has become a cause of price volatility. Market participants would be well advised to stay informed about these developments.

Offset Potential

Carbon and greenhouse gases are unique among atmospheric pollutants in that several sources create and mitigate them. A wide variety of CO_2-absorbing sinks and GHG-destruction technologies act as offsetting avenues to GHG emissions.[32] This situation led to the development of an offset market in which offset allowances generated from GHG-reducing projects are used, within regulatory

---

[32]A carbon sink is a natural or artificial reservoir that accumulates and stores some carbon-containing chemical compound for an indefinite period.

limits, to meet compliance targets. Examples of technologies for sourcing offsets include energy-efficiency, renewable energy (wind, hydro, and biomass), changes in industrial processes, and methane destruction from animal manure, among others. (Offset opportunities did not exist for acid rain pollutants.)

The EU ETS did not allow for offset credits to be generated internally within the EU. The program did, however, allow for the use of Kyoto compliance instruments, such as Certified Emission Reductions (CERs) for compliance in the EU ETS. CERs, a type of carbon allowance or credit, were meant to assist developing countries in achieving sustainable development and contribute to the ultimate goal of stabilizing GHG concentrations in the atmosphere. In theory, EUA prices can be affected by CER supply and other regulatory issues. In reality, however, EUA pricing remained unaffected by the CER link in the EU ETS. CERs were not used in Phase I because not many were actually issued until 2008. In Phase II, the EU imposed an explicit annual cap (13.4% of total CERs outstanding) on the proportion of CERs that could be used for compliance. Also, some sovereign risk was embedded in the CERs, depending on the country of origin and type. Given these factors, the link did not significantly affect EUA prices.

Carbon as Innovation Catalyst in Europe

As a direct result of the EU ETS, several innovative technologies were deployed in the EU. In some cases, these technologies generated new products and new revenue streams for the companies that produced them. Three examples of such innovative approaches are presented here.

Example 1. Fuel Switching in the Paper and Pulp Industry

The paper and pulp industry is a significant contributor to GHG emissions. This sector covers about 7% of mandated entities under the EU ETS. The EU ETS was a key reason for reducing emissions and energy use in Sweden's paper and pulp industry. Estimates suggest that improvements in energy use and fuel switching in that sector have led to emission reductions worth $12 million to $35 million annually in Sweden alone.

Sweden's Södra Cell Värö pulp mill has been successful in fully switching all of its fossil fuel energy sources to carbon-neutral sources. Specifically, to generate steam, the paper mill uses a by-product from the digestion of pulpwood called "black liquor," together with waste bark. These biofuels generate 99% of the mill's power. The mill also exports nearly 65 gigawatts of electricity to the electric grid and provides energy to meet nearly half of the heating needs of a nearby town.

Chemrec, another Swedish paper and pulp company, has gone further with its black liquor. The company produces renewable motor fuels and electricity with this industrial by-product. Chemrec claims its black liquor motor fuel can satisfy the energy needs of up to half of Sweden's trucks. This example illustrates how innovative companies have used the EU ETS not only to transform their own energy use but also to develop additional products and business streams that add to their bottom line.

Example 2. Carbon Dioxide Fertilization for Horticulture

Carbon dioxide is an important energy source for plants, and CO_2 fertilization has important applications in agriculture. Royal Dutch Shell's refineries have creatively used CO_2 emissions from smokestacks to promote commercial horticulture in the Netherlands.

Shell's oil refinery in Rotterdam is the largest refinery in Europe. It emits about six million tons of CO_2 annually and accounts for nearly 3% of the Netherlands' GHG emissions. This unit captures about 350,000 tons of CO_2 from its smokestacks and uses it to fertilize 500 large greenhouses for horticulture. The recycled CO_2 is used as a substitute for about 95 million cubic meters of natural gas that otherwise would have been used annually for heating the greenhouses. This technology is not new, but it was economically feasible only because of the carbon price imposed by the EU ETS. For Shell, redirecting its smokestack emissions means capturing surplus EUAs, and for greenhouse operators, it means savings in heat used. This trade is a win–win situation for both Shell and the greenhouse operator and is in operation even though ETS rules affecting the project have changed.

Example 3. Use of Waste Heat for Energy

A by-product of fossil fuel combustion is heat. The EU ETS has provided companies with the incentive to capture this waste heat and use it as a resource. Twence, a regional waste company in the Netherlands, captures the steam generated from its waste incineration and uses it to generate power. Furthermore, to reduce its CO_2 emissions and energy use, Twence and AkzoNobel, a salt company, teamed up in an innovative project involving steam. In their agreement, Twence transports its steam to the AkzoNobel salt factory via a pipeline. The steam is used by AkzoNobel in salt production to evaporate brine water and as a substitute for natural gas. AkzoNobel saves about 40 million cubic feet of natural gas every year and was able to cut its emissions by 72,000 tons of CO_2 per year as result of the project. This project was another direct result of the EU ETS.

Investing in GHG as an Asset Class

The EU ETS has given rise to several new kinds of investment opportunities in carbon. The most direct way is by taking a position in carbon allowances. This strategy can be accomplished via numerous carbon brokerage houses or exchanges that facilitate carbon trading. Fund managers and individual investors can respond to carbon risks and opportunities in a number of ways.

The first and most visible opportunity involves analyzing the carbon profiles of companies or investments and identifying the costs associated with their carbon footprints. Naturally, sectors that are more exposed to fossil fuel combustion (such as utilities, oil and gas companies, and the cement sector) will be exposed to more carbon risk than the others. Similarly, the analyst may find geographical or regional variations in carbon exposure arising from regulatory and operational differences. A multinational company, in particular, has to manage a wide range of carbon regimes that are determined by the location of the multinational's operations. Carbon liabilities in portfolios can be managed by shifting positions from more carbon-intensive holdings to less carbon-intensive holdings within a sector. By doing so, the sectoral allocation remains unaltered. Investors can also follow a carbon-weighting approach to their portfolios and rebalance regularly to optimize their holdings from a carbon-exposure standpoint. A variety of index products exist that provide carbon-optimized exposure, including the S&P U.S. Carbon Efficient Index, UBS Europe Carbon Optimized Index, DB Platinum CROCI Carbon Alpha TR Fund, and BNP Paribas EasyETF Low Carbon 100 Europe.

As discussed in the following subsections, investors can access carbon investments in numerous ways, ranging from the commodity markets to carbon project development funds.

Commodity Markets

The most direct way to get exposure to the asset class of carbon-related investments is by taking a position in spot, futures, or options markets for EUA allowances. The major exchanges trading EUA spot and futures contracts are, in this order, the Intercontinental-Exchange (ICE), Chicago Mercantile Exchange, European Energy Exchange, and NASDAQ OMX. ICE, which has emerged as the primary marketplace for European emissions, has a market share of more than 90% of the exchange-traded fund (ETF) volume in the EUA futures market. An interesting note is that the EUA futures volume on ICE now surpasses that of Brent oil futures.

Equity Vehicles

Stock picking based on climate risk exposure can have an impact on the overall portfolio return as well as on risks. It is becoming increasingly important for investors to assess environmental performance as they would assess financial performance. Important factors include a company's EUA exposure, its emissions, its energy-efficiency, its position on alternative energy, and available alternatives to reduce emissions. An analysis of the carbon risks in UK equity funds conducted by Trucost, an environmental cost accounting organization, found significant differences in carbon costs across individual equities, sectors, and regions.[33] Trucost analyzed 2,380 listed companies held in 118 equity portfolios and found overall exposure of 134 million tons of CO_2 equivalent (or CO_2e) and £1.6 billion to £7.6 billion in carbon potential allowance costs.[34] The carbon footprint of the aggregate portfolios was 582 tons of CO_2e per £1 million invested, on average, although significant variation was found among individual funds. Sectors with significant carbon risk included utilities, basic resources, construction, oil and natural gas, and food and beverages. Overall, the top four contributors to a portfolio's carbon footprint were RWE AG, International Power, American Electric Power, and BP.

Exchange-Traded Funds and Notes

ETFs and exchange-traded notes (ETNs) exist for retail investors interested in EUAs. Most of these instruments provide exposure by holding EUA futures contracts. Some of them are as follows:

- *iPath Global Carbon ETN (NYSE Arca:GRN)*. This product, launched in June 2008, tracks the Barclays Capital Global Carbon Index Total Return.[35] The index currently includes two carbon-related credits: EUA allowances (88%) and CERs (12%).

---

[33] Trucost, "Carbon Risks in UK Equity Funds." Trucost (6 July 2009); available online at http://www.trucost.com/_uploads/downloads/Carbon_Risks_in_UK_Equity_Funds.pdf.

[34] Carbon dioxide equivalency is a relationship that describes the amount of CO_2 for a given mixture and amount of greenhouse gas that would have the same global warming potential when measured over a specified timescale (generally, 100 years). Please see Appendix B for the definitions and calculations of CO_2 equivalency.

[35] The Barclays Carbon Index is discussed in Chapter 8.

- *ETFS Carbon ETC (LON:CARB and CARP).*[36] These products are designed to track the price of carbon emissions allowance futures. They track the ICE ECX EUA futures contract, which is traded in London on the ICE Futures Market. CARB and CARP are backed by matching fully funded swap contracts purchased from an entity of the Royal Dutch Shell Group. The product has been listed since October 2008 and trades in British pounds (CARP) or euros (CARB).

Clean Technology Companies

Picking companies that supply clean energy technologies allows investors to gain direct exposure to carbon as an asset class. In recent years, rapid increases in clean energy deployment have occurred in response to climate and renewable energy policies. In 2012, the clean energy sector recorded 88 gigawatts of additional generating capacity and $269 billion in investments. Investing in clean technology can take the form of investing in, specifically, solar, "smart grid," wind, biofuels, and similar companies.

Solar, in particular, has been drawing much attention because of the drop in panel-manufacturing costs combined with third-party financing and retail investments. With $126 billion invested, solar technologies attracted more investments than any other clean energy technology in 2012. Top names in the sector include Suntech Power (OTCBB:STP), which is the largest producer of silicon panels; First Solar (NASDAQ:FSLR), which produces low-cost thin-film solar panels; Sharp Solar (TYO:6753); and Yingli Green Energy (NYSE:YGE). China, Europe, and the United States were the top markets for solar investments in 2012.

Wind energy has long been an important component of the clean energy mix. In 2012, the sector attracted about $73 billion in investments. Top wind-generation companies by market share are Dutch-based Vestas Wind Systems (CPH:VWS); China's Sinovel Wind (SHA:601558) and Goldwind Global

---

[36]LON is the London Stock Exchange.

(HK:2208); Spain's Gamesa (MCE:GAM); Germany's ENERCON (AU:PVT company) and Siemens (NSE:SIEMENS); India-based Suzlon Energy (BOM:532667); and General Electric Wind Energy (NYSE:GE) from the United States.[37]

Another exciting development is smart grid technology. A smart grid allows utilities and consumers to communicate with each other through intelligent technologies that result in better energy use and reliability. Several companies have jumped into development of this emerging technology and associated infrastructure. Major players include the Swiss company ABB (NYSE:ABB); Aclara Technologies (FRA:ET7), a smart grid facilitator that also develops advanced metering infrastructure; Alstom Grid (pvt), which provides equipment and services to the power sector; General Electric (NYSE:GE), which provides smart grid hardware and software services; and Siemens, whose smart grid portfolio includes switches and protection gear, substation automation, and wind and solar power products.

Companies involved in developing and building carbon capture and storage technologies form another class of investment opportunity. Most large companies that service the power sector are involved, including Halliburton (NYSE:HAL), KBR(NYSE:KBR), Shell (LON:RDSA), Fluor (NYSE:FLR), ABB(NYSE:ABB), and Mitsubishi Heavy Industries (TYO:8058).

Companies that are involved in improving energy-efficiency include Siemens, United Technologies (NYSE:UTX), Johnson Controls (NYSE:JCI), and ABB.

Related opportunities exist in the transportation space. Transportation, the second-largest source of emissions after power generation, has been shifting to cleaner forms of energy. Electric automotive companies (e.g., Tesla Motors (NASDAQ:TSLA)), natural gas transportation (e.g., Clean Energy Fuels NASDAQ: CLNE), and fuel efficient air transportation (European Aeronautic Defence and Space Company and Boeing (NYSE:BA) are all

---

[37]SHA is the Shanghai Stock Exchange, CPH is the Copenhagen Stock Exchange, and BOM is the Bombay Stock Exchange.

worthy of attention. The EU ETS does not include transportation, so, given the focus of this chapter, we do not delve in great detail into these companies and technologies.

Climate Funds

Investors can also consider investments in the climate solutions field. This category includes the subcategories of energy-efficiency, clean technologies, and renewable energy supplies. Examples of funds that invest specifically in companies that provide solutions are the following:

- *Jupiter Climate Change Solutions* (FGV7:FSX; ISIN:LU03 00038618).[38] An open-end fund incorporated in Luxembourg, Jupiter's objective is long-term capital growth from investment in companies worldwide. The fund invests in equities and equity-related securities of companies providing products or services that contribute to environmental improvement and facilitate adaptation to the impact of climate change. The fund is listed in Frankfurt.
- *F&C Global Climate Opportunities Fund* (ISIN:LU031845-1738). This fund aims to achieve long-term capital appreciation by investing at least two-thirds of its total assets in equities and equity-related securities of companies that have substantial activities in alternative energy, energy-efficiency, sustainable mobility, waste management, advanced materials, forestry and agriculture, water, acclimatization, and support services.

Listed Climate Companies

Another direct way to get carbon exposure is to take a position in listed initial public offerings (IPOs) of companies active in the

---

[38]FSX is the Frankfurt Stock Exchange; visit http://www.boerse-frankfurt.de/en/funds/jupiter+climate+change+solutions+fonds+LU0231118026 for more details.

carbon allowance space. Several companies issued listed IPOs at the height of the EUA market. They include companies that have an interest in generating and holding emission allowances or offsets — that is, project developers and funds — as well as companies engaged in ancillary services to the emissions trading industry. (Commodity exchanges are among the ancillary services.)

Listed Carbon Project Development Funds

The broad class of funds in this category includes originators and developers of carbon allowance–generating projects and traders of carbon credits. The investment strategy in these funds involves deploying capital to either purchase carbon credits at reasonable prices or gain exposure to assets whose value is closely linked to the carbon credit price. This strategy includes (1) making investments through equity and debt instruments and (2) purchasing forward emissions contracts and interests in clean energy projects and companies. Investments in clean energy projects include ownership interests in waste-to-electricity projects, hydroelectric power, biodiesel manufacturing, carbon-trading brokerages, agricultural manure digesters, and wind power projects.

These funds manage a diverse set of assets with carbon exposure. Such assets include CERs, private equity investments, and cash and other assets. The portfolio companies seek to commercialize their carbon portfolios through derivatives markets and over-the-counter contracts.

In the past, several of these funds depended on carbon revenues to maintain a healthy balance sheet. The global carbon market, however, experienced major policy uncertainties that were triggered, in part, by lack of U.S. action on climate change under Kyoto, the financial crisis, and the accompanying economic slowdown. These macro events caused severe losses for carbon portfolios during the 2008–2013 period. Price declines in the carbon allowance market, for CER prices in particular, led to losses in many of these entities.

In retrospect, investors would have benefited from shorting these funds.[39]

The core lesson for many of the listed carbon funds was that a high degree of correlation between the company's asset base and carbon prices presents a risk.

Listed Exchanges

Another environmental investment worthy of mention is the listed exchanges. Note that the exchanges' valuations are related to transaction volumes rather than transaction prices. When market volatility rose, the exchanges typically experienced greater transactions and more revenues. One such opportunity was Climate Exchange.[40]

Climate Exchange (CLE) owns spot and derivatives exchanges globally, on which major classes of environmental financial products are traded. The company began in 2004 as the Chicago Climate Exchange. Exchanges held by Climate Exchange include the Chicago Climate Exchange, Chicago Climate Futures Exchange, and European Climate Exchange as well as Environmental Derivatives Exchanges in Canada, Australia, and China. The exchanges held by CLE have the largest market share and most diverse set of financial products in the environmental finance sector. CLE was listed in the alternative investment market division of the London Stock Exchange (LSE). CLE also was the first exchange to list environmental derivatives contracts on North American domestic carbon programs, such as the Regional Greenhouse Gas Initiative and the California project (this will be discussed later).

At its height, CLE was valued at more than $2.2 billion with a share price of a little more than £20 per share. The stock price declined in late 2009 because of uncertainty about U.S. climate

---

[39] Although many of these funds have not been financially successful, this observation should not be interpreted as a recommendation to either buy or sell them. The future performance of these funds cannot be inferred from past performance.

[40] Richard Sandor, one of the authors of this book, is a Founder and Chairman of Climate Exchange PLC and its associated companies/subsidiaries.

Figure 4.6. CLE Stock Prices on the LSE, 2003–2010.

policy. Its European business had a market share of more than 90% in the EU ETS, however, with significant latent growth potential. In 2010, ICE bought CLE for $600 million, causing CLE's initial investors to experience a return of seven times the initial investment over an eight-year period. Figure 4.6 is a graph of CLE's stock price from 2003 to 2010.

The CLE story is an example of the diverse opportunities that exist for gaining exposure to the carbon market without directly holding carbon allowances. Given the CLE experience, readers can see that listed financial exchanges are an interesting way to gain exposure to environmental assets. Seven exchanges cater to the EUA market. ICE, with more than 90% of the liquidity, is the predominant marketplace for EUAs. Others include the NASDAQ OMX and Chicago Mercantile Exchange (CME).

As emerging economies consider markets for carbon allowances or other environmental derivatives, such investments as CLE may emerge in those economies. In large growing economies — for example, India and China — that are introducing financial reforms and innovations into their derivatives industry in parallel with environmental policy considerations, new exchanges for trading of environmental derivatives may arise.[41] Already, exchanges in Tianjin in northern China and Shanghai exist exclusively for environmental allowance trading. The China Emissions Exchange in Shenzen started trading carbon intensity in June 2013.[42] Other exchanges, such as the Multi Commodity Exchange of India and the National Stock Exchange of India, have experience with environmental contracts. The state of these emerging markets will be further discussed in Chapter 5.

Conclusion

This chapter provided an overview of today's major program to reduce GHG emissions — the European Union Emissions Trading Scheme. The market mechanism and the nature of risk and opportunity should be the focus for the reader. This knowledge will assist in evaluating other emissions markets and products that emerge in the future.

The success of the EU ETS, in spite of the current debate about EUA prices, has led to emissions trading programs getting off to promising starts around the world. The next chapter will discuss the characteristics and state of regional and emerging trading programs around the world.

A wide variety of sectoral and regional policies has emerged to manage GHGs and other energy and environmental objectives. For example, in addition to reducing GHG emissions, renewable energy facilities have value in creating energy diversity and a cleaner electrical grid. The cap-and-trade framework is central to the design of these markets. Both developed and developing economies have employed the framework according to individual country goals and growth aspirations. Australia announced a nationwide cap-and-trade scheme, expected to start in 2015, that will cover 60% of the

---

[41] For a detailed review, see Sandor, *Good Derivatives, op. cit.*

[42] China Emissions Exchange; available online at http://www.cerx.cn/cn/index.aspx.

country's annual GHG emissions. Mexico and South Korea have their own comprehensive climate bills, each passed in April 2012. India and China have set up markets that may be precursors to carbon trading. India is tackling its GHG emissions via a national renewable energy trading program and a scheme for trading energy efficiency called "Perform, Achieve and Trade." Some cities around the world — Tokyo, for one — have prepared or are preparing their own schemes. Simultaneously, we are witnessing state and regional programs emerge in many parts of the world. GHG markets in California and the Northeastern Region in United States are good examples. All of these efforts are essential to achieve the kind of GHG reductions required to comply with recommendations from global climate policymakers.

The most recent goal of the UN Framework Convention on Climate Change, agreed to in Doha, Qatar, in 2012, is a limit on GHG emissions intended to be achieved by 2020 and designed to hold the cumulative total global temperature rise to 2° Celsius or less.[43,44]

These targets were set by international negotiations after careful consideration of the stage of economic growth of each mandated country. However, although about 90 countries have indicated plans for reducing emissions by 2020, the gap between current GHG emissions and the desired goal is widening. Even with the best efforts, global emissions by 2020 are expected to reach 49 billion tons (against an admissible level of 42 billion tons). Unless a variety of mitigation and adaptation strategies is used soon, the world will fall short of required emission reductions.

Therefore, there is an urgent need for a broad range of GHG management strategies across the economy. This will create risks and opportunities that will lead to GHG reductions in the most cost-effective manner. Because of the increasingly evident effects of

---

[43] The 2° Celsius limit has been determined as a critical threshold to prevent further negative impact from climate change.

[44] Note that Phase I and Phase II have major differences both in terms of membership as well as mandated gases.

climate change, governments will be unable to ignore this need, even if progress is challenging. Confronting climate change will require technology, regulation, human resources, capacity building, and adaptation.

The emissions trading model, when structured properly and deployed as an overall framework for climate mitigation, provides several opportunities for emissions to be "priced" efficiently by the market The efficient market does not care what method for reducing GHGs is used and, therefore, selects a portfolio of mitigation avenues that optimizes the tradeoffs between attaining the emission-reduction goals and the cost of achieving them.

Appendix B. Standardizing Greenhouse Gas Emissions[45]

The Kyoto Protocol seeks to limit emissions from 6 greenhouse gases implicated in global warming. These are as listed below:

1. Carbon dioxide (CO_2)
2. Methane (CH_4)
3. Nitrous oxide (N_2O)
4. Sulfur hexafluoride (SF_6)
5. Hydrofluorocarbons (HFCs)
6. Perfluorocarbons (PFCs)

Each of the above gases contributes differently to overall global warming. Scientists measure this relative difference in global warming potency using Global Warming Potential or GWP. The GWP of a gas refers to how much heat it is able to trap over a standard period of time relative to carbon dioxide. The international measure for the time period is 100 years and the reference

---

[45] Intergovernmental Panel on Climate Change, "IPCC 4th Assessment Report on Climate Change 2007." (2007); available online at www.ipcc.ch/publications_and_data/ar4/wg1/en/ch2s2-10-2.html.

gas, carbon dioxide, has a GWP of 1. For example, the GWP for methane is 25, which means that methane emissions are 25 times more potent than CO_2 over a 100 year period in trapping atmospheric heat. From an emissions accounting standpoint, emitting one ton of methane emissions is equivalent to emitting 25 tons of carbon dioxide. This is commonly denoted as "carbon dioxide equivalent" or CO_2e and bears a 1:1 relationship with the GWP.

The GWP of all greenhouse gases is given below, along with the equivalent quantity of emissions in CO_2e terms:

Gas	GWP	CO_2e tons
Methane	25	25
Nitrous oxide (N_2O)	310	310
Sulfur hexafluoride (SF_6)	23,900	23,900
Hydrofluorocarbons	140–11,170	140–11,170
Perfluorocarbons	0.10–0.57	0.10–0.57[46]

From a trading standpoint, the unit of account for emissions credits or GHG emissions allowances trading programs around the world is usually 1 ton of CO_2e. Hence, in the methane example, emitting one ton of methane would require 25 CO_2e or 25 carbon emissions allowances to offset it. If this offset was done on 26 February 2013 using European Union Allowances based on market determined prices, then it would cost (25 EUA × €4.30/EUA) = €107.50. This example uses closing EUA prices for the March 2013 EUA futures contract from the IntercontinentalExchange.

---

[46] Hydrofluorocarbons and perfluorocarbons describe general classes of compounds, and the various gases that fall under these categories have different GWPs. Therefore, we present the range of GWP that they take.

Chapter 5

EMERGING GEOGRAPHIES FOR GREENHOUSE GAS EMISSIONS MARKETS

With the success of the European Union ETS and Acid Rain Programs, the use of markets to combat environmental challenges has been firmly established. The world is now witnessing the adoption of the environmental market framework in several emerging economies. In tandem, we are also witnessing the emergence of several regional markets in developed economies. Many of these markets are already in early stages of development. These programs exhibit different environmental objectives, mandated entities, compliance schedules, and cap-and-trade designs.[1] Interestingly, some of these markets are already exploring the potential for market linkages, which if successful, will create a plurilateral[2] market solution to manage global warming. The development of multiple markets in different geographic regimes aimed at solving global warming suggests that, in the short-term, a host of tradable emission products and risk management tools could exist in parallel.

---

[1] Details of environmental market design and cap-and-trade systems is provided in Chapter 2 of this book.

[2] A plurilateral treaty is a treaty between a limited number of states with a particular interest in the subject of the treaty. First expressed in Richard Sandor, "A Limited-scale Voluntary International Greenhouse-gas Emissions Trading Program as Part of the United States Environmental Policy in the Twenty-first Century." In David L. Boren and Edward J. Perkins, eds., *Preparing America's Foreign Policy for the 21st Century* (Norman: The University of Oklahoma Press, April 1999). A more detailed discussion appeared in Richard Sandor, "The Case for Plurilateral Environmental Markets." Environmental magazine (September 2001).

This development, while theoretically complex to visualize, could signal several opportunities. This is the focus of this chapter. The objective of this chapter will be to explore the GHG market mechanisms, risks, and opportunities as it pertains to emerging GHG markets both in the developed and developing world. A wide range of new geographies where environmental market models are being experimented will be included. These include Australia, Canada, Brazil, China, and Korea among others. In addition, promising regional programs in the United States, namely, in Northeast and California, will be discussed at length. Figure 5.1 presents a snapshot of some of these regions where programs are actively being pursued.

Understanding these emerging markets is important for financial analysts, corporates, investors, and entrepreneurs for several reasons. First, as witnessed in earlier discussions on the Acid Rain Program and the EU ETS in Chapters 3 and 4 respectively, there are advantages in building market knowledge and readiness in early stages of evolution in environmental markets. For example, the EU ETS from 2005–2007 was established for that express purpose. During the course of market evolution, several of these markets have seen emission allowance prices fall due to factors such as regulatory uncertainty, economic conditions, or competition. However, it is undeniable that during early stages of market development these markets have witnessed impressive growth. Such opportunities for early entrants may still exist in the emerging markets. This is especially true for those market participants who are not compliance buyers but traders.

On the other hand, experience with acid rain and EU ETS markets has shown that those companies that are mandated to reduce emissions, and therefore maybe buyers of emission allowances, may benefit from waiting to purchase longer-term requirements of allowances. Second, given the development of several regional markets, the opportunistic investor can gain from both locational and programmatic arbitrage opportunities across these environmental markets. Third, a point that will be discussed in further detail, several of the emerging markets, especially in Asia and Latin America, are

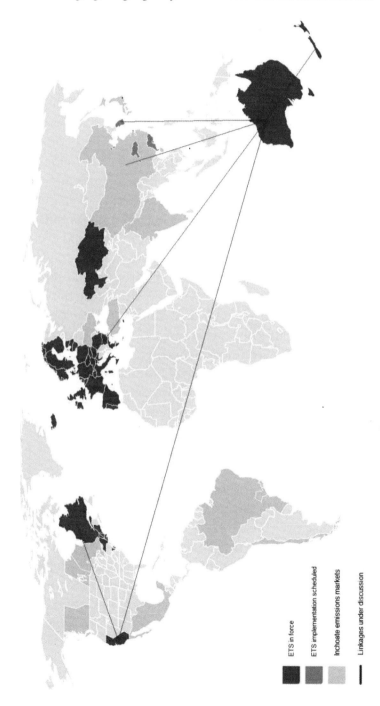

Figure 5.1. Worldwide Cap-and-Trade Programs.

Source: Adapted from ICAP Carbon Action.

located in key geographies which have the potential to be growth engines of futures.[3] Several corporates are strategically positioning themselves in these regions and increasing the level of manufacturing and industrial activity. Increased industrial and manufacturing activity closely correlates with higher energy use. Further, the dependence of fossil fuels for energy translates as these centers have potential increased emissions growth. This along with a combination of increased confidence in environmental markets, alongside building of financial and trading capacity in these regions augments a bright future for emissions trading in emerging markets. Other markets, such as California and Regional Greenhouse Gas Initiative (RGGI), which are located in developed economies, could eventually represent the framework for national systems in these countries. Fourth, these markets represent new areas for product and business innovation in environmental finance. As witnessed during the evolution of other environmental markets, opportunities to develop financial products, trading platforms and exchanges, project development and advisory services, environmental funds etc. could be interesting avenues for value creation, both from an investment and new business standpoint. In addition, the factors on why financial analysts, corporates, and investors should pay attention as mentioned in Chapters 3 and 4 of this book are valid to this chapter.

Since these markets are in early stages of development, a full suite of financial products, such as the ones described in the EU ETS and acid rain chapters, is not yet available for these markets. The expectation is that with further maturity in these markets, those products will evolve over time.

This chapter is divided into five sections. The first section will describe the different market approaches that are being employed in the emerging GHG markets. The second and third sections will focus on North American programs and emerging international programs respectively. The next section will describe voluntary

---

[3]Antonia Guerrero, "Looking Back, Moving Forward: Emerging Markets." *Global Finance* (16 July 2012); available online at http://www.gfmag.com/archives/155-25th-anniversary/11836-emerging-markets.html#axzz2qP19huVL.

markets and the final section will conclude with some highlights and lessons learned.

Market Approaches to Mitigating Climate Change

A host of market based approaches have been employed in response to environmental and public policy goals to combat climate change and meet energy demands. While the cap-and-trade framework is the predominant underlying operational mechanism, different programs have variations in the underlying tradable commodity, the policy objective and trading framework reflecting the local policy need. To illustrate, the EU ETS and Acid Rain Programs targeted absolute emissions reductions of the respective pollutants, whereas the Perform, Achieve & Trade program in India targets the policy objective of increasing energy-efficiency, and emerging programs in China target reducing carbon intensity. All of these approaches can lead to credible decreases in GHG emissions and employ the cap-and-trade design. Similarly, several other such approaches co-exist and drive carbon efficiency gains along with other policy objectives. For example, the EU has 2020 targets of 20% improvement in energy-efficiency, 20% energy from renewables, and 20% reductions in its carbon emissions from 1990 levels. Considering the considerable emissions gap in achieving the goals of containing global warming to a 2°C increase, all of these approaches and other complementary efforts may be required to meet the environmental objective.

Before proceeding to define the two broad approaches to managing emissions, it may be worthwhile to explain the core underlying mechanism differentiating the approaches. These approaches, while different in the programmatic target, may achieve similar overall objectives. In that sense they complement each under. There are three main program designs that form the basis for most global programs:

(1) Absolute GHG reductions: This approach is the most direct and widely applied method for reducing GHG emissions in most

developed economies. The approach mandates covered entities in select sectors to reduce actual tons of GHG emissions as defined in the reduction targets. Allowance trading programs trade in emission rights corresponding to a quantity of GHG emissions. Depending on the program's scope, a wide variety of carbon offsetting programs, such as renewable energy projects, may be linked to these programs. This approach, due to its requirement of reducing actual GHG emissions, may incentivize covered entities to adopt clean energy sources, improve energy-efficiencies, and invest in carbon offset projects. The best examples of this approach are the European Union Emissions Trading Scheme, discussed in great detail in Chapter 4 of this book and the Acid Rain Trading Program discussed in Chapter 3.

(2) Reductions in Carbon Intensity: Carbon intensity is defined as the amount of carbon emitted per dollar GDP produced, or per unit of production. In other words, it is a measure of carbon emitted as economies produce goods and services. When economies have high carbon intensity, it suggests that they are producing very little in comparison to the carbon emitted in the production process. Recall that carbon in the production process is largely from the fuel used. Thus when coal is the primary fuel for economic activity, carbon intensity tends to be high. Changing the fuel type to renewable energy or other clean sources, or alternatively improving the production efficiency can lead to reductions in carbon intensity. Programs that focus on reducing carbon intensity are another approach to reducing GHG emissions. This approach has a particular appeal in developing countries which particularly have to balance environmental goals with growth concerns. A carbon intensity target links the environmental objective with the economic aspirations. The most promising country that has adopted this approach is China although it has been tried earlier in developed economies as part of regional programs such as Alberta in Canada. Under a carbon intensity approach, covered entities are given a carbon intensity

target. These targets may be benchmarked to specific sectoral goals based on that sector's reliance on a certain fuel, best available technology, and other economic factors. In theory, a carbon intensity target will motivate covered entities to move towards less carbon intensive fuels, improve energy-efficiency, and other activities that can lead to reducing absolute GHG emissions. When the regulator sets rigorous carbon intensity targets, substantial real reductions in GHG emissions can be achieved. It is also important to note that a carbon intensity cap-and-trade program need not necessarily lead to absolute reductions in GHG emissions. It is especially true in growing economies witnessing rapid growth in manufacturing and industrial processes and GDP. In other words, a carbon intensity approach guarantees containing the level of carbon emissions per unit of economic activity but does not limit the aggregate level of carbon emissions or economic activity. From a policy standpoint, this method can be a good pre-step prior to taking on absolute emissions reductions targets for high growth economies.

(3) Reductions in Energy Intensity: Energy Intensity refers to the amount of energy consumed per unit of GDP or unit of production. It is therefore a measure of energy-efficiency in an economy. An economy with high energy intensities suggests that its production systems consume too much energy in relation to production of goods and services. In other words, the production process is energy-inefficient and may also involve energy losses. Trading in energy intensity is the third approach that leads to directly improving energy-efficiency and indirectly reduces GHG levels and improves carbon intensity as co-benefits.

This is because given the reliance of global economy on fossil fuels for meeting energy demands, reducing energy intensity can directly lead to reducing carbon emissions. The largest proposed programs targeting energy intensity as the programmatic goal is the Perform, Achieve and Trade program in India. This program sets energy intensity targets for large GHG emitting sectors and allows them to trade the energy intensity targets among sectors. The program requires benchmarking of energy intensity in each sector. Covered entities are incentivized to improve their energy-efficiencies as a result of this approach. The significant GHG reductions that accrue from improving energy-efficiency are well documented in Chapter 7 of this book. Similar to a carbon intensity approach, an energy intensity approach is of special value in developing economies due to their growth concerns with absolute GHG targets. In addition, demand for energy is already significant in these economies providing a stimulus to energy conservation and efficiency. Similar to the discussion in a carbon intensity approach, while an energy intensity cap-and-trade program will promote energy conservation and efficiency measures per unit of economic activity, it does not guarantee a reduction in overall GHG emissions levels. As a policy tool, this approach is focused on promoting judicious use of energy at the corporate level and any GHG emissions benefits are secondary co-benefits. An economy following this approach may witness overall increases in aggregate fossil fuel energy use and therefore GHG emissions. Similar to the carbon intensity approach, it may be a practical first step prior to taking on absolute GHG emissions reductions.

Broadly, from a policy perspective, the various trading approaches described above can be categorized as those focused on energy usage and those focused on emissions:

(1) Energy Policy Measures: These approaches are outcomes of policy responses to multiple needs in addition to climate change. Many regions in the world are still energy- and electricity-deprived. As these economies strive to provide these basic needs to their citizens and develop, a key policy goal is to provide these amenities under a low-carbon sustainable pathway. Other energy policy objectives include energy security, national energy diversification goals, costs reduction and affordability, and increased efficiency in power production and delivery.

The primary mechanisms employed have been promotion of renewable energy generation and energy-efficiency. These have been achieved either by mandate, preferential tariffs or market based renewable energy, or energy-efficiency trading programs. These mechanisms have been discussed at length elsewhere in this book and will not be discussed in this chapter.

(2) Emissions Policy Measures: These approaches are primary outcomes of policy responses to tackle global warming. Depending on the program design, they can include a wide variety of sectors that are sources and sinks for GHG emissions. Depending on these designs, they contribute to energy policy measures above as well as climate adaptation and rural development. The predominant mechanism employed is cap-and-trade mechanisms that seek to reduce absolute GHG emissions. Other variants employed include cap-and-trade models that seek to reduce carbon intensity. Theoretically, a hybrid model that seeks to initially reduce carbon intensity followed by absolute reductions may be realistic in certain developing economies. This section discusses programs that fall under both categories.

North American GHG Emissions Markets

There are four regional programs currently underway in U.S. and Canada: (1) California, (2) Northeast region — Regional Greenhouse Gas Initiative (RGGI), Canadian provinces of Quebec and Alberta. Other regions are also actively in the process of designing their own GHG reduction measures.

California's Cap-and-Trade Program: The California program has the potential to be one of the world's largest and most influential carbon trading programs. Given the size of the California economy, the 8th largest[4] in the world and accounting for 13% of U.S.

---

[4]Center for Continuing Study of the California Economy, "California Poised to Move Up in World Economy Rankings in 2013." (July 2013); available online at http://www.ccsce.com/PDF/Numbers-July-2013-CA-Economy-Rankings-2012.pdf.

gross domestic product, rivaling large economies such as India,[5] the program can have significant global impact on the economy and the environment. In addition, with its tendency to foster entrepreneurship, California has been the center of innovation in the United States for technology and to some extent for the agricultural, automotive, and other sectors. California has a history of leading the world in setting the policy and standards. Many of the policies set in California have been replicated and adopted in the rest of the country and later the world. This is especially true in the case of environmental policy. California was one of the early adopters of renewable energy and energy-efficiency policy and the state led the nation in mandating energy-efficiency standards for appliances, buildings, and furnaces which was later adopted by rest of the country. Similarly, the national new fuel economy standards have their roots in a 2002 law passed by California to slash vehicle tail pipe emissions.[6]

California has already been ahead of the nation when it comes to energy-efficiency and per capita electricity consumption. To illustrate, nationally the per capita electricity consumption is 13,000 kiloWatts (kW) per year while Californians only consume 7,400 kW/year. When it comes to GHG emissions, California's efforts are significant. If California was a country, it would rank 18th among GHG emitters. It also ranks among the cleanest, measured by GHG emissions per $1,000 GDP, alongside France and Japan. California, in a global context, represents about 1.3% of the total global GHG emissions. In that sense, its emissions are within range of comparison to Australia's and South Africa's national GHG emissions. Given California's impressive record, it is not surprising that in their first 12 months of trading in 2013, the California Carbon Allowances traded on IntercontinentalExchange has already more than surpassed in open interest for the same period of the long established Random Length Lumber futures

---

[5]The GDP of California is $1.9 trillion and is greater than that of India (where the latter is not purchasing power parity adjusted).

[6]Coral Davenport, "California's New Cap-and-Trade Law: A Model for the Country?" *National Journal* (13 December 2012); available online at http://www.nationaljournal.com/magazine/california-s-new-cap-and-trade-law-a-model-for-the-country-20121213.

contract.[7] Post futures and options expirations for December 2013, the open interest for the Oats futures contract, and Random Length Lumber contracts on the Chicago Mercantile Exchange (CME) stood at 9,397 and 3,746 respectively. The California carbon allowances futures (CCAR) on the primary trading venue, the IntercontinentalExchange, recorded an open interest of 19,663 contracts. Prior to December futures and options expirations, the open interest for CCAR futures peaked at 46,090 contracts.[8] The post expiration open interest figures are representative of the significant interest in the California emissions allowances contract. Market participants in emission futures traditionally trade the December month expirations contract as it is indicative of the annual calendar environmental compliance requirements. This trading activity suggests open interest in emissions contracts to fall during the December expirations as market participants sell their December long positions to take long positions in future listed expirations. This process of rolling forward the futures position explains the fall in open interest in the month of December.

The California emissions trading program that started operating in January 2013 is currently the largest and most comprehensive emissions program in the U.S. The designed program includes the largest GHG emission tonnage from most of the sectors and requires the most ambitions emissions targets. The program has its roots in 2006, with passage of the California Global Warming Solutions Act or AB 32, which mandates the state's GHG emissions return to 1990 levels by 2020.

In absolute terms, California's emissions in 1990 were about 427 $MMTCO_2$ and projected to be around 600 $MMTCO_2$ by 2020. AB 32 is requiring that by 2020, California reduces its emissions by 172 $MMTCO_2$ or roughly by 30%. Further, by 2050, the Act is expected to drive California GHG emissions 80% below the 1990 levels. This is comparable to the ambitious goals set by the European Union,

---

[7] As of 22 July 2013, California Allowances futures and options open interest on ICE was 27,403 compared to Random Length Lumber futures and options of 6,990.

[8] IntercontinentalExchange (ICE) Data; available online at https://www.theice.com/market_data.jhtml.

which has resolved to reduce its GHG emissions by 80% to 90% from 1990 levels. Meeting these goals will require impressive effort and technological innovation.

As typically seen in most developed economies, about 85% of California GHG emissions are due to CO_2 emissions primarily from fossil fuel combustion. About 6% to 7% GHG emissions are methane from landfills, manure digestion, and fermentation. Another 7% to 8% are from nitrous oxide primarily from soil management practices involving fertilizer applications. Fluorinated gases constitute the remaining 2% to 3% of the state's GHG emissions. These statistics are important as they provide information on where significant emissions and least cost reductions can occur. Understanding the dynamics of the underlying source of GHG emissions can help in predicting market movements, and demand and supply for allowance credits. California's case clearly indicates that in-state emissions reduction requires targeting fuel combustion followed by industrial process emissions, agriculture and forestry, and other sources.

The GHG emissions from fuel combustion are primarily from sectors such as transportation and electricity generation which together accounted for over 50% of California's GHG emissions. The sector wise breakdown of California's GHG emissions along with a forecast for 2020 emissions is presented in Figure 5.2 below.

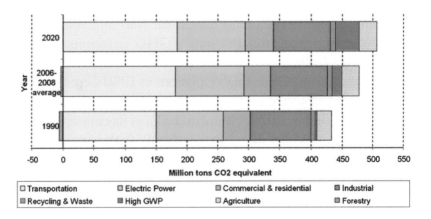

Figure 5.2. California Greenhouse Gas Emissions Forecast.
Source: California Environmental Protection Agency; available online at www.calepa. ca.gov.

The California Air Resources Board (CARB) was charged with developing rules and regulations for implementation of the program. The program covers 85% of the state's GHG emissions, includes all six GHGs, and trades through an emissions currency called the California Carbon Allowance or CCA. Together with the Public Utilities Commission, the California cap-and-trade program, or AB 32, requires CARB to cooperate with stakeholders in the business community and civil society and ensure that implementation:

(1) Minimizes cost and maximizes benefits for California's economy;
(2) improves and modernizes California's energy infrastructure;
(3) maintains electric system reliability;
(4) maximizes environmental and economic co-benefits; and
(5) complements state efforts to improve air quality.

In order to achieve the AB 32 mandated emission reductions, CARB promulgated several actions. First, it set in motion a mandate for reporting and verification of GHG emissions from large industrial sources. As seen under the Acid Rain Program and the EU ETS, having a reliable monitoring and tracking process for GHG emission is critical for program success. Second, CARB identified GHG reduction activities that could benefit from early action. Third, advisory committees were developed to provide input for environmental justice issues as well as economy and technological advancement issues.

The first compliance period is 2013–2014, in which large stationary sources in industry and electrical power generation emitting 25,000 tCO_2e/year are covered, including imports of electricity. In aggregate these represent about 350 businesses in California. The first commitment period seeks to achieve a reduction of 2% each year. The allowance budget for 2013 is about 162.8 million tons, which puts the market value of the allowances at $2.38 billion assuming a $15 price per allowance.

The second compliance period is 2015–2017, in which the targeted rate of emissions reduction rises to 3% per year. In addition, it now applies to distributors of fuel for transportation as well as residential and commercial use. The third compliance period is 2018–2020, with the targeted rate of reduction remaining at 3% per year.

The allowance allocation process followed by California involved large industrial facilities being allocated free allowances, much like the Acid Rain Program. However, in later stages of the program, allowances must be procured via auctions. Electric utilities are provided free allowances in an effort to benefit rate payers. Electric sector and industrial sector allowances are set at 90% of the average emissions. The industry sector benchmark allows for rewarding efficient facilities.

In addition to regular allowances, offset credits may also be used to fulfill up to 8% of each facilities compliance obligations. Such offset credits can be generated by GHG emission reductions or carbon sequestration projects involving forestry, urban forestry, methane destruction from animal manure, and destruction of ozone depleting substances. Offset projects are subject to rigorous independent verification requirements and must be located within the United States, though international offset projects are anticipated in the future.

Covered industries are required to report GHG emissions annually and register with CARB for the emissions trading market. Reported emissions are verified by independent third-party entities. CARB maintains an accreditation and oversight program to enroll qualified verification firms as well as individual verifiers[9] to conduct verification services. A list of verification firms and the required qualifications[10] to become eligible verifiers have been made publically available by the CARB.

---

[9]California Environmental Protection Agency Air Resource Board, "Accreditation of GHG Verifiers Bodies." (September 2013); available online at http://www.arb.ca.gov/cc/reporting/ghg-ver/ghg-ver-accreditation.htm.

[10]California Air Resources Board, "Accreditation Requirements for Verifiers and Verification Bodies in California's Mandatory GHG Reporting Program." (January 2012); available online at http://www.arb.ca.gov/cc/reporting/ghg-ver/acc2.pdf.

Each compliance period is 2 or 3 years (2013–2014, 2015–2017, and 2018–2020), though allowances sufficient for 30% of the previous year's emissions are to be surrendered annually. In the event of non-compliance within the allowed deadline, four allowances must be surrendered for each allowance shortfall.

In addition to ordinary allowance trading, CARB permits banking of allowances to control compliance costs. Banking, a concept that was introduced in Chapter 3, allows unused emission allowances to be retained between compliance periods for use or trade at a later time.

CARB also maintains a strategic reserve of allowances that are sold at set prices. The CARB strategic reserve comprises of about 120 million allowances — about 4% of the total emissions until 2020. These can be purchased by program participants at three different price points of $40, $45, and $50 per ton with up to 40 million allowances available under each price point. These reserve allocations provide some relief in case prices rise too quickly. Over-the-course of the program, the prices of these reserve allowances may be raised.

In addition, CARB also administers quarterly auctions that allow eligible participants to purchase allowances directly from the Air Resources Board. As seen in the Acid Rain Program, provision for having auctions at pre-determined auctions ensures that transparent price signals exist for markets as well as prevent supply restrictions. CARB auctions allow for 2013 compliance year allowances and advance allowances to be made available. Table 5.1 presents the summary statistics of auctions results from the first auction in November 2012 to the last auction in November 2013. The current compliance year allowances have all been sold out in each of the auctions. Prices have ranged between $10 to $14 per allowance for 2013 allowances and around $11 per allowance for 2016 allowances.

Participants in these auctions have included a wide variety of businesses and government agencies. The number and kind of participants have increased over time, indicating a healthy trend for the program. Participants include energy companies such as DTE energy, Dynegy, Exelon; transportation companies like BNSF;

Table 5.1. California Allowances Auctions Bids Summary Results.

	Month	2013 allowances			Advance auction		
		Allowances available	Allowances sold	Settlement price	Allowances available	Allowances sold	Settlement price
I Auction	November-12	23,126,110	23,126,110	$10.09	39,450,000	5,576,000	$10.00
II Auction	February-13	12,924,822	12,924,822	$13.62	9,560,000	4,440,000	$10.71
III Auction	May-13	14,522,048	14,522,048	$14.00	9,560,000	7,515,000	$10.71
IV Auction	August-13	13,865,422	13,865,422	$12.22	9,560,000	9,560,000	$11.10
V Auction	November-13	16,614,526	16,614,526	$11.48	9,560,000	9,560,000	$11.10

banks like Citigroup, J.P. Morgan, Morgan Stanley, and Royal Bank of Canada; industries such as Dow Chemicals; brokers such as Evolution Markets, Amerex, and TFS; and Californian cities such as Anaheim, Banning, Needles, and Colton.

In addition to auctions, California allowances can also be procured through futures and options contracts on ICE and CME. The predominant trading venue for environmental derivatives, including the California emissions contract, is ICE. As of 9 January 2014, ICE commanded an impressive 100% of the market share of exchange-traded CCAR futures trading volume. From a historical perspective, the Chicago Climate Exchange was the first to launch a regulated market for trading California carbon. As early as 2007, the exchange setup a venture called the California Climate Exchange to promote a transparent and regulated marketplace for California carbon. In addition, several environmental brokers also broker these allowances over-the-counter. Figure 5.3 presents historic prices, volumes, and open interest for California allowances from the ICE futures market. Interest in California allowances has been rising given the positive policy developments discussed earlier in this section. As mentioned earlier, in the three months since listing of the contract on ICE, the open interest in California allowances is greater than that of the lumber contract that was listed on CBOT, and is rising quickly.

In conclusion, the California GHG program has several of the design mechanisms that were introduced in the earlier chapter being incorporated into its program. First, California allows for a range of offset credits to be eligible for environmental compliance.[11] Compliance Offset Credits can be bought from projects anywhere in North America. Second, California allows banking of CCAs future use, but not borrowing of credits. Third, California allows for international offset linkage for projects in developing countries in selected sectors, such as tropical deforestation and forestry. The program permits purchasing credits from other regulatory programs that may institute their own system. There is a possibility of linking

---

[11] Up to 8% of CCAs may be accounted for by offsets, which fall under several categories.

of the California cap-and-trade program with other international emission systems. As of April 2013, California announced the linkage of its carbon program with the Canadian province of Quebec. With this bold initiative it became an international program.

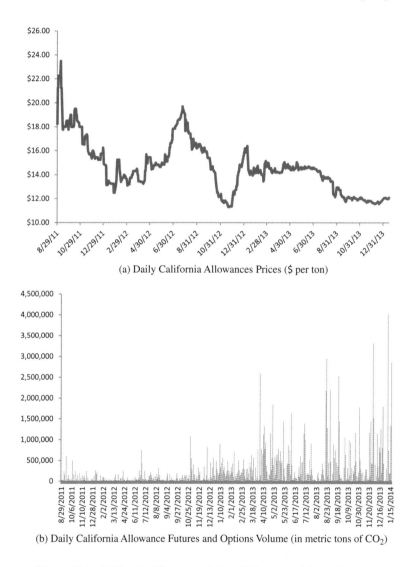

(a) Daily California Allowances Prices ($ per ton)

(b) Daily California Allowance Futures and Options Volume (in metric tons of CO_2)

Figure 5.3. California Allowance Prices, Volume, and Open Interest.

Source: ICE

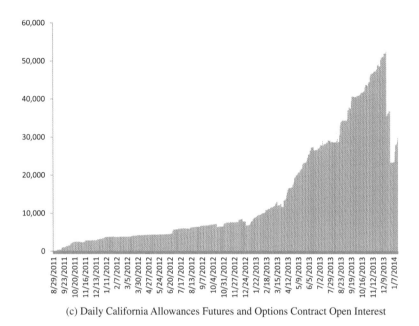

(c) Daily California Allowances Futures and Options Contract Open Interest

Figure 5.3. (*Continued*)

Furthermore, California has already taken steps to potentially link its program with China and Australia. In September 2013, California signed a two-year agreement with China to share expertise and experience with low carbon development and emissions trading.[12] A year earlier, it agreed in principle to work with Australia to develop regional and global carbon markets and share experiences with low carbon growth.[13]

These developments suggest the evolution of a global carbon market via linking of regional systems rather than through national systems. The next section describes the other major regional

---

[12] Ari Phillips, "China and California form Unlikely Parternship to Address Climate Change." *Climate Progress* (6 September 2013); available online at http://thinkprogress.org/climate/2013/09/16/2626181/california-china-climate-deal/.

[13] Department of the Environment, Australian Government, "Australia and Canada to Work Together on Carbon Markets and Emissions Trading Links." [Press Release]; available online at http://www.climatechange.gov.au/ministers/hon-greg-combet-am-mp/media-release/australia-and-california-work-together-carbon-markets.

carbon trading program that exists among a coalition of states in Northeastern U.S., namely, the Regional Greenhouse Gas Initiative.

Regional Greenhouse Gas Initiative (RGGI): The Northeastern U.S. has also been a center for implementing policies that foster environmental objectives. The region was among the first to launch mandates for renewable energy and energy-efficiency. Similarly, for carbon, the region launched the Regional Greenhouse Gas Initiative (RGGI) — the first mandatory CO_2 emissions trading program within the United States in 2009. The program was a significant step in U.S. domestic climate change mitigation efforts using market based mechanisms. The program size is by no means trivial. The nine states that form RGGI as a whole account for 13% of the U.S. population, 7% of U.S. CO_2 emissions, and 16% of U.S. GDP. While the region covering RGGI is comparable to California in population and U.S. GDP contributions, California accounts for 7% of all GHG emissions in the U.S. while RGGI accounts for a similar contribution for carbon dioxide alone. Clearly, the California program is much more ambitious in its scope. California covers all six GHG emissions while RGGI covers only carbon dioxide; California covers a wide range of GHG emitting sectors versus RGGI coverage of the utility sector alone. Lastly, California has a wide range of emissions offsets in comparison to very limited options under RGGI.

RGGI is a CO_2 trading program formed by agreement between nine Northeastern and Mid-Atlantic states in United States. RGGI covers only the electric power sector within these states which are mandated to reduce only their CO_2 emissions as per individual state regulations. RGGI is therefore a program focused on reducing the largest GHG, CO_2 from its biggest emitting sector, i.e., electric power generation. In 2010, CO_2 emissions from the power sector in RGGI states were 137 million short tons, or 5.5% of the U.S. emissions from that sector.

Another point of interest is that RGGI is composed of several individual state cap-and-trade programs with common trading instruments allowing trading across member states. The states currently under RGGI currently are Connecticut, Delaware,

Massachusetts, Maryland, Maine, New Hampshire, New York, Rhode Island, and Vermont. Under RGGI, participation is at the discretion of the states, which have the option to opt out of or to opt into the program. To illustrate, New Jersey withdrew its membership in 2011 while Maryland entered it in 2007. Given that RGGI is a compilation of several state mandates, the program established a set of model rules whereby individual states established their CO_2 limits on power plants, allocated carbon allowances, and participation in the RGGI auctions.

Some of the key features of the program are discussed next, starting with environmental compliance. These program features are discussed in terms of aggregate RGGI states rather than individual state programs.

Compliance Mechanism

The RGGI CO_2 compliance period consists of three phases comprising three years each. The first compliance period operated from the beginning of 2009 through the end of 2011 with a CO_2 emissions cap of 188 million tons.[14] The total number of emitters that RGGI covered in this period was 211 electric generating units. Over the first compliance period, the actual emissions of the aggregate participating states were about 121 million metric tons of CO_2 while the allowance cap was set at 188 million metric tons. The second compliance period operates from the start of 2012 through the end of 2014. As stated earlier, New Jersey opted out of RGGI in 2011. To account for this, the second RGGI compliance period operated with a reduced emissions budget of 165 million tons. Total covered entities also decreased to 171 following New Jersey's withdrawal. As part of its 2012 review, observing actual emissions levels in relation to the RGGI cap, the participating states decided to substantially reduce the cap, starting from 2014, to 91 million tons. The third compliance period is expected to start from 2015 and run until the end of 2018. During this period, the annual emissions

---

[14] Refer to short tons.

Table 5.2. RGGI State Emissions Budget.

State	Budget (tons)	Budget (%)
New York	64,310,805	38.93
Maryland	37,503,983	22.70
Massachusetts	26,660,204	16.14
Connecticut	10,695,036	6.47
New Hampshire	8,620,460	5.22
Delaware	7,559,787	4.58
Maine	5,948,902	3.60
Rhode Island	2,659,239	1.61
Vermont	1,225,830	0.74
Total Emissions Budget (tons)	**165,184,246**	

are expected to reduce by 2.5% annually for a total reduction of 10% by the end of 2018.

The state-wise share of the CO_2 emissions budget is presented above in Table 5.2. Major manufacturing and population regions of New York, Maryland and Massachusetts account for the bulk of the emissions budget. Figure 5.4 presents the RGGI emissions cap alongside the actual emissions from 2009 through 2013.

At RGGI's inception, the emissions cap was set about 4% above the average CO_2 emissions from the electric power sector in years 2000 through 2002. The policy assumption was that the actual emission would rise over time to match the established cap of 188 million tons. It is evident that the actual emissions have been far below the set emissions cap. This means that the emissions cap by itself may not compel the covered entities to make internal emissions reductions or purchase offsets. Specifically, during the first compliance period, actual emissions were 36% lower than the cap, causing a severe oversupply of RGGI credits. The over-allocation problem led the allowance prices to reflect the annual price floor that was established for the first compliance period.

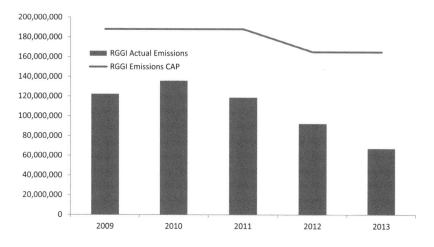

Figure 5.4. RGGI Emissions Cap and Actual CO_2 Emissions (Short Tons).

Several studies indicate that the RGGI emissions are not projected to reach the 2005 levels until 2020. The reasons for the lower emissions include fuel switching, energy-efficiency measures, and the weather. This is partly based on assumptions on economic recovery but also due to fundamental structural changes in electricity generation. The region has been witnessing a shift to greater energy-efficiency and low carbon in electricity generation. To illustrate, in 2005, RGGI states generated 32% of their electricity from coal, petroleum, and other CO_2 rich sources. In 2011, these sources generated 12% of the RGGI electricity supply. However, covered entities may undertake such measures anticipating further cuts, for corporate social responsibility purposes or other strategic reasons.

The excess of allowances issued in relation to the cap led to mandated entities banking allowances, up to 57 million allowances in aggregate, for use in future compliance years. In responding to the over-allocation issue, RGGI included some rectifying measures in its updated model rules established in 2013. The primary measure for managing over-allocation involved decreasing the emissions budget. The methodology involved each state adjusting its emission budget based on the amount of allowances that have been banked by its emitters in the previous periods. This adjustment would effectively reduce the overall cap down, over the course of seven years, to the total number of allowances banked in previous years. A second measure involves states not offering, and in some cases retiring, allowances that were undersubscribed in the RGGI auctions. These policy measures essentially are designed to reduce the cap and allow the market to price the allowances. From a practical view, this measure is more efficient as the pricing mechanism is left unaltered, thereby allowing the market to respond to the fundamental underlying demand, supply, and risks associated with the program.

The tradable allowance under the program is one short ton of CO_2 issued by RGGI. These allowances are held and tracked by an allowance registry and tracking system called RGGI COATS.[15] This electronic platform monitors each state's CO_2 Budget Trading Program and allows for transfers from one account to another, enabling efficient trading. Individual states issue the allowances allocated to them among covered entities. Trading however could be done across RGGI states.

Flexibility Mechanism

The RGGI program had several flexibility provisions all of which helped control allowance prices. First, the program included price collars including a reserve price on auctions. RGGI also credited early reduction efforts. These provided benefits to those entities that achieved emissions reductions prior to the program's inception in the years 2006 to 2008. The decision by RGGI to use a three-year compliance mechanism rather than annual compliance provided for added flexibility. In addition, RGGI has a novel price trigger mechanism that allowed the states to extend the compliance period. Under this setup, if the RGGI allowance price exceeds $10 per allowance for a period of 12 months on a rolling average basis, the program can extend the compliance period by three one-year periods. So far

---

[15] Regional Greenhouse Gas Initiative, "CO_2 Allowance Tracking System"; available online at https://rggi-coats.org/eats/rggi/.

there has been no need to employ these measures. Thirdly, RGGI allows use of specified offsets credits generated within its program states. The use of offsets is restricted to 3.3% of each individual entity's compliance obligation. RGGI also allows unlimited banking of allowances for future use.

Allocation of Allowances

The RGGI program allocates the majority of its allowances (over 90%) through quarterly, regional auctions. The auctions serves as the primary issuance and price discovery mechanism for RGGI CO_2 allowances prices. The proceeds from these auctions are returned back to the states to be used for various energy-efficiency, strategic energy purposes, renewable energy, and GHG mitigation schemes. In the first compliance period, these proceeds were around $952 million and in the second compliance period, the proceeds exceeded a billion dollars.

The RGGI auctions are designed as single round, uniform price auctions. Industrial and financial players are free to participate as long as they meet the eligibility conditions, which include financial eligibility. In a single auction, qualified buyers are restricted to a maximum of 25% of the auctioned allowances. As mentioned earlier, RGGI auctions also had a floor price; the initial floor price was set at $1.86 per allowance and later increased to $1.98 in 2013. Given that the RGGI cap has so far been higher than the actual emissions, the reserve price has served the role of an emissions fee.

RGGI has so far conducted 22 quarterly auctions. Summary data on each of the auctions is presented in Table 5.3. On average about 36 million RGGI allowances have been offered each quarterly auction. While most of the quantity offered has been procured at each auction, compliance years 2011 and 2012 saw successive auctions being undersubscribed. States have not re-offered these unsold allowances and retired them. This undersubscription denotes the over-allocation problem that plagued RGGI since its inception. The over-allocation was a result both of slagging economy that caused decreased output and hence emissions, as well as RGGI's success

Table 5.3. Summary Data on RGGI Quarterly Auctions.

Date	Auction number	Quantity offered	Quantity sold	Clearing price ($)	Number of bidders	Allowances won by compliance entities (%)	Total proceeds ($)
9/25/2008	Auction 1*	12,565,387	12,565,387	3.07	82	82	38,575,738.09
12/17/2008	Auction 2	31,505,898	31,505,898	3.38	84	87	106,489,935.24
3/18/2009	Auction 3	31,513,765	31,513,765	3.51	63	78	117,248,629.80
6/17/2009	Auction 4	30,887,620	30,887,620	3.23	67	85	104,242,445.00
9/9/2009	Auction 5	28,408,945	28,408,945	2.19	59	77	66,278,239.35
12/2/2009	Auction 6	28,591,698	28,591,698	2.05	74	65	61,587,120.90
3/10/2010	Auction 7	40,612,408	40,612,408	2.07	61	85	87,956,944.56
6/9/2010	Auction 8	40,685,585	40,685,585	1.88	53	92	80,465,566.78
9/10/2010	Auction 9	45,595,968	34,407,000	1.86	56	92	66,437,340.00
12/1/2010	Auction 10	43,173,648	24,755,000	1.86	49	97	48,224,220.00
3/9/2011	Auction 11	41,995,813	41,995,813	1.89	49	85	83,425,588.47
6/8/2011	Auction 12	42,034,184	12,537,000	$1.89	47	91%	25,477,200.00
9/7/2011	Auction 13	42,189,685	7,487,000	1.89	41	94	14,150,430.00
12/7/2011	Auction 14	42,983,482	27,293,000	1.89	49	99	51,583,770.00
3/14/2012	Auction 15	34,843,858	21,559,000	1.93	34	99	41,608,870.00
6/6/2012	Auction 16	36,426,008	20,941,000	1.93	35	95	40,416,130.00
9/5/2012	Auction 17	37,949,558	24,589,000	1.93	29	100	47,456,770.00
12/5/2012	Auction 18	37,563,083	19,774,000	1.93	34	100	38,163,820.00
3/13/2013	Auction 19	37,835,405	37,835,405	2.80	43	69	105,939,134.00
6/5/2013	Auction 20	38,782,076	38,782,076	3.21	55	68	124,490,463.96
9/4/2013	Auction 21	38,409,043	38,409,043	2.67	52	53	102,552,144.81
12/4/2013	Auction 22	38,329,378	38,329,378	3.00	55	43	114,988,134.00

*Six states participated in Auction 1.

in reducing emission levels. The clearing prices in these auctions have ranged from $1.89 to $3.38, with an average of about $2. The over-allocation problem meant that for substantial periods, the RGGI auction clearing price was the set reserve price. This situation has recently changed with auction clearing prices nearing $3 per allowance in auctions conducted in 2013. Historically, a significant majority of the allowances procured in the auctions have been by the covered entities. This is not surprising given that the primary procurement avenue for covered entities, which represent the natural buyers in market, has been the auction, whereas non-covered entities may purchase some allowances in auctions with the hope of selling them for a higher price in the secondary market. In more recent auctions in 2013, this covered entities' share of auction sales has fallen to about 50%, suggesting that there is interest from other organizations and this is encouraging.

The other avenue for entities to buy or sell RGGI allowances is the secondary market. This avenue allows participants to buy or sell RGGI allowances in the three months in between auctions. The secondary market also provides firms a means to hedge themselves against the allowance price volatility of future auction clearing prices. As emphasized throughout this book, the price signals from the secondary market are valuable tools to assist firms in making investment decisions in markets affected by the cost of RGGI compliance. The secondary market includes trading in RGGI allowances through spot, futures, and options contracts. These are listed on regulated exchanges such as ICE and CME. In addition, several emission brokers such as Evolution Markets, Amerex, and Tradition Finance also broker in RGGI trades. In the case of futures markets, market participants have the option of taking to delivery a long position in RGGI futures to take possession of allowances. In most cases, participants primarily use the futures market to hedge price risks. Figure 5.5 is a depiction of historical RGGI prices. As seen in Figure 5.5, the RGGI prices in the secondary market have closely mirrored the auction clearing prices. The perception in the market over-allocation of credits is a major factor.

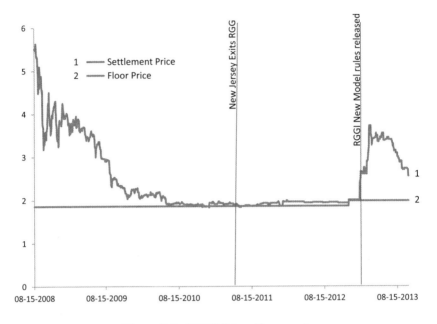

Figure 5.5. RGGI Prices ($ per ton).

Source: ICE

In conclusion, the RGGI program is significant as the first mandatory regional carbon market in the U.S. In spite of it being a program that was limited in its scope and coverage, it set in motion the idea that a regional carbon mandate within the U.S. could be viable. From a policy standpoint, there are numerous lessons from RGGI that are valuable for design of other regional and national markets. RGGI's first phase was fraught by policy and design flaws. This phase was marked by the effects of severe over-allocation of RGGI carbon allowances and a weak cap. Mandated emission limits never rose to the levels of the target due to weak economic conditions, weather, and other energy-efficiency measures. As a result, mandated companies were never compelled to purchase additional RGGI allowances or make internal changes. RGGI prices tracked the auction floor prices. Recognizing the policy and design failures, the RGGI market designers enacted a model review process to correct some flaws. This marked the second phase of RGGI.

The comprehensive model review process set in motion in 2012 acted to address the oversupply issue by a series of measures. Significant measures include lowering the emissions cap to align with the current level of emissions, addressing the banked allowances problem, and recommending states not re-offer unsold RGGI auction allowances back into the market. These steps have re-invigorated the market in 2013. It is important to note that RGGI chooses to address the over-allocation problem not with an allowance pricing measure but with reducing the allowance quantity and stricter target measures. This allows efficient market pricing as per the fundamental market demand and supply rather than introducing extraneous allowance price which could cause market distortions. These are important lessons immediately for the EU ETS which is reeling under a similar over-allocation problem and for other emerging emissions trading programs.

Canadian Emission Markets

This section describes the other major North American GHG reduction initiatives that exist in several provinces of Canada. The earliest among these initiatives was in the Province of Alberta which has seen impressive growth in its energy industry. The other province that will be discussed is Quebec, where the opportunity to link with the California carbon program has been negotiated.

Alberta

The Canadian Province of Alberta accounts for about one-third of all the Canadian GHG emissions and ranks second in per capita national emissions. The growth in Alberta GHG emissions is driven by the province's reliance on coal fired generation and more recently as a global supplier of energy. Alberta accounts for the third largest supply of crude oil behind Saudi Arabia and Venezuela.

The Alberta GHG emissions trading program has its origins in early 2002 when the province complete a comprehensive climate strategy. In the following year, the Climate Change and Emissions

Management Act required facilities emitting over 100,000 metric tons to reduce emissions, which set the province among the early leaders in establishing a GHG compliance market in North America.

With regards to the program design, unlike the EU ETS, the Alberta program is a GHG intensity program. For facilities existing in the year 2000 and emitting over 100,000 tons of CO_2, the program seeks to reduce emissions intensity by 12% below 2003–2005 average emissions per year. Beginning from the 4th year of operation in 2006, the program requires an additional 2% emissions reductions annual intensity goal each year until the facilities reach the required 12% mandate. The program does not have a declining target for mandated entities over time but requires them to meet a constant emissions intensity target each year. The program includes all six GHGs and includes 106 multi-sectoral facilities with an aggregate emissions budget of 108 million metric tons of CO_2. The program mandates GHG emission intensity targets to sectors contributing roughly half of Alberta's total GHG emissions.

The program allows for a variety of compliance options. Facilities could either improve their emissions intensity, purchase an emissions offset from qualified offset projects, purchase an emission Performance Credit which represents surplus emission intensity units from covered units, or pay a fee — fixed price of CAD $15 per ton — to an Alberta Technology fund. The fixed price combined with the unlimited nature of the technology fund effectively established a price ceiling for the Alberta GHG program. The purpose of the fund is innovation in new technologies that lead to GHG emission mitigation and adaptation.

Since its implementation in 2007 till 2011, the program has achieved 33 million tons of CO_2 reductions and raised CAD $312 for the Technology Fund.[16] This is a good example of how a GHG emissions intensity program can lead to credible decreases in actual

---

[16]Environmental Defense Fund and International Emissions Trading Associations, "The World's Carbon Markets: A Case Study Guide to Emissions Trading." (May 2013); available online at http://www.edf.org/sites/default/files/EDF_IETA_Alberta_Case_ Study_ May_2013.pdf.

Table 5.4. Specified Gas Emitters Regulation (SGER) Operational Results (Selected).

Compliance cycle	Offset credits (in megatons)	Fund payments (CAD)	EPC credits retired (in megatons)
2007 (half year)	1	43 millon	0.25
2008	2.7	82 millon	0.57
2009	3.8	63 millon	1.2
2010	3.9	70 millon	1.9
2011*	5.3	55 millon	1

*denotes unaudited results.
Source: IETA, "Greenhouse Gas Market 2012." (2012); available online at http://www.ieta.org/assets/Reports/ieta%20greenhouse%20gas%20market%202.

GHG emissions. About half of these funds have been invested in various low-carbon projects in Alberta and research and development. In 2010, 42% of the compliance was achieved through payment to the technology fund. This serves as an indirect avenue for achieving environmental compliance with the program rules. Operational improvements accounted for 14% and buying emissions offsets for about 28% of compliance. Trading in emission performance credits accounted for 16% of achieved compliance.

Table 5.4 presents the historical breakdown of the various compliance mechanisms in the Alberta GHG program.[17]

Future challenges for the Alberta program include its interaction with the proposed federal oil and gas sector regulations. Multiple policy uncertainties exist on the flexibility and stringency of the federal sectoral mandates and their congruence with the Alberta program.

Quebec

In November 2009, the Canadian province of Quebec adopted a target of achieving 20% reductions in GHG emissions by 2020

---

[17]International Emissions Trading Association, "Greenhouse Gas Market 2012." IETA GHG Market Report (2012).

from 1990 levels. Interestingly, the program has been initiated in a province where the majority of power generation is from hydro-electric power. The program has been developed with the intention of harmonizing future linkages with other regional programs such as California, Ontario, and British Columbia.

The Quebec program comprises of three compliance periods. The first period, from 2013 to 2014, covers 80 facilities from the industrial and power sectors that exceed 25,000 metric tons of annual CO_2 emissions. The second compliance period, from 2015 to 2017, extends the emissions cap to fossil fuel distributors. With this extension, the program is expected to cover 85% of the Quebec's GHG emissions. The third period, from 2018 to 2020, will require an annual reduction of 4% each year. As seen previously in the EU ETS and the Acid Rain Program, Quebec intends to freely distribute emission allowances to covered entities in the first compliance period. However, fuel distributors who are required to comply starting from 2015 will not be distributed free allowances. After initial free allocation, Quebec will auction off remaining allowances periodically to market participants with a floor price of CAD 15 per ton. Proceeds from auctions will be transferred to a Green Fund, with similar objectives as Alberta's technology fund.

The Quebec program allows for limited offset credits and credits from early action to be used for compliance. At the time of writing of this chapter, the eligible offsets include agricultural methane destruction, small landfill methane destruction, and ozone depleting substances. Furthermore, there is an 8% quantitative limit on offsets usage for individual compliance by covered entities. There are several other finer programmatic aspects of the Quebec program that are not relevant to this publication.

The main challenge to the Quebec program is that there are few reduction opportunities in the electric power and industrial sectors. As stated earlier, 96% of Quebec's electric power generation is sourced from hydro-electric power. This leaves the onus on the transportation, manufacturing, and construction sectors to achieve the bulk of the GHG reductions. In addition, Quebec also lacks sufficient offset sources and depends on its linkage with California for offset supply. A delay in the linkage with California is therefore expected to increase the costs of compliance, at least in the short-term in Quebec.

In this section, the active programs to manage GHG emissions in North American have been discussed. The discussion revealed a diversity of program designs in the continent. While most of the programs in place focus on reducing the absolute emissions, variation exists with provinces like Alberta choosing an emission intensity approach. In addition, coverage of GHGs has variations with large regional programs like RGGI focusing on carbon dioxide alone. Most North American programs have incorporated carbon offset usage of some form although on a limited basis. Table 5.5 presents a comparison of various programs in North America. The next section of the chapter will focus on international low carbon initiatives.

Emerging International Programs

Prior to describing several international programs, a description of some unique macroeconomic aspects of the regions in which the programs are in place must first be presented. First, some international locations are uniquely important as new centers for global economic growth. Among these, China and India are economies in various stages of economic growth and liberalization. The financial analyst has to bear in mind that in these geographies, environmental financial instruments are developing in parallel with traditional financial tools. As such, the institutional, governance, and compliance mechanisms are still maturing. Second, the potential for economic growth and development in these regions also means significant opportunities for environmental markets. This is partly due to the strong correlation that exists between industrialization and

Table 5.5. Comparison of Low Carbon Cap-and-Trade Initiatives in North America: Emissions Reductions, Carbon Intensity, and Energy Intensity Programs.

	California cap-and-trade	Regional Greenhouse Gas Initiative (RGGI)	Quebec	Alberta
Gases covered	All greenhouse gases	Carbon dioxide	All greenhouse gases	All greenhouse gases
Program type	Cap-and-trade with absolute emission reductions	Cap-and-trade with absolute emission reductions	Cap-and-trade with absolute emission reductions	Cap-and-trade based on emission intensity
States participating	California; efforts to link with Quebec	Nine Northeastern States: Connecticut, Delaware, Massachusetts, Maryland, Maine, New Hampshire, New York, Rhode Island, and Vermont	Province of Quebec, efforts to link with California	Province of Alberta
Sectoral scope	Electricity generation and industrial units producing more than 25,000 metric tons of carbon dioxide equivalents, and transportation	Fossil fuel-powered electric generating units over 25 megawatts in size	Electricity generation and industrial units producing more than 25,000 metric tons of carbon dioxide equivalents, and transportation	Covers all sectors that have emitted 100,000 tCO$_2$ per year from 2003 onwards

(Continued)

Table 5.5. (*Continued*)

	California cap-and-trade	Regional Greenhouse Gas Initiative (RGGI)	Quebec	Alberta
Effective date	• 1 January 2012 for generators and industrials • 1 January 2015 for transportation	1 January 2009	1 January 2013	1 January 2007
Established emissions CAP	• 2013 and 2014 cap of 162.8 million tons of CO_2e • 2015: Cap increased to 394.5 million tons CO_2e	165 million short tons	65.3 million tons	
Reduction commitment	9% reduction from 2005 levels or stabilize at 1990 levels by 2020	10% reduction in emissions by 2018 below estimate of 2009 emissions	20% below 1990 levels by 2020	Each covered facility is obligated to achieve a 12% reduction below its 2003 to 2005 average net emissions intensity baseline each year

(*Continued*)

136 Sustainable Investing and Environmental Markets

Table 5.5. (*Continued*)

	California cap-and-trade	Regional Greenhouse Gas Initiative (RGGI)	Quebec	Alberta
Compliance period	• Three compliance periods: (1) 2013–2014 (2) 2015–2017 (3) 2018–2020 • Annual compliance: 30% of compliance obligation is due 1 November each year; balance obligation for compliance period is due no later than 1 November following end of compliance period (i.e., 2015, 2018, and 2021)	Three compliance periods: (1) 2009–2011 (2) 2012–2014 (3) 2015–2018	• Three compliance periods: (1) 2013–2014 (2) 2015–2017 (3) 2018–2020 • Compliance obligations no later than 1 October of year following the end of each compliance period	• Compliance period of 1 year duration from 2007 through 2014 • Plan to be reviewed in 2014 • Annual compliance date 31 March of each year
Compliance unit	• Emission allowances issued by CARB • Offsets credits issued by CARB • Early Action Credits issued by ARB	• RGGI carbon unit issued by states • Offset credits issued by states	• Emission allowances issued by Quebec • Early reduction credit issued by Quebec • Offsets issued by Quebec	• Emission Performance Units • Emission offsets

(*Continued*)

Table 5.5. (*Continued*)

	California cap-and-trade	Regional Greenhouse Gas Initiative (RGGI)	Quebec	Alberta
Regulator	California Air Resources Board (CARB)	• Individual states regulate the program • RGGI Inc., a not for profit administers the program	Ministry of Sustainable Development, Environment and Parks	Government of Alberta
Allocation	• Minimum 10% auction in first compliance period (2012–2014), minimum 25% auction after 2020 • Quarterly auctions with reserve price	~90% of 2009 allowances to be auctioned, remainder used for state-specific objectives	• Free allocation to eligible emitters • Quarterly auctions with reserve price	Not applicable
Banking provisions	Banking of allowances allowed	Banking of allowances allowed	Banking of allowances allowed	Not applicable
Offsets	Limited use of approved offsets allowed	Approved offset originating within U.S. allowed	Approved offsets issued by regulator allowed	
Penalty for non-compliance	Four allowances for each missing one	Penalties are decided by individual states and are in order of 3:1	Three allowances for each missing one	Up to CAD 200 per ton of CO_2e

environmental damages. The leadership, both government and corporate, in many of these regions has shown interest in low carbon and sustainable growth pathways. This is in congruence with the concept of Kuznets curve, introduced in Chapter 2 that states that environmental attributes and quality become more important as GDP increases. In addition, these regions also represent huge centers for global population and population growth. This obviously has implications on resource scarcity, allocation, and prioritizations, all of which have an impact on the state of the environment. It is also interesting to note that several of these regions possess significant reserves of important energy and commodity resources that are huge parts of their national economies. This, combined with the economic structure and stage in economic development, demands different market structures than the ones exposed so far in this book. For example, economic growth is of paramount importance in the developing world — both from social and fairness perspectives. Environmental interventions must hence take into account these factors in their design.

As many of these programs are in the nascent stages of their development, the focus of the chapter is more on the fundamental environmental challenges and the opportunities therein for use of market instruments. As illustrated in the previous chapter, the development of a sound, credible, and transparent marketplace for environmental assets paves the way for the creation of asset classes both physical and financial. The EU ETS and the Acid Rain Program have clearly demonstrated this premise. Lessons from the market history of these early environment markets also suggest that early entrants have better opportunities for value generation. In that sense, financial analysts, investors, and corporates should keenly watch developments in the emerging environmental market space.

The first international programs to be discussed are from the large Asian economies of China and India. This is followed by

Australia, South Korea, and Brazil where GHG reduction initiatives have been proposed.

China

The rapid emergence of China as an economic powerhouse is well documented. The Chinese economy has been growing at an average rate of 10% since 2000 and its unprecedented growth rate has helped the country establish itself as the second largest economy after the United States. Much of the Chinese economic growth has been fueled by heavy dependence on fossil fuels. China is the world's largest consumer of energy and its economy is heavily dependent on coal and oil which make up 70% and 19% of its total energy consumption respectively. Natural gas demand is also rising quickly. The Chinese economic growth has been accompanied by significant pressures on natural resources, environment, and society in general. Air pollution is a major problem in Chinese cities, with four Chinese cities figuring in the top 10 most polluted cities in the world. In 2008, China surpassed the United States as the world's largest emitter of GHG emissions. China emits more than 31 million tons of SO_2 emissions and 9.5 million tons of NO_x emissions. In comparison, the United States emits about 9 million tons of SO_2 and 3 million tons of NO_x. More than 400,000 Chinese die prematurely of respiratory illnesses every year and health care costs associated with respiratory illness account for 3.8% of the GDP.

The extent of environment damage witnessed so far is only the beginning. Vast regions in China are yet to be urbanized and rural electrification is proceeding at a rapid pace. In addition to population growth pressures, Chinese population is expected to peak at 1.47 billion between 2030 and 2040,[18] and rapid urbanization will lead to one billion Chinese living in urban areas.

---

[18] China's Second National Assessment Report on Climate Change (2011).

The Chinese government realizes the importance of environment to its economic growth and is starting to take steps to
transition to a more sustainable, environmentally friendly growth
path. More importantly, the Chinese government has been open
to the idea of using market mechanisms to manage some of
its environmental challenges. For market participants and financial analysts, understanding China's environmental issues and risks
becomes an important area of focus. Given the contribution of
China to the global economy, any environmental risks it faces
can have huge ramifications on the rest of the globe. In addition, environmental regulations and markets that the Chinese government implements could represent the biggest environmental
markets in the world. China is already taking steps to curb its
GHG emissions and this will be further explored in the sections
below.

The Chinese government in its 11th five-year plan (2006–2010)
announced a series of energy security and climate polices including
efforts to reduce GHG emissions. The overall goal was to reduce
energy intensity by 20% and increase the share of renewables in the
energy mix from 6% to almost 10% by 2010. Rapid economic growth
accompanied by rising fossil fuel energy consumption resulted in
increased GHG emissions. The Chinese government embarked on
new ambitious goals in its 12th five-year plan (2011–2015). The
current five-year plan (FYP) calls for establishment of a national
carbon trading system by 2015 and as a first step, China's National
Development and Reform Commission has initiated carbon trading
pilots in seven provinces and cities. A host of measures, including
reducing energy intensity by 16% below 2010 and increasing forest
cover by 12.5 hectares are planned. The seven pilots, when operational, will cover over 700 $MtCO_2$ and will be the second largest
GHG emissions program behind the EU ETS. At the end of 2013,
five of the seven proposed GHG trading programs in China were
operational.

The pilot programs are to be established in the following jurisdictions (see Table 5.6).

Table 5.6. China Pilot GHG Trading Programs.

Municipality	2015 energy intensity target, baseline: 2010	2015 carbon intensity target, baseline: 2010	Status
Beijing	17%	18%	Pilot ETS approved; Carbon Trading program launched in November 2013[19]
Tianjin	18%	19%	Pilot ETS approved; Carbon Trading program launched in December 2013[20]
Shanghai	18%	19%	Pilot ETS approved; Carbon Trading program launched in November 2013[21]
Hubei	16%	17%	Pilot ETS approved
Chongqing	16%	17%	Pilot ETS approved
Guangdong	18%	19.5%	Pilot ETS approved; trading commenced in China Emissions Exchange in December 2013[22]
Shenzhen	19.5%	21%	Pilot ETS approved; was the first province to launch Carbon Trading in June 2013[23]
PRC Central Government	−16%	−17%	

[19] Kathy Chen and Stian Reklev, "Beijing Carbon Trading Starts as China Acts on Climate." *Reuters* (28 November 2013); available online at http://www.reuters.com/article/2013/11/28/us-china-carbon-beijing-idUSBRE9AR07C20131128.

[20] Cui, "Tianjin Starts Carbon Trading Market." *crienglish.com* (26 December 2013); available online at http://english.cri.cn/6826/2013/12/26/2701s805326.htm.

[21] Luan, "Shanghai Starts Carbon Emission Trading." *english.news.cn* (26 November 2013); available online at http://news.xinhuanet.com/english/china/2013-11/26/c_132919150.htm.

[22] Ari Phillips, "The Second-Largest Carbon Market In The World Just Opened In China." *Climate Progress.* (19 December 2013); available online at http://thinkprogress.org/climate/2013/12/19/3088811/chinas-biggest-carbon-market-guangdong/.

[23] "First Chinese Pilot Emissions Trading Scheme Starts in Shenzhen." [Press Release]. Wall Street Journal (June 2012); available online at http://online.wsj.com/article/PR-CO-20130618-908499.html.

It is important to note that Beijing, Shanghai, and Tianjin set up emissions trading exchanges as early as 2008. Of these, Beijing and Shanghai announced the first carbon exchange platforms in August 2008;[24] Tianjin followed with the Tianjin Climate Exchange (TCX) which was the first to setup an integrated environmental derivatives platform in China and launched on 25 September 2008. The Tianjin Climate Exchange was established as a joint venture with the Chicago Climate Exchange (CCX) and benefitted from the intellectual inputs and market expertise of the Chicago Climate Exchange. They helped establish capacity building measures, voluntary standards, and other infrastructure necessary for a vibrant emissions marketplace.

With the establishment of the pilot trading programs, China aims to gradually establish a national trading market. A wide variety of International Emissions Trading frameworks alongside domestic experience is being used in structuring these markets. Of interest is that several Chinese cities have shown intentions to start their own carbon markets. The city of Qingdao in February 2014 its plans to impose CO_2 caps on its biggest companies and to adopt a market based framework. Similarly, the city of Jining in Shandong also proposed city-wide emissions market.

Of the seven pilot regions, Guangdong is the largest and covers about 508 $MtCO_2$, which accounts for 72% of the total aggregate baseline for all seven regions. As of now, only the Shenzhen pilot has been operational via the China Emissions exchange. Interestingly, Shenzhen is located inside Guangdong and is subject to its own ETS and the Guangdong ETS. A national unified emissions trading scheme based on lessons from the pilot is expected to be launched between 2016 and 2020.

The Chinese ETS is unique in that it is being built bottom-up, incorporating lessons learnt from local regions and international experiences. The next section describes India's initiatives on GHG

---

[24]"Environment and Energy Exchanges Launched." *China Daily* (6 August 2008); available online at http://www.china.org.cn/business/2008-08/06/content_16143784.htm.

reduction. The Indian program relies more on renewable energy and energy-efficiency as the route to a low carbon economy.

India

India is laying the foundations for environmental markets. It has already established a national renewable energy trading program and is getting ready to launch an ambitious energy-efficiency trading program. India presents a clear economic and environmental case where market based intervention can succeed. The Indian economy, the 4th largest in the world, has posted impressive economic rates of growth through this decade, averaging above 7% since 1997 and reaching 8.5% in 2008. Capitalizing on a well-skilled work force, entrepreneurship, democratic governance, and competent legal and business institutional structures, the Indian economy is well positioned for economic expansion in the coming years. Rapid rates of economic growth have manifested in all major sectors of the Indian economy.

Just as we have seen in the Chinese case, the steady growth of the Indian economy has also come with its share of challenges, both from an environmental as well as social standpoint. India still supports 298 million citizens, 26% of its population, who live in absolute poverty. Environmental and natural resource use challenges are widespread, and the country faces increasing demand for energy along with a host of social and developmental challenges. Key threats to continued economic growth process include challenges from environmental degradation along with other factors.

The rapid Indian economic progress, made possible by growth in its energy intensive manufacturing base, has been well complemented by a high rate of growth in its fossil fuel energy sector. India remains one of the leading primary energy producers in the world and is one of the largest consumers of energy. Indian energy use has grown faster than GDP for the last 20 years. Most notable is the case of the electricity sector, where electricity consumption has grown at a rate higher than GDP for the past two decades; this trend has become remarkably pronounced in recent times. In addition, India's power capacity has risen at the rate of 5.87% per annum over the last 25 years. The total supply of electrical energy has risen at the rate of 7.14% over the same period.

This trend is a direct result of fossil fuel based energy demand, especially coal, which accounts for roughly 52% of Indian power generation. India is ranked third in the world for both coal production and consumption.

The demand for energy resources is expected to grow further as the economy grows and there is an increase in urbanization, population growth, rural electrification, and per capita incomes. This is evident from projections in the 11th five-year plan where utility-based generation capacity is expected to increase to 78,000 MW, largely from thermal-coal based power generation. In similar lines, the Integrated Energy Policy report of the Planning Commission of India states:

> To deliver a sustained growth of 8% through 2031, India would, in the very least, need to grow its primary energy supply by 3 to 4 times and electricity supply by 5 to 7 times of today's consumption. By 2031–2032 power generation capacity would have to increase to 778,095 MW and annual coal requirement would be 2040 metric tons, if we do not take any measures to reduce requirement.

This history of fossil fuel dependence by major energy intensive sectors like power generation, steel, cement, chemical, fertilizer, and transport, has had its environmental repercussions. While still low in per capita terms, India's absolute GHG emissions have almost doubled since 1990 to 1.3 billion metric tons of carbon dioxide. Ranked fourth in the world after China, United States, and the European Union, Indian GHG emissions, growing at a rate of about 6.5% annually, are major impediments to sustainable economic growth. Closely associated with climate change are threats to the fragile Himalayan ecosystem, water security, particulate pollution as well as expected sulfur dioxide and nitrous oxide emissions with increased fossil fuel generation.

While none of these challenges are insurmountable and traditionally have been part of the economies in transition, India is cognizant of the critical need to initiate the process of sustainable economic growth that is sensitive to the social and environmental aspects.

To this effect, India has been active in the UNFCCC negotiations and benefitted from the UN Clean Development Mechanism (CDM) program. India, along with nearly 200 other countries, has ratified the United Nations Framework Convention on Climate Change (UNFCCC), which entered into force in 1994.[25] In August 2002, India became a party to the Kyoto Protocol to the UNFCCC.

As regards CDM, the Government of India (GoI) has taken a leadership role in facilitating large-scale promotion and adoption of CDM projects in the country. This, combined with multifaceted human resource talent, especially entrepreneurship capital, has led to India's emergence as important hub for CDM activity. As of April 2009, India accounts for 15.7% of total CER issuances from 415 projects accounting for an underlying notional value of U.S.$4.5 billion.

More recently, the Government of India (GoI) has initiated a forward looking policy framework that seeks to sustain future economic growth while ensuring minimum damage to the environment as well as ensuring improvement in the lives of its citizens. The Prime Minister's National Action Plan (NAP) on Climate Change, first announced in 2008, outlines existing and future policies that address India's position on climate mitigation and adaptation. These initiatives form part of a broad cohesive policy on energy, environment, and economic development as outlined in the Prime Minister's National Climate Action Plan, 11th FYP, and the Integrated Energy Policy Report to name a few. These goals are to be achieved through the establishment of eight core national missions through an approach described as one representing a multi-pronged, long-term, and integrated strategy for achieving the key goals in the context of climate change.

---

[25]For more details on the Status of Ratification of the Kyoto Protocol, visit http://unfcc.int/kyoto_protocol/status_of_ratification/items/2613.php.

Pertinent to this proposal are two initiatives proposed in the NAP:

(1) Under the auspices of the Ministry of New and Renewable Energy (MNRE): Establish a dynamic and escalating minimum renewable purchase standard per year and in addition allow for a tradable Renewable Energy Certificate (REC) program.

(2) Under the auspices of the National Mission for Enhanced Energy Efficiency: Establish a market based mechanism and tradable certified Energy-Efficiency Credits to enhance energy-efficiency in energy intensive large industries and facilities.

Both these above initiatives take into account inherent strengths of the Indian economy and its future aspirations. They are concurrent with the Indian Government's objective of establishing an approach to climate change based on the principle of common but differentiated responsibilities and respective capabilities, as enshrined in the United Nations Framework Convention on Climate Change (UNFCCC). In addition, from the perspective of India's energy security they present opportunities for enhancing the internal ability for generating clean power while yielding other social co-benefits.

Renewable Energy Certificate Scheme: India has already one of the highest percentages of renewable energy relative to its overall generation capacity. The country is ranked fifth in the world for wind power generation with an estimated generation potential of 45,195 MW. Total renewable energy is currently generating about 13,878 MW, contributing about 8% of total installed capacity and contributing 3% to the electricity mix, with wind power having the largest share. This suggests a huge latent potential that is yet to be tapped. To this effect, the GoI has deployed one of the world's largest programs for deploying renewable energy products and systems. Demand for renewable energy is high and it is regarded as a key solution to rural electrification, as expounded by the Ministry of Power's Accelerated Rural Electrification Programme, in the country.

India's private sector has been playing a major role in the production of renewable energy. This includes important roles in establishing manufacturing capacity, power generation, and GHG allowance trading. The market for renewable energy in India is estimated at U.S.$500 million, with an annual growth rate of 25% and investment in renewable energy of about U.S.$3 billion per annum. With increased activity from venture capitalists, India remained among the countries with the highest levels of annual investment in renewable energy in 2007 along with Germany, China, USA, Spain, and Japan. India also has established financial institutions, such as the Indian Renewable Energy Development Agency, which provides dedicated services to finance renewable energy projects.

The 11th FYP of the GoI states the need to increase the renewable power to 10–12% of installed capacity, contributing about 5% of the electricity mix. Out of the overall target of 70,000 MW power generation installed capacity addition during the 11th FYP period, a 14,500 MW (about 20%) capacity addition is proposed from renewables.

In March 2010, pursuant to the 11th FYP guidelines and the NAP, India introduced the REC mechanism to support the Renewable Purchase Obligations (RPO). These obligations require that electric power generators produce 5% of the nation's share of electricity sourced from renewable energy in 2010, increasing at a rate of 1% for the next 10 years. Mandated entities may buy or trade RECs, each equivalent to 1 MW of electricity. The mechanism involves RECs being issued to renewable energy operators and purchased at monthly auctions by entities that do not meet the RPO requirement. Figure 5.6 provides the monthly renewable energy credits issued to eligible entities which could then be sold to obligated entities which are covered by the REC mandate. Two electricity exchanges in India, namely, (1) The India Energy Exchange (IEX) and (2) Power Exchange India Ltd (PXIL) conduct the monthly auctions. Separate auctions for RECs from solar power and all other RECs are conducted.

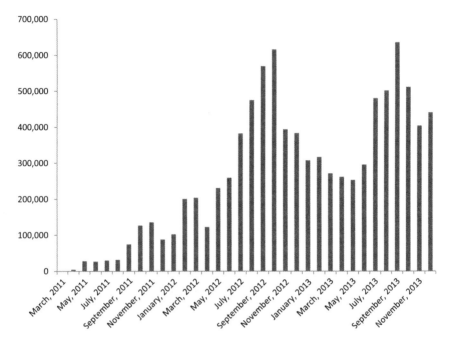

Figure 5.6. Renewable Energy Certificates Issued.

The trading mechanism is designed to promote interstate REC transactions. The trading mechanism allows regions with high renewable energy potential to produce to their full capacity and trade with regions with low renewable energy capacity. As of December 2013, 915 renewable energy projects have been accredited by State Nodal Renewable energy agencies. This corresponds to a combined 1,890 MW or 9.5% of national renewable energy installed capacity.[26] From a renewable energy technology standpoint, about 44% of the renewable generation is from wind power, 28.5% from bio-fuel cogeneration, 22.6% from biomass, 4.2% from small scale hydro, and 0.4% from solar generation.

---

[26]Data compiled from REC registry of India; available online at https://www.recregistry india.nic.in/index.php/general/publics/index.

Table 5.7. Growth of REC Market in India.

	REC issued	REC traded	Average price[27] ($)	Notional value ($)
2011	547,340	438,249	38	20,625,596
2012	3,432,615	1,982,614	35	121,628,992
2013	4,679,485	1,200,591	25	116,987,125
Total	8,659,440	3,621,454	30	259,783,200

Sources: REC Registry of India; available online at https://www.recregistryindia. nic.in/indexphp/general/publics/recs. REC traded and Average Price are from Power Exchanges of India Monthly REC Auction Data: (1) India Electricity Exchange; available online at http://www.iexindia.com/marketdata/recdata.aspx; (2) Power Exchange of India Limited; available online at https://www.powerexindia.com/PXIL Report/pages/RECMVPReport.aspx.

India maintains a fully electronic renewable energy registry with issuance, monitoring, and transfer capabilities for its Renewable Energy Certificates. In 2011, the first year of operation, 546,808 RECs were issued and 438,249 were traded on Exchanges. Based on the average clearing price, the underlying notional value was about U.S.$20 million. Table 5.7 presents the growth of the REC market in India. To date, 8,659,440 RECs have been issued at an average price of $30 per REC with the underlying notional value of $259 million.

As of April 2012, the Central Electricity Regulatory Commission which regulates the REC market has implemented a floor price of 1,500 Indian Rupees or about $25 per REC. This floor price will remain in place for a period of five years and is intended to provide market participants long-term planning alternatives in lieu of the weak prices prevailing for CDM credits.

The next subsection covers the energy-efficiency program termed Perform, Achieve and Trade. This scheme is expected to be India's answer to combating global warming and improving energy efficiency.

---

[27] Conversion to USD made using constant exchange rate of 1 U.S. $ = 60 Indian Rupees (as of April 2014).

Perform Achieve and Trade (PAT): The PAT scheme was announced as the flagship program of the National Action Plan on Climate Change (NAPCC) in 2008. The scheme covers eight industrial sectors of the 15 energy intensive sectors identified by the NAPCC. PAT mandates specific energy consumption reduction targets to 478 Designated Consumers (DCs) of energy within these sectors. Together, these DCs account for 60% of India's primary energy consumption and 25% of national GDP. The energy-efficiency measures envisaged under the PAT scheme are expected to reduce carbon emissions by 26 million tons and contribute to the national goal of 20% to 25% reduction in carbon intensity from 2005 levels by 2020. Salient features of India's PAT scheme are presented in Table 5.8.

The first compliance period of the PAT scheme is from 2012 to 2015. Under the scheme, participating plants are designated a specific energy reduction (SEC) consumption target to be achieved by the end of 2015. SEC is the energy consumed per unit of production and expressed in tons of oil equivalent (TOE) per ton of product. The baseline established for SEC was average energy consumption per plant for years April 2007 through March 2010. The energy targets set by the PAT scheme are not sector specific but plant specific with an average energy reduction requirement of 4.8% SEC by 2015. This keeps in view the wide range of energy-efficiencies that exist within a sector.

The PAT scheme will be regulated by the Bureau of Energy Efficiency (BEE) under the Ministry of Power. Designated Consumers who overachieve their target are issued certified and tradable Energy Savings Certificates or ESCerts annually. The measurement, reporting, and verification of the energy savings will be done by BEE designated verifiers. DCs that do not meet their reduction obligations may purchase ESCerts available for trading. The trading may be done bilaterally or through established platforms in the Power exchanges. The trading is restricted to DCs and no financial institutions or other participants are allowed. A full set of trading infrastructure and rules are yet to be established by the BEE. As of now, the program status has

Table 5.8. India PAT Market Design Elements.

ESTABLISHING LEGISLATION	Energy Conservation Act 2001, modified by the Energy Conservation Amendment Act 2010, Article 14 (August 2010).
REGULATOR	Bureau of Energy Efficiency (BEE) of India's Ministry of Power, under supervision of the Central Electricity Regulatory Commission.
ADMINISTRATOR	BEE.
COVERAGE	– Selected DCs in B energy intensive sectors (478 DCs): Thermal Power plants, Iron & Steel, Cement, Fertilizer, Aluminum, Textile, Pulp & Paper, Chlow alkali. – Possible sectoral extension in the second compliance periods.
COMPLIANCE PERIOD	– First PAT cycle going from 1 April 2012 to 31 March 2015. – Fulfillment of compliance obligations subsequent to first cycle termination.
BASELINE	– Defined as the average total energy input per production unit over 2007–2010. – All energy sources are considered and converted to metric ton of oil equivalent (MTOE).
TARGET	– Specific energy consumption (SEC) target assigned to each DC, in percentage of the baseline. – Overall reduction of 4.2% equivalent to 6.6 milion MTOE. – Revision in each subsequent PAT cycle.
MONITORING AND VERIFICATION	– Based on a "Baseline Energy Audit" (BEA). – Performed by "Designated Energy Auditors" (DENA) accredited by BEE. – First BEA at the end of the first PAT cycle (2014), possible annual BEA thereafter.
ENFORCEMENT	Penalty of 10 lakhs (U.S.\$20,000) in addition to the value of compliance.
TRADING	– ESCert issued to any DC exceeding own SEC target. – Bilateral transactions or cleared through the two national power exchanges, i.e., Power Exchange India, India Energy Exchange. – Market design elements (e.g., banking) under consideration.
MARKET READINESS	– Target setting by March 2012 (completed). – Rules and procedures completed. – Trading infrastructures and rules to be announced soon (ongoing).

Source: World Bank, Bureau of Energy Efficiency.

been bogged with efforts to promote capacity-building among DCs, implementation delays, and establishment of baseline audits for DCs.

The next subsection describes the GHG program being proposed in South Korea. Unlike China and India, the South Korean economy is closer to developed economies. Its large manufacturing base and technology services are primary emission sources.

South Korea

South Korea was the first Asian country to pass a national emissions trading scheme. Korean emissions have been on the rise since 1990 and now exceed 600 MMTCO$_2$. South Korea ranks as the seventh largest GHG emitter in the world and among the fastest growing emitting nations. Korea enacted what is known as the Framework Act on Low Carbon and Green Growth in 2010. The objective of this Act is to reduce the country's GHG emissions by 30% by 2020. It includes provisions for a nationwide emissions trading program to achieve this goal. As of 2011, the country was building the infrastructure required to implement the program including measuring, reporting, and verification procedures. The program is expected to begin by 2015. Table 5.9 presents the salient features of the program.

To achieve its targets South Korea needs to reduce its industrial emissions by 83 MtCO$_2$, electricity sector emissions by 68 MtCO$_2$, building sector emissions by 48 MtCO$_2$ and transportation emissions by 37 MtCO$_2$ to achieve 236 MtCO$_2$. The country will execute the plan under three phases: Phase I will run from 2015 through 2017, Phase II from 2018 to 2020, and Phase III from 2021 to 2026. The program is expected to begin on 1 January 2015 with the participation of 490 of South Korea's largest emitters and 60% of the annual GHG emissions. The covered entities include mandatory as well as voluntary participants. The threshold for the mandatory cap is emissions over 125,000 tCO$_2$ per year. Similar to the Australian program, South Korea will allow flexibility mechanisms through a limited use of offsets, called Korean Certified Emission Credits or KCERS. Offsets are limited to 10% of entities' compliance obligations.

Having discussed the major Asian programs, the discussion proceeds to examples of initiatives in Australia and Brazil.

Table 5.9. Salient Features of the Framework Act on Low Carbon and Green Growth.

GHG	CO_2, CH_4, N_2O, HFCs, PFCs, SF_6.
Sectoral scope	– 60% of the national total GHG emissions. – Inclusion threshold: Entities emitting more thatn 125,000 tCO_2e; individual facilities emitting over 25,000 tCO_2e.
Compliance periods	– Compliance periods (CP): CP1 2015–2017, CP2 2018–2020. – CPs to last five years from CP3.
Allocation	– Over 95% free allownaces in CP1 and CP2. – 100% free for energy-intensive trade-exposed sectors. – Future allocation by Presidential decree.
Auctions	Early auctioning allowed.
Banking and borrowing	– Banking allowed over a CP and first year of the folowing CP. – Borrowing allowed over a CP only.
Other cost containment	A maximum of 25% allowances will be reserved for the new entrant.
Offsets	Applicable standards (e.g., CDM and/or own standard) and utilization limit for international offsets to be specified by Presidential decree (expected in 2012)
Penalty for non-compliance	Up to three allowances for each allowance not surrendered (at most) with the maximum cap of 10 million Korean Won (KRW) per allowance (U.S.$8,800).
Linking	Considered in the future.

Source: World Bank, Presidential Committee on Green Growth.

Australia

A nationwide cap-and-trade program, the Clean Energy Future Package, is expected to bring 60% of the countries emissions under cap by 2015. The included sectors are electricity generation, industrial facilities, fugitive emissions,[28] and landfill sector. The objective of the plan is to reduce Australia's carbon emissions by 5% by 2020 and 80% by 2050 from 2000 levels. Salient features of the Clean Energy Future Package are presented in Table 5.10. Under the proposal, a national cap for the first five-year phase starting from 2015 will be announced in May 2014. The government proposes to announce the cap for the next undefined years in advance, providing a five-year advance notice to covered entities. This mechanism is also expected to allow the government to take due consideration for its national and international environmental obligations, state of economy etc. in its decision making. To manage the risk of the government being unable to make a decision, the law allows the minimum achievement of the 5% target.

The program covers four of the GHGs and has provisions for use of CERs for compliance. Salient features of the program are provided in Table 5.10.

Entities covered in the Australian program included power generation, oil and gas, and industrial entities for sources whose annual emissions exceed 10,000 tCO_2 per year. While transportation and agriculture have been excluded from the program, voluntary measures are in place to promote climate mitigation in those sectors. Notable is the Carbon Farming Initiative (CFI), which allows for sale of offset credits to covered entities. It is proposed that under the CFI, both domestic and Kyoto projects will be considered. The transportation emissions are expected to be curbed via a fuel tax equivalent to carbon price.

An interesting feature of the Australian program is its phased pricing policy. Under the system, the first phase of the program will feature a fixed price of AU\$23 per ton of CO_2,[29] adjusted for inflation. A flexible phase from 2015 to 2018 will allow for market prices with a price ceiling of AU\$20 above the EU ETS

---

[28] Fugitive emissions are emissions of gases or vapors from pressurized equipment, pipes etc. due to leaks and other unintended or irregular releases of gases, mostly from industrial activities.

[29] As of 27 February 2014, the exchange rate between AU\$ to U.S.\$ was 1:1.14.

Table 5.10. Salient Features of the Clean Energy Future Package.

Indicator	Detail
Objective	• Help to lower Australia's carbon emissions by 5% by 2020 (relative to 2000 levels) and by 80% (also relative to 2000 levels) by 2050.
Commencement	• Fixed price period: 1 July 2012; • Flexible price period: 1 July 2015; and • Floating price: 1 July 2018.
Coverage	• Four Kyoto Protocol GHGs: carbon dioxide (CO_2), methane (CH_4), nitrous oxide (N_2O), perfluorocarbons (PFCs). Sulphur hexafluoride (SF_6) and hydrofluorocarbon-23 (HFC 23) will be regulated by non-trading legislation and broad coverage. Forestry, agriculture, and some transport not covered.
Compliance basis	• Annual, based upon 30 June year-end.
Caps	• Caps will be set by May 2014 for the first five years of the flexible price period of the CPM; • Each year thereafter a further year's cap will be determined such that there will always be caps set five years in advance; and • Eligible from 1 July 2015 (up to 50% of annual obligation for liable entities).
International offsets	• Qualitative restrictions apply to some CERs; and • Subject to a "surrender charge" during the flexible price period.
Assistance	• Households to be the largest recipients of assistance; and • The bulk of sectoral assistance will be provided primarily in the form of free permits to trade exposed industries.

price, rising 5% annually. Post-2018, a floating phase will have the price ceiling removed and allow greater access to international offset credits. This combined with the ability of the Australian government to change the emissions trajectory according to international efforts and economy makes it a unique system among proposed programs.

Brazil

In 2009, Brazil established a National Climate Change Policy (NCCP) that set a voluntary GHG reduction target of 36.1% to 38.9% by 2020. The vast majority of these reductions were to be achieved through reducing emissions from tropical forest deforestation, land use change, and agricultural and livestock activities. Other measures include gains in energy-efficiency, use of biofuels, and increased hydroelectric generation.

Other initiatives underway in Brazil include the state and city of Rio de Janeiro proposing to establish what would be the first legally binding cap-and-trade program in the nation. The first phase of the program targeted to operate as a pilot between 2013 to 2015, will be extended to three subsequent five-year phases. Covered entities will include sectors from energy, steel, chemicals, and cement. In addition, an Environmental Asset Exchange, BVRio has also been setup as a public–private partnership. BVRio is expected to serve as a carbon market platform for participants of the Rio de Janeiro program. The Brazilian Securities, Commodities and Futures Exchange (BM&F BOVESPA) has also played an early and active role in promoting environmental finance.

The state of Sao Paulo has also announced a mandate to reduce its GHG emissions by 20% by 2020 from 2005 levels. This would result in Sao Paulo's emissions going from the present 140 $MtCO_2$ to 112 $MtCO_2$. The public relations from the 2014 World Cup are also driving several private companies in Brazil to take on voluntary emission reduction commitments. In addition, Brazil has also developed its own carbon emissions standards, namely, Brasil Mata Viva for forest certification and Social Carbon Standard.

This section concludes with a comparison of various programs discussed so far. The national programs show diversity in their targets, included sectors, and program types. Table 5.11 presents an overview of the international proposed and launched cap-and trade programs.

Table 5.11. Comparison of Global Cap-and-Trade Environmental Programs.

	Australia	South Korea	China	India
Program type	GHG absolute reduction	GHG absolute reduction	Carbon intensity	Energy-efficiency
Sectoral scope	• All six GHGs • Covers all high emissions industrial sectors • Mandate covers 60% of Australian GHG emissions	• All six GHGs • Covers high emitting sectors. Emission threshold for inclusion of 125,000 metric tons of CO_2 per year for entities and 25,000 tons of CO_2 per year for individual facilities • Covers 60% of Korean GHG emissions	• Includes high emitting sectors. Each pilot program has a list of mandated companies defined	• Eight high energy intensive sectors
Commitment	• 5% GHG reduction by 2020 • 80% GHG reduction by 2050 • Relative to 2000 level emissions	• 30% GHG emission reduction below Business as Usual by 2020	• Individual pilots have specific targets • Overall national target of 17% cut in emission intensity per unit of GDP by 2015	• Reduce specific energy consumption • Overall reduction of 4.2% or 6.6 million MTOE's of energy
Tradable units	Carbon units	KCERS		ESCERTS
Regulator	Australian Government	Korean Ministry of Environment	National Development and Reform Commission	Bureau of Energy Efficiency, Ministry of Power

Voluntary Carbon Markets

In addition to the mandated regional programs described above, there exists a market for GHG credits generated through projects approved under various voluntary programs. These credits are purchased mainly by corporations for their corporate social responsibility, carbon neutrality, and other green commitments. The most prominent of these programs is the Verified Carbon Standard (VCS). A wide range of GHG offset projects globally source allowances to the VCS and trade through Verified Carbon Units or VCUs. The price of these credits is determined by a wide range of factors including project type, country, nature of GHG reducing activity, and other social and environmental attributes, although they can also be affected by the international CER price. These credits are mainly bought and sold through carbon brokers or intermediaries who purchase allowances from brokers and sell them to businesses and individuals.

The voluntary carbon market caters to an interesting class of offset projects, which mainly exist outside or in advance of the UN CER system, that foster biodiversity, pursue social goals such as the empowerment of women, and alleviate poverty. One such project category is worth describing: Carbon projects that seek to preserve tropical rain forests. A market called Reducing Emissions from Deforestation and Degradation (REDD) operates by generating REDD allowances that can be used as carbon offsets or efforts promoting corporate social and environmental responsibility. By purchasing such REDD credits, corporates not only prevent carbon loss from deforestation, but also promote socially responsible and environmental goals such as preventing deforestation and promoting biodiversity, waterways, indigenous people and their habitats, and a wide variety of other ecosystem assets. For example, mining companies that degrade tropical forests could purchase REDD credits to demonstrate their commitment to offset their environmental activity.

Countries such as Peru, Indonesia, Congo, and Brazil are leading the development of these projects. Peru is already a leader in the emerging environmental markets as evidenced by the protection of its rich tropical forests. REDD projects in Peru are in advanced stages of development compared to those of its peers. Peru currently hosts four REDD projects under the Verified Carbon Standard, which have generated roughly nine million carbon credits in the aggregate. Peru also has been ahead of others in terms of REDD readiness. A detailed description of the REDD markets and opportunities therein is presented in Chapter 6 of this book.

Conclusion

This chapter described several domestic and international emerging climate mitigation initiatives. It provided an overview of several developed and developing economies as well as regional and state programs where market-based structures are being used to combat global warming, and promote renewable energy and energy-efficiency. These markets are of different designs, growth stages, and policy focus but they yield a common environmental dividend for the planet. The experience from early implementation of such models in the United States and Europe provides valuable lessons for these programs. California, with comprehensive GHG reductions and trading programs, is leading the way in the United States. It is a testimony to how powerful individual state action can be in tackling a global problem. The RGGI program, in its second phase has made important changes that have added vigor and strength to the Northeast's efforts to tackle carbon emissions. Canada has taken a multi-pronged approach in its long standing commitment to tackle global warming. Provinces like Quebec have designed their programs in close consultation with California and they have taken on absolute GHG reduction commitments. Others such as Alberta enacted GHG intensity targets as the initial approach.

The international scene provided even greater optimism on the future of environmental markets. Among the major developing countries, diverse actions are being taken to transform to a low-carbon pathway. China, the world's largest GHG polluter has taken a major step in combating global warming through its carbon intensity trading program. India, predicted to be the world's third largest economy, has a national renewable energy program in place and will soon launch an energy-efficiency trading program. Brazil has a combination of internal measures to reduce tropical deforestation, and promote clean fuels alongside small cap-and-trade pilots proposed in Brazilian cities. Elsewhere in the developed world, Australia and South Korea have plans to initiate trading programs that reduce absolute GHG emissions. All of these mandated environmental markets exist alongside a vibrant voluntary market for GHG emissions reductions.

It is remarkable to note that some form of environmental marketplace exists in these countries which account for 70% of the global GHG emissions in total. From the standpoint of an investor, corporation, financial analyst, or entrepreneur, these emerging programs offer multiple opportunities to create economic value. These programs are also testament to the fact the carbon management is becoming mainstream risk management wherever corporations operate in the world. Due cognizance to corporations' choice of energy use, and its implications on emissions and cost are key enterprise risk management themes.

The future is bright for all types of environmental markets. The promise from an efficient market standpoint that could reap enormous economic value is the ultimate linking of these diverse markets to create a global carbon market. This would create for the first time, a parallel set of environmental programs that are compatible with each other and provide opportunities similar to foreign exchange markets. Multiple product innovations and efficiency gains can flow out of such a system.

Previous chapters have discussed a wide variety of sectoral and regional policies that have emerged to manage GHGs and other energy and environmental objectives. The next chapter discusses yet another emerging environmental market that assists in the development and maintenance of tropical forest conservation projects. A market called Reducing Emissions from Deforestation and Degradation (REDD) operates by generating REDD allowances that can be used as carbon offsets. By purchasing REDD credits, corporations not only prevent carbon loss from deforestation but also prevent deforestation itself and promote such environmental goals as biodiversity, waterway preservation, the protection of indigenous people and their habitats, and the conservation of a wide variety of other ecosystem assets. Given the magnitude of the climate change issue, forest carbon markets are important sources for mitigating climate change alongside other ecosystem benefits. The next chapter discusses the opportunities in the forest carbon sector and the environmental markets that preserve forests.

Chapter 6

FOREST CARBON AS AN ASSET CLASS

The world's forests play an important role in sustainable economic development. With 30% of the global land area under forestry and an estimated 1.6 billion people depending on forests for food, fuel, and medicinal plants, preserving forests is an important economic and environmental goal. Forests play two major roles in mitigating climate change. First, new growing forests help by absorbing CO_2 from the atmosphere and second, mature forests help by storing absorbed carbon as biomass for a long period. In fact, forests are the biggest reservoirs for carbon storage more than the atmosphere and the world's oil reserves.

However, unsustainable exploitation of forests is causing serious economic, social, and environmental damages. Each year an estimated 13 million hectares are deforested and degraded due to land conversion, catastrophic weather events, and unregulated timber logging. Deforestation causes between 12–15% of global greenhouse gas emissions,[1] more than the emissions from worldwide transportation.[2] But perhaps more importantly, forest exploitation occurs at the expense of biodiversity, indigenous tribes that

---

[1] Based on 2013 estimates of global GHG emissions of ~39 billion tons, this represents 4.68 to 5.85 billion tons of CO_2.

[2] Conservation International, "Center for Environmental Leadership in Business." (2014); available online at http://www.conservation.org/global/celb/Documents/2013_REDD_Corporate-Primer.pdf.

inhabit forests, and ecosystem health, especially soil and water. Tropical forests are also important factors in the global climate and hydrological cycles. Rapid deforestation and land use change can turn forests into a massive source of carbon emissions with catastrophic results. It is therefore not surprising that the international community, including climate change advocates have been devising avenues that incentivize forest preservation.

Global environmental challenges, such as climate change, are providing opportunities for forestry to serve as suppliers of a global environmental service — the removal of CO_2 from the atmosphere. Emission reduction and trading markets, that were the subject of Chapter 4 of this book, are supplemented by credits from projects that result in sequestration of carbon dioxide. These new markets are causing a transformation in the traditional role of forestry activities as suppliers of food, fiber, and recreational services. Not only do forest offset projects offer low-cost greenhouse gas (GHG) mitigation options but they also help channel financial support to rural economies, enrich biological diversity, and yield other social and economic benefits. The multiple benefits that accrue from forest preservation have been commoditized via the greenhouse gas markets. It is important to emphasize that price discovery for forest carbon credits should theoretically represent not only the carbon offsetting service but also the social, biodiversity, and ecological services that are concomitantly enhanced by forest preservation. In that sense, the climate, community, and biodiversity benefits that accrue from these credits make them unique and preferred amongst certain constituents of the environmental marketplace.

Inclusion of forest carbon into national cap-and-trade programs as mandatory compliance instruments is being discussed in several emerging markets. Carbon credits sourced from forestry has already been the fastest growing segment of the voluntary carbon market in recent times. In 2011, forest credits accounted for 6.8 MtCO$_2$ and were the third popular choice among voluntary buyers. High quality forestry projects command a price of $7 to $10, well above the market price for most other offsets.[3] As environmental markets mature, there is also the potential for separate markets for ecosystem and biodiversity services emerging, where forest carbon can play a prominent role. The unique risks and opportunities in forest ecosystem services has led to growing interest among the financial community into creation of a separate asset class.

The purpose of this chapter is to provide a primer on ecosystem services from the forest sector and the emerging market for forest carbon. The topic is of interest to corporations, investors, and financial analysts. For corporations, the opportunities and risks from forests are huge, given the vast number of inputs and products that are sourced from forests. Corporations can also find interesting opportunities to offset their carbon emissions through forest credits and enhance their linkages with local communities and concerned citizens. To date, this has been a big driver of demand for forest carbon credits and this will be discussed in detail in this chapter. Financial analysts need to understand the specific nature of risks and opportunities from forest ecosystem services. Just as they would analyze the fundament drivers for value creation and risk within any asset class, the same approach is essential in analyzing forestry as an asset class. The fundamental factors that affect forests and their protection ultimately impact the value in forest carbon.

The state of forest landscape also provides new business challenges, commodity risks and opportunities, and importantly, trading opportunities. Entrepreneurs in finance, forestry, and forest-based industries, such as paper and pulp, can reap important investment opportunities. This chapter is divided into six sections. The first section explains the dynamics of forest carbon sequestration, its potential, and the drivers for deforestation and degradation. This is followed by a section that explains the different activities that assist in sequestering and storing forest carbon; Section 3 presents the

---

[3] Molly Peters-Stanley, Katherine Hamilton and Daph Yin, *Leveraging the Landscape: State of the Forest Carbon Markets 2012* (November 2012); available online at http://www.forest-trends.org/documents/files/doc_3242.pdf.

policy response and origins of forest carbon trading via the Kyoto framework, various national, regional, and individual corporate programs; and Section 4 explains the existing market framework for forest credits. Section 5 presents trends in the voluntary market for forest carbon; the last section presents private sector participation in forest carbon; and this will be followed by the conclusion.

Dynamics of Forest Carbon Sequestration and the Problem of Deforestation

The problem and consequences of climate change have been discussed in great length in Chapter 4. To reiterate, GHGs are growing at an unprecedented rate and implicated in causing climate change, a phenomenon commonly called global warming. Forests play an integral role in mitigating climate change. Half of all the photosynthesis globally takes places in forests, enabling the sector to be a huge repository for global carbon. This section discusses the role of forestry in the global carbon cycle and its potential for carbon sequestration. Further, it also discusses the common drivers of deforestation. The section begins with an account of the forest carbon cycle.

Forest Carbon Cycle

A simple account of the carbon cycle in a forest involves two chemical reactions that vegetative systems undergo on a daily basis: photosynthesis and respiration. Photosynthesis converts atmospheric CO_2 into carbon and oxygen using energy from sunlight. Respiration combines carbon and oxygen to create CO_2 and energy. The two do not balance, and the net carbon uptake is stored in the form of biomass in leaves, branches, stems, and roots of the growing plant.

Land cleared of vegetation will often slowly revert to a forest over time. First, weeds, bushes, and fast-growing species appear. Over time, slower growing, taller species may also become established. Once established, these eventually dominate. The taller trees continue to flourish until the canopy closes over at the eventual maturity of the stand. At each stage of development there are cycles within the forest. Some plants grow, die, and fall to the forest floor along with leaves that appear and fall regularly. This litter eventually rots and releases their stored carbon to the atmosphere and the soil. If trees are cut, their roots die and become underground litter, which releases carbon into the soil and atmosphere as it decomposes. Carbon in the soil is slowly released into the air through respiration of microscopic organisms. If the amount of carbon entering the soil through decomposing litter is greater than the amount being released to the atmosphere then the soil carbon pool increases. As the forest reaches maturity, the litter and growth come into balance and the forest reaches steady-state with respect to carbon stored in biomass. A forest that has reached maturity will stop storing additional net carbon until a disturbance like a fire or harvesting starts the cycle over again.[4] Figure 6.1 provides an illustration of the global forest carbon cycle.

The following equation presents an overview of the global carbon cycle. The earth's annual atmospheric flux of carbon in billion metric tons is characterized as:[5]

Atmospheric increase (billion metric tons of carbon)	= Fossil fuel emissions	+ Emissions from net deforestation and land use changes	− Oceanic uptake	− "missing sink"
3.4 (+/− 0.2)	5.4 (+/− 0.5)	1.6 (+/− 1.0)	2.0 (+/− 0.8)	1.6 (+/− 1.4)

In 1990, carbon emissions arising from changes in land use were equal to approximately 23% of all global human-induced emissions (i.e., deforestation and fossil fuel emissions) and 29% of annual global fossil fuel emissions. This amount reflects the net difference between forest carbon absorption and the release of carbon from

---

[4]Food and Agriculture Organization, *Global Forest Resources Assessment* (2005); *Progress towards Sustainable Forest Management* (2005).

[5] *Ibid.*

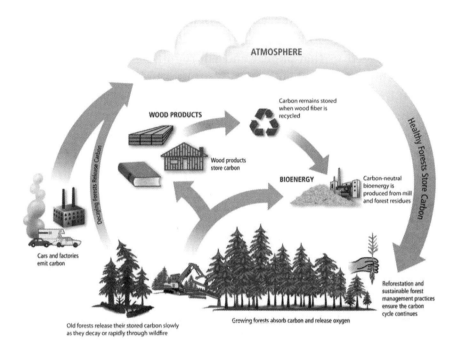

Figure 6.1. Illustration of Global Forest Carbon Cycle.[6]

land use change, primarily a result of forest destruction. A large amount of forests are cleared and burned each year — over 11 million hectares annually during the 1990s and 17 million hectares annually during the 1980s.[7]

Other studies estimate annual carbon emissions from land use change in the tropics in the range of 1.2–2.2 billion metric tons[8] and 1.5–3.0 billion metric tons.[9] On the other hand, growing forests remove carbon from the atmosphere. Some analysts have suggested

[6] Illustration courtesy of World Resources Istitute.

[7] Food and Agriculture Organization, *Global Forest Resources Assessment* (2005); *Progress towards Sustainable Forest Management* (2005).

[8] Sandra Brown, Louis R. Iverson and Anantha Prasad, "Geographical Distribution of Biomass Carbon in Tropical Southeast Asian Forests: A Database." *Geocarto International*, Vol. 8 (1993): 1–59.

[9] Richard A. Houghton, "Revised Estimates of the Annual Net Flux of Carbon to the Atmosphere from Changes in Land Use and Land Management, 1850–2000." *Tellus B*, 55B: 378–390.

that at least a part of the very large "missing sink" reflects an underestimation of sequestration occurring in forests. The significant role played by forests as an emissions sink suggests the critical need to incorporate forestry in any initiative to tackle climate change.

The Intergovernmental Panel on Climate Change (IPCC) reported in its third assessment that 10–30% of human-induced global GHG emissions are due to Land Use, Land Use Change, and Forestry (LULUCF).[10] The IPCC concluded that globally, changes in forest management could induce future carbon sequestration adequate to offset an additional 15–20% of CO_2 emissions. Within the U.S., LULUCF activities in 2004 resulted in a net carbon sequestration of 780.1 million tons CO_2 equivalent.[11] This represents an offset of approximately 13% of total U.S. CO_2 emissions, or 11% of total GHG emissions in 2004. U.S. CO_2 emissions amounted to approximately six billion tons in 2004. With LULUCF carbon sequestration activities, roughly 13% could be offset as they are banked in soil and biomass. The forest sector has the potential to mitigate 8 Giga tons of CO_2 annually primarily through avoided deforestation and forest degradation (65%), reforestation (18%), afforestation of marginal pastureland and croplands (13%), and improved forest management (7%).[12]

In addition, forest carbon projects offer a practical and credible low-cost option to mitigate CO_2 emissions. In their research report, The Conference Board recently reported that about 44% of surveyed companies in the United States are either involved in sequestration

---

[10]Intergovernmental Panel on Climate Change, "Climate Change 2001: Synthesis Report." (September 2001); available online at http://www.ess.uci.edu/researchgrp/prather/files/2001IPCC_SyR-Watson.pdf.

[11]U.S. EPA, "EPA Inventory of US Greenhouse Gas Emissions and Sinks: 1994-2004. USEPA #430-R-06-002, Table ES-5. Washington, D.C." U.S. Environmental Protection Agency (April 2006).

[12]McKinsey & Company, "Pathways to a Low-Carbon Economy: Version 2 of the Global Greenhouse Gas Abatement Cost Curve." (January 2009); available online at https://solutions.mckinsey.com/climatedesk/default.aspx.

projects or considering them to offset GHG emissions.[13] Forestry based sinks provide an immediate opportunity to channel financial support for biological diversity that may lead to multiple social and economic benefits. Forest carbon projects also expand the range of international participation in the carbon market in places such as Africa where CO_2 reduction opportunities are very limited due to low levels of fossil fuel use.

The next section discusses the primary drivers for deforestation and forest degradation. This section is important as it provides potential risks from holding forest assets. In other words, the nature of the deforestation driver and its impact on the forest ultimately impacts forest carbon stocks. Understanding the fundamental impact of the deforestation drivers is therefore important in understand the nature of risks and opportunities the forest asset faces.

Drivers of Deforestation and Degradation

Deforestation is a consequence of interaction between social, economic, and environmental drivers. It is a complex, dynamic, and interconnected phenomena with multiple actors. This section describes the general framework under which deforestation occurs along with specific geographic drivers when appropriate. This section is important both to provide an understanding of the causes of deforestation but also to understand the phenomenon from a risk management standpoint. The risk management aspect is important not only for forest managers who are interested in sustainable growth in their forest parcels but also for financial analysts who value the forest assets for their timber, biodiversity, and carbon assets. The nature of deforestation drivers will play a role in the valuation of forest environmental attributes and ultimately the riskiness of asset. First, we explain the difference between deforestation and degradation.

According to the IPCC, deforestation is the direct human induced conversion of forested land to non-forested land.

---

[13]The Conference Board, "Carbon Footprint: An Increasing Management Concern." Executive Action Series No. 213 (October 2006).

Degradation occurs when there are changes within the forest class that negatively affect the stand or site and, in particular, lower the production capacity.[14]

In other words, deforestation results in the absence of land that was previously forested and degradation results in the reduction in the quality of existing forested land. Continued degradation may in fact lead to deforestation.

It is hard to pinpoint any single driver for deforestation but for explanatory purposes we categorize the drivers as direct and indirect drivers (See Figure 6.2). The most important direct driver for deforestation is clearing and conversion of forests for commercial agriculture, accounting for about 67% of total deforestation. This kind of activity is particularly prevalent in Latin America where forest clearing for pasture land and soybean cultivation are major drivers of deforestation. Globally, forest clearing for cultivation of oil palm, sugar cane, and corn are major drivers of deforestation. However, agriculture is not always the

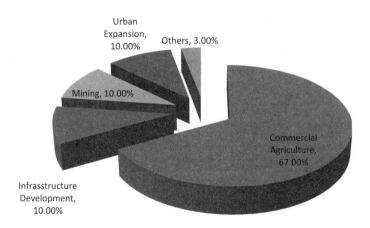

Figure 6.2. Global Drivers for Deforestation.

[14]Jim Penman, Michael Gytarsky, Taka Hiraishi, Thelma Krug, Dina Kruger, Riitta Pipatti, Leandro Buendia, Kyoko Miwa, Todd Ngara, Kiyoto Tanabe and Fabian Wagner, "Good Practices Guidance for Land Use, Land-Use Change and Forestry." Intergovernmental Panel on Climate Change (2003); available online at www.ipcc-nggip.iges.or.jp/public/gpglulucf/gpglulucf_files/GPG_LULUCF_FULL.pdf.

driver that leads to deforestation; in many instances land deforested for other purposes is subsequently converted to agricultural use as a result of government policy (e.g., Brazil). Other direct drivers include mining, urban expansion, and forest clearing for infrastructure development, which account for 10% each. Urban expansion was a significant factor in Asia while mining and infrastructure development were major factors in Africa and Latin America.

Indirect drivers result from interaction between demographic, economic, technological, policy, and socio-cultural factors. From an economic standpoint, increasing global demand for timber and agricultural products are major indirect factors. "Embedded deforestation" via international trade in agricultural and wood products is a leading indirect driver of deforestation. The European Union is the largest net importer of embedded deforestation through soy imports from Brazil, Argentina, and Paraguay, meat products from Brazil, palm oil from Indonesia and Malaysia, and cocoa from Ghana and Nigeria. This phenomenon is similar to the concept of virtual water discussed in Chapter 8 of this book. Export of forest products also includes "virtual" export of resources such as water which may lead to ecosystem impacts such as water depletion.

Others include, weak forest governance and institutional framework in many countries, population growth, ill-defined land property rights and insecure land tenure, and other macro factors such as commodity prices, foreign direct investment etc. Expanding road infrastructure in many developing countries is providing access to loggers, migrants, and farmers, thereby exacerbating the problem of deforestation.

Geographically, over half of the world's deforestation takes place in two countries — Indonesia and Brazil. Largely due to emissions attributed to deforestation, these countries rank among the top five GHG emitting nations.

As far as forest degradation is concerned, timber and logging activities accounted for more than 70% in Latin America and Asia. In Africa, fuel wood collection and charcoal production was the main driver of forest degradation. Degraded forests often end up in alternate non-forest uses.

Mitigating deforestation therefore can play a major role in mitigating climate change. The sink capacity of global forests alone suggests that it will be hard to solve the climate problem, without inclusion of forestry. However, forestry (and other land-based offsets) have had a difficult route to inclusion in GHG markets. The next section, discusses the policy response to inclusion of forestry as a legitimate source for climate mitigation.

Categorizing Forest Carbon

There are several different kinds of project activities that qualify under forest carbon rules and can be credited with carbon allowances. Further, the nature of the project type has an impact on the volume of carbon tons, nature of underlying risks, eligibility requirements etc. All of these variables ultimately have an impact on market price. This section provides an overview of the most common types of forest carbon projects in the market:

(1) Reducing Emissions from Deforestation and Forest Degradation (REDD): These projects are focused on preserving existing tropical forests given the impact of deforestation and degradation on GHG emissions. Compared to other land-based strategies, REDD has the greatest potential to generate large volumes of carbon benefits in the near term. Typically, REDD projects are quite large (100,000–1,000,000 ha) and have the potential to generate significant volumes (100,000–1,000,000 tons CO_2e/year) of emissions reductions. REDD also has the greatest potential to produce major biodiversity and social co-benefits, given the natural capital, and goods and services associated with intact native forests.

(2) Afforestation/Reforestation (A/R): These projects refer to planting trees in land that was not recently forested, i.e., afforestation and reforestation in previously forested land.

These projects are among the earliest to participate in GHG emissions markets. This is partly due to the accounting methodologies for such projects being straightforward and proven. While relatively easy, the quantity of carbon accrued in such projects is also lower and needs to build up with the growth of trees. Nonetheless, A/R sequestration activities have great potential to draw down carbon that has already been released into the atmosphere, making them an important longer-term carbon mitigation strategy.

(3) Improved Forest Management (IFM): Improving how forests are managed can generate climate benefits, potentially both in terms of reducing emissions and sequestering carbon. Broad activity types include: Shifting from conventional to low-impact logging; protecting forests that would have been logged; increasing rotation age; and converting marginal forests into highly productive forests (e.g., through replanting). Most timber operations are commercially managed, which can simplify IFM carbon transactions and project activities. However, the short-term profit motivation can also present challenges with ensuring that the carbon benefits are maintained over the long-term, especially in the face of rising opportunity costs. Regardless, unless demand for timber and other wood products rapidly declines it will be important to develop forest management strategies that benefit, or at least do not harm, the global climate. As a best management practice, this category is critical for enhancing or maintaining carbon stocks and sustainably managing commercial forestry and timber plantations. The Chicago Climate Exchange[15] (CCX) was the first program to incorporate forest carbon in its program. CCX members from the commercial forest sector not only took a binding emissions reductions target but also committed to IFM. In

---

[15]The Chicago Climate Exchange was the first market based, multi-sectoral program for trading greenhouse gas emissions in the world. The program was voluntary but legally binding and involved over 400 members including offsets from forestry and agriculture projects.

addition to practicing best management practices, this involved obtaining sustainable forestry certification and committing to stability in forest carbon stocks. Leading forest companies such as International Paper (NYSE:IP), Stora Enso (HEL:STERV), and Meadwest Vaco (NYSE:MVW) took a leadership role in the program.

In addition to the above described avenues, there exists a wide range of carbon sequestration opportunities in agriculture. These are described below.

The environmental marketplace has provided an opportunity for global agriculture to provide environmental services. Specifically, the main sources of opportunity are sequestering carbon in soil by practicing conservation tillage, grassland cultivation, and tree planting. These opportunities allow farmers to diversify their income streams, improve productivity, and reduce production risks while promoting long-term sustainability and health of farmland. For example, these practices improve water quality and enhance local environmental conditions. The multiple gains that can accrue to farmers can be substantial.

The Chicago Climate Exchange (CCX) was also the first program to include agricultural soil sequestration as a legitimate source of carbon offset in a transparent, monitored, and verified greenhouse gas trading program. CCX felt the important need to position agriculture to realize a major new income stream through the provision of global environmental services. Under the program, CCX members who could not reduce their own emissions could purchase credits from those who make extra emission cuts, or could buy offsets from individual mitigation projects, such as agricultural projects, including no- and low-till farming, grass, or tree plantings. The concept of conservation tillage or no-till farming involved leaving the soil undisturbed from harvest to planting except for strips of less than 30% of the row width. Planting is accomplished in a narrow seedbed or slot created by disk openers. This kind of tillage promotes growth in soil carbon because crop residues from previous years are left on the soil surface, and root systems from previous crops are left to decay in the soil, thereby maintaining or increasing the organic carbon content of the soil. No-till practices can be verified through confirmation of plant residues left on the soil surface from previous years as well as evidence that the soil has not been significantly turned, mixed, or disrupted. A properly designed program could then credit farmers by issuing them carbon offset allowances for the quantity of additional carbon sequestered during a period of time, usually a year. The CCX program registered, verified, and transacted carbon allowances from over 16 million acres of conservation tillage, grassland, and tree planted acres in North America. This effort was supported by the National Farmers Union and Farm Bureau in the United States.

Tree planting is another avenue that farmers could participate in the global GHG market. The program works similar to the soil program with carbon sequestration attributed to woody biomass from tree growth. Senator Richard Lugar, Republican from Indiana, was among the first participants in such a program via CCX. In May 2006, Senator Lugar enrolled his 604 acre hardwood tree farm, Lugar Stock farms, in Indiana into CCX. Each year, carbon sequestered via tree growth was computed and carbon allowances issued. The amount of carbon sequestered varies based on the farm's management practices, tree type, density, and age group. The carbon allowances accrued may then be monetized by selling them on the CCX GHG marketplace.

The Policy Response: Origins of Forest Carbon in Greenhouse Gas Emissions Trading

The 1992 "Earth Summit" (more formally known as the United Nations Conference on Environment and Development) at Rio de Janeiro witnessed the opening for signature of the Convention on Biological Diversity as well as the United Nations Framework Convention on Climate Change (UNFCCC) and a treaty on desertification. In 1997 the climate convention culminated in the adoption of the Kyoto Protocol with a central goal of slowing human contribution to increased atmospheric concentrations of carbon dioxide. Both the climate and biodiversity treaties have at their heart the preservation of ecological systems and both explicitly espouse the goal of environmentally sustainable economic development. Moreover, slowing the pace of rapid climate change would, on its own, provide an enormous service towards the preservation of biological diversity.

From its inception, the UNFCCC has recognized the importance of flexibility by targeting multiple greenhouse gases, encouraging the use of all sources and sinks as mitigation options (e.g., forest biomass and soil sequestration), and allowing flexibility and economic efficiency. These principles were reflected in the UNFCCC's Kyoto Protocol which established a comprehensive approach to address global warming.

As expounded in Chapter 4, the Kyoto Protocol introduced four forms of international flexibility allowed in realizing compliance with its quantitative emission reduction commitments. Notably, Article 3 of the UNFCCC clearly states that policies and measures to be adopted by all Parties should cover "all relevant sinks and reservoirs." This is reaffirmed in the Kyoto Protocol, Article 2, which states that Annex I Parties shall implement policies and measures for "the protection and enhancement of sinks."

However, several restrictions were placed on carbon credits sourced from forestry and other land use change activities, including under the Kyoto Protocol. For example, under the Kyoto Protocol, the inclusion of credits from forestry is limited to afforestation and reforestation projects under the CDM. Here again, the UNFCCC issues forestry a variant of the CER[16] called temporary CER (tCER) or long-term CER (lCERS). Both these forms of carbon credits had to be replaced by the buyers at some point in the

---

[16]For a detailed explanation on CER, refer to Chapter 4.

future to stay compliant under the UNFCCC rules. The uncertainty and additional cost involved in procuring forest tons due to this mechanism generated limited interest and investment in afforestation and reforestation activities. In addition to such constraints from design elements, the inclusion of forest carbon under the UNFCCC has also faced long standing philosophical disagreements. Part of the reluctance to include forestry arises from a perception of inadequate methods for quantifying carbon uptake by forests and assuring long-lasting carbon storage. In addition, there is in some quarters a concern that use of forest sequestration as a mitigation option should be de-emphasized as it is somehow less attractive than reductions in emissions. There are also differences in the nature of financial assistance and compensation to incentivize developing countries that are endowed with tropical forests to preserve the resource as a global asset.

The United Nations negotiations were not the only platform where forest carbon faced roadblocks. The EU Emissions Trading Scheme (EU ETS), which was the first large scale demonstration of the trading approach to realizing commitments under Kyoto, has also been hesitant. The EU excluded credits from forestry and other land-use change activities from the linking directive that allowed for CDM credits to flow into the EU ETS. The primary reason for the exclusion was EU policymakers' focus on the energy sector and fear that large quantities of forestry credits would flood the market thereby causing collapse in EU allowance prices. The fall in EUA prices, due to reasons explained in Chapter 4, did not help with the argument to include forest-based sinks. Current thinking within the EU is to not allow for new offset types, including forestry, before 2020.

In spite of slow progress at the international front, several bilateral agreements among nations, emerging domestic trading programs, and individual corporate action has resulted in significant support and nurturing of the market for forest carbon. Past efforts for a U.S. GHG emissions reduction program, such as

Waxman–Markey and McCain–Lieberman,[17] within the United States have prominently included a forest and agriculture sourced component. However, most of the optimism for REDD in the United States is from state level efforts. Here climate policy leadership has continued in California, with its Global Warming Solutions Act (AB 32) moving forward. California's cap-and-trade regulations specifically (and only) identify REDD as a potential international sector that could generate offset credits. If this proposal is enacted, it will establish the world's first compliance market for REDD. Analysts suggest that based on California emissions, offset caps, and abatement opportunities, REDD demand could be more that 40 Mt between 2015 and 2020 at an average price of $30/ton.[18] California has already moved ahead and partnered with the Brazilian state of Acre and Mexican state of Chiapas to develop REDD supply. California is also the only U.S. state that is still active in the Western Climate Initiative, which includes several Canadian provinces. This holds the promise for additional demand for California compliance REDD credits from Canadian emitters to comply with their GHG obligations.

In the absence of mandatory markets that allow forest carbon, the voluntary market and corporate demand has remained the primary driver for these credits. When discussing the voluntary markets, it is important to provide some discussion on the major voluntary standard and certification process for REDD credits. As discussed in other chapters, the pricing of environmental credits to a large extent depends on the underlying nature of the program (mandatory versus voluntary) and robustness of the certification standard. Given the multi-dimensional nature of REDD credits, robust standard, and

---

[17] Senator John McCain, Republican from Arizona and Senator Joseph Lieberman, Democrat from Connecticut.

[18] Toby Janson-Smith and Helene Marsh, "A Corporate Primer on Reducing Emissions from Deforestation and Forest Degradation (REDD). The Context, Key Technical and Policy Issues, and Private Sector Involvement." Conservation International (August 2013); available online at http://thereddesk.org/sites/default/files/resources/pdf/%5Bite-date-yyyy%5D/REDD%20Corporate%20Primer.pdf.

certification attesting to the environment, social and biodiversity attributes of the project are important from a market perspective. Recent years have seen rapid growth in the standardization of best practices in REDD and assessment of environmental, social, and environmental outcomes. This has directly led to growth in the demand for REDD credits boosted by market confidence.

The global REDD market has converged around two standards for ensuring best practices in forest preservation, namely, (a) Verified Carbon Standard (VCS) and (b) Climate, Community & Biodiversity Standards (CCBA):

(a) Verified Carbon Standard: The VCS has emerged as the leading standard to ensure carbon accounting in REDD projects. VCS, which was established in 2005 by several leading organizations working for climate change, is now managed as a non-profit Verified Carbon Association. While forestry is not its lone focus, VCS has developed several REDD methodologies appropriate to particular types of deforestation and forest enhancement activities. As of April 2013, VCS had registered over 70 land use projects including forestry. The carbon credits from VCS protocol are called Verified Carbon Units or VCUs and represent one metric ton of verified carbon. As of April 2013, over 8.5 million VCUs have been issued from agriculture, forestry, and other land use change activities. The pipeline of REDD projects in development indicates that the volume of VCUs from such activities is increasing rapidly. Developing a robust voluntary and mandatory demand for REDD is essential to ensure continued funding for such projects. VCS is actively engaged with several emerging markets to potentially utilize VCUs as the underlying compliance standard. The outcomes of these efforts are uncertain at the time of writing of this report.

(b) Climate, Community & Biodiversity Standards (CCBA): The CCBA standard focuses on ensuring the best practices in REDD projects are followed for social, biodiversity, and community aspects. This standard does not issue credits and is combined with other carbon accounting standards as the auxiliary standard. The most common combination in the market is VCS+CCBA dual certification. The CCBA Standards assess a variety of social and environmental dimensions for demonstrating that a project will mitigate climate change, conserve biodiversity, improve the well-being of local communities and also ensure that: The rights of indigenous peoples and local communities are recognized and respected; local stakeholders are effectively involved in project design and implementation; carbon property rights are clear and there are no unresolved land tenure disputes; and positive and negative social and environmental impacts are monitored and the results are made public. As of April 2013, 65 projects have been validated under the CCBA, with another 22 projects undergoing validation. 74 of these projects are in developing countries.

Industry surveys indicate that there is a strong preference for the CCBA standard.[19] This is indicated by the market willingness to pay a premium for projects that in addition to VCS carbon certification had CCB accreditation. Surveys conducted in 2011 indicate that the premium paid for CCB certification over VCS was $0.50 per ton.

Having described the predominant voluntary standards, the next section presents an overview of the market volumes and prices.

Market Size and Price

Markets for forestry projects internationally are very modest but growing at a rapid rate, primarily in the voluntary carbon market place. Given the significant role that voluntary markets play in forestry, this section will predominantly focus on voluntary market

---

[19] Janson-Smith and Marsh, "A Corporate Primer on Reducing Emissions from Deforestation and Forest Degradation (REDD)." (August 2013).

Table 6.1. Volume, Value, and Prices in Forest Carbon Markets.

Market	Historical	Volume (in millions) 2010	2011	Value (in million U.S.$) 2010	2011	Average Price (in U.S.$ per ton) 2010	2011
Voluntary OTC	76.4	27.8	16.7	157.8	172	5.6	10.3
California/WC pre-compliance	2.0	0.5	1.6	—	13	—	8.1
CCX	2.9	0.1	0	0.2	—	1.2	—
Voluntary Total	**81.4**	**28.4**	**18.3**	**158**	**185**	**5.6**	**9.2**
CDM/JI	15.3	1.4	5.9	6.3	23	4.5	3.9
NSW GGAS	6.3	2.3	—	13	—	—	—
NZ ETS	0.9	0.2	—	0.3	—	13	—
Other/ Unknown	1.9	0.4	1.5	—	29	—	19.7
Compliance Total	**24.5**	**4.4**	**7.3**	**25.0**	**52**	**4.6**	**7.2**
GRAND TOTAL	**105.9**	**33**	**26**	**177**	**237**	**5.5**	**9.2**
Primary Market	*95*	*32*	*21*	*143*	*143*	*5.5*	*8.1*
Secondary Market	*11.3*	*1.2*	*4.9*	*4.8*	*54.7*	*7.6*	*12.1*

Notes: Based on 965 observations in 2011; >1,000 total historical observations. "Other" category includes markets with fewer than three data points. 2008–2010 values for the NSW GGAS market should be considered conservative due to limited market price data.
Source: Ecosystem Marketplace (2012).

transactions. We start with a discussion of market volume and value and proceed to pricing. A separate section on trends in the voluntary market follows:

1. Market Volume and Value: Table 6.1 presents historical volumes and prices from forest carbon markets and Figure 6.4 presents the cumulative volume and market transactions in the forest carbon market. Since 2005, the cumulative volume of forest carbon transacted is about 106 MMTCO$_2$e from about 451 forest carbon projects. About 77% of these transactions were

conducted in voluntary or pre-compliance credits and 23% trans-actions were conducted under mandatory markets.

Historically, much of the volume has been in the brokered market. To illustrate, over 72% of voluntary market transactions happens through this mode. While the relative delay in development of technical protocols, platforms, and forest specific tradable carbon products may be one reason to explain this, the predominant rational is the difficultly in the standardizing a forest carbon product given the unique set of attributes under each forest project. Proper due diligence on both the environmental and socio-cultural aspects of the forest project are therefore critical for potential investors.

In 2011, the total value of forest carbon market was about U.S.$237 million, a 30% increase from the previous year and 540% increase from pre-2005 market emergence. Part of this increased valuation of the market is attributed to the emergence of scientific techniques to measure forest carbon and assess ecosystem risks and partly to capacity building and market readiness efforts. With continued progress on these fronts alongside greater acceptance of land use change and forestry as legitimate supplies of GHG credits, this trend is expected to grow.

While the largest portion of the value was from voluntary markets (72%), it is noted that the greatest jump in value year to year was in the CDM/JI category followed British Columbia Carbon Neutral Directive. In these cases, the large increases in transaction value can be attributed to high "fixed prices"[20] under the British Columbia market and higher transaction volume under the CDM market.

2. Pricing: There can be wide variance in the pricing of credits sourced from forestry due to their unique set of environmental and social attributes, project specific risks, locational attributes, and other variables. In addition, the volume of transactions, type

---

[20]The British Columbia Scheme had a fixed price of $25 per tCO_2.

Figure 6.3. Annual Volume and Value of Forest Carbon Transactions.

Source: Adapted from Molly Peters-Stanley, Katherine Hamilton and Daphne Yin, *Leveraging the Landscape: State of the Forest Carbon Market 2012* (Washington, DC: Ecosystem Marketplace, 2012).

of contract (forward versus spot), and forest carbon standard also play a role in price determination. For example, in 2011 the price range for forest carbon ranged from less than $1 per ton to over $100 per ton. On average, the forest carbon was priced at $9.2 per ton/$CO_2$ in 2011 compared to $5.2 per ton/$CO_2$ in 2010 (see Figure 6.3).

The next section discusses more on the trends on voluntary markets which have a profound influence on the price determination.

Trends in the Voluntary Market

The motivation for purchasing voluntary carbon of any kind, including forestry, includes voluntary offsetting, public relations,

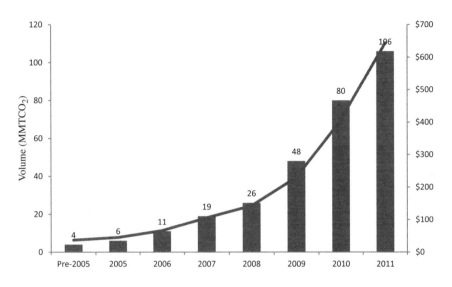

Figure 6.4. Cumulative Volume and Forest Carbon Market Transactions.

Source: Molly Peters-Stanley, Katherine Hamilton and Daphne Yin, *Leveraging the Landscape: State of the Forest Carbon Market 2012* (Washington, DC: Ecosystem Marketplace, 2012).

and corporate social responsibility etc. In turn, forest carbon assets purchased in voluntary markets may have pre-compliance value in mandatory markets either nationally, regionally, or internationally. The demand for forest carbon is subject to global and specific industry economic conditions, other competing offsets, and expected national and regional policy outcomes of GHG emissions mandates. The segmented nature of market and lack of standardization increase transactions cost for procurement of these credits. Some of the factors are discussed below.

Forest Project Type Matters

Forest carbon accounted for about 24% market of all voluntary carbon and was the second most preferred category in 2011. Voluntary carbon sourced from renewables accounted for the bulk of the market demand (45%). Here again, it is important to note that the type of forest carbon project mattered to the demand side. Forest projects from REDD and afforestation and reforestation accounted for 10% each, which improved forest management accounted for 4% of the market share of total voluntary carbon market. It is noted that, REDD projects contracted the highest value of any project type in the voluntary markets, owing to the above average prices paid for newly issued tonnage. Being the first projects in the market, afforestation and reforestation projects saw continued demand from earlier projects and new entrants. Some of the voluntary market demand is also attributed to buyers who want to take an early position anticipating acceptance of forestry within the California cap-and-trade program.

Forest Standards and Technical Protocols have Market Implications

While great progress has been made, the scientific community continues to develop quantification measures and best practice guidance for forestry projects. Project developers and buyers of forest carbon have adjusted through new protocol requirements, and incurred additional costs and time in implementing forest carbon projects and in some cases faced bureaucratic delays to get projects governmental sanction. Market participants could greatly benefit from greater transparency and standardization of quantification standards and verification protocols regarding the costs and time required to pass project milestones. This will provide greater certainty to commercial transactions and increase liquidity in the marketplace.

In addition, the lack of clarity regarding carbon rights, land tenure, and best practice stemmed from slow progress in developing national and international rules, safeguards, and clear processes that market participants could reference to guide their engagement with communities. In its absence, the market place will continue to be plagued and in some cases negatively impact legitimate activities and increase the real or perceived risk of project activities and investments

The State of International Climate Negotiations

Support for carbon market in general and forest carbon in particular has suffered from global economy as well as regulatory uncertainty in international climate negotiations. Here we note that forest carbon projects usually require a longer developmental time period than other projects such as renewables. This makes them especially vulnerable to uncertainty in regulations and changing rules on eligibility. The state of climate negotiations has increased the burden of project developers in procuring funding for forestry projects. Not only is there a lack of agreement on emerging regulations but also a failure to maintain existing regulations and markets rules which have an impact on forest carbon market development and price discovery. In addition, uncertainty regarding market specifications in California and other emerging markets regarding forest carbon as well as a lack of clarity, recognition, or regulation of carbon rights in some developing countries has an impact on project timelines.

The Great Recession, the European Debt Crisis, and the Substitution Effect

In Chapter 4, we discussed how economic slowdown resulting from the great recession led to a decrease in price for EUA allowances resulting from reduced GHG emissions and demand for EUA. While that logic does not hold true for voluntary forest carbon, the economic pressure created from the great recession forced buyers to choose among available offset tons. Here voluntary carbon from renewable sources is relatively cheaper compared to carbon from forest and other land use change activities. This substitution to lower-priced voluntary offsets reduced demand for forest carbon in 2011. European corporates have prominent sources of forest carbon procurement (50%) and this had a significant impact on forest carbon demand.

Private Sector Participation: What Does the Demand Side Want?

As discussed earlier, much of the demand, development, and financing for forest carbon arises from the private sector including corporate buyers, conservation organizations, retail participants, and others. For example, private sector buyers procured about 12.3 $MtCO_2$ from the total 26 $MtCO_2$ forest carbon tons transacted. This included participants acting on CSR and PR objectives, procuring pre-compliance tons as well as conservation objectives. The forest carbon offset market is therefore determined by preference, unique motivations, and the business case for each buy side participant. These are discussed under various categories in this section.

Corporate Social Responsibility and Public Relations

This category of buyers is the most prominent subset of the demand side. Typically these buyers have relatively lower GHG emissions and are not participants in any mandated GHG emissions reductions program. These participants typically possess major brand presence and customer exposure. These buyers are also motivated to set aggressive corporate climate goals (e.g., carbon neutrality) to appeal to their customers, employees, and shareholders, as well as to differentiate themselves from competitors. Other motivations include extended GHG commitments such as greening the supply chain. In addition, several of these buyers have a history or culture of such leadership on climate and social issues. In 2011, about 30% of all forest carbon transacted was a result of this category of participants.

Under this set, forest offsets are purchased if these corporate climate goals go beyond what is achievable through internal emissions reduction efforts. To take full advantage of these benefits, companies often prefer to be associated with a particular, early-stage project. Most CSR-motivated buyers invest directly with project developers (typically major NGOs) rather than buy off-the-shelf credits. Examples include companies such Disney, Dell, Marriott, GM/Chevy, NAVTEQ, Home Depot, and eBay who have all procured or committed to procure forest carbon tons.

Another motivation under this category includes companies that have a strong connection with land-based activities which may be seen as being synergistic with other business goals. For example, there are opportunities for agricultural companies to accelerate and support sustainable production practices (e.g., conserving forests that may provide pollination and natural pest control services to nearby farms, maintaining forest canopy for shade grown coffee, and maintaining soil health through conservation practices) through forest activities. In addition, paper and pulp companies may find certain forest projects useful to building alternate income streams for their small farmer suppliers and adapting to a changing climate. In a similar fashion extractive industry (e.g., oil and gas, and mining) companies may find forest strategies helpful for sustaining conservation and rehabilitation activities with a carbon revenue stream.

Retail Carbon Offset Markets

Some corporate buyers, especially the transportation industry, have established consumer or business facing programs through which their customers can buy forest carbon credits to offset the GHG footprint associated with their product use. A number of airlines, hotel chains, parcel shippers, car rental, and computer companies have established customer facing offset programs. Unfortunately, few of these programs have experienced significant uptake rates, often due to implementation issues. Some programs such as Dell's "Plant a Tree for Me" program allowing its consumer and business customers to offset (through tree planting efforts) the energy use associated with running their Dell computer for three years have done reasonably well. Other examples include Pacific Gas & Electric which has run a successful offset program for their California customers interested in offsetting their energy use emissions through forest restoration projects in the state. Several other companies including Hyundai, Chevrolet, and Motorola have retired forest carbon offsets to make a newly launched product carbon neutral for all life cycle emissions or just those from a year's worth of operation.

Forest Carbon Project Development and Investments

There are three groups of entities that are involved in the business of developing forest carbon projects. The first group includes NGOs interested in conservation that have played a prominent role in forest preservation long before the emergence of carbon markets. This group, with the primary motivation of forest and biodiversity preservation, seeks finance from environmental markets as a sustainable means to attain those goals.

With the development of environmental markets, carbon market standards, and best practices, a second group consisting of an increasing number of private companies is engaged in developing forest carbon projects. Some of the leading private developers of forest carbon projects include Terra Global Capital, Wildlife Works, and Infinite Earth.

A third group comprising of investors are directly involved in project development, such as Floresta and Macquarie bank. However, it is more typical for investors to simply fund existing projects or work with third parties to develop new projects. Major forest carbon, especially REDD+ investors include Althelia, Merrill Lynch, and Ned Bank.

These investors develop or invest in forest carbon projects to generate large volumes of carbon credits, which they look to sell for a profit within the voluntary, pre-compliance, or compliance markets. In addition, over the past two years, a number of new REDD focused investment funds have been established, including Althelia ($275m target capitalization), Macquarie-IFC ($25m+), and Terra Global Capital ($50m+). These funds are hoping to profit from the voluntary carbon market's rapidly growing appetite for forest carbon credits, while positioning themselves to take advantage of emerging compliance market demand for forest carbon.

Pre-Compliance Demand

Unlike CSR motivated buyers, compliance-driven buyers are typically major emitters that expect to be operating under climate regulations that credit forest carbon activities. They act under the belief that future global climate agreements, either internationally, nationally, or regionally, will credit forestry activities in some fashion. This category of purchase can be highly speculative given the significant uncertainties associated with inclusion of forest carbon in emerging GHG trading programs. As discussed earlier, California is predicted to become the world's first compliance market for REDD+ credits. In addition, these types of credits can also find a place in Australia's new climate legislation, Japan, and South Korea. Each one of these compliance markets could be worth hundreds of millions of dollars annually for forest carbon, especially REDD.

Some major GHG emitters (including BP, American Electric Power (AEP), and Duke Energy) have funded forest carbon projects developed by conservation organizations in an attempt to build capacity building and education. Others are making early strategic investments in forest carbon. For example, BP has pledged $5 million to the Carbon Fund of the World Bank's Forest Carbon Partnership Facility (FCPF), which expects to generate verified emission reductions for participating donor countries and investors.

Offsets in general can be valuable to compliance-driven companies as a means to: reduce regulatory risk exposure (e.g., through securing future rights to carbon credits); reduce costs; and facilitate long-term business planning. Forest carbon projects can be particularly appealing due to their potential to generate large volumes of inexpensive emissions reductions and provide an effective diversification strategy given that they are decoupled from energy and industrial developmental costs.

Carbon Credit Trading and Retailing

Although the forest carbon market has grown substantially over the past few years, the project pipeline is still relatively immature and there are not yet many verified credits in the system. This, combined with demand being concentrated with few major buyers, has resulted in only a small number of companies focused on trading or retailing forest carbon credits. Most transactions occur bilaterally with the project developer transacting directly with the investor or carbon buyer. Examples of companies trading/retailing REDD+ credits include Carbonfund.org and the Carbon Neutral Company.

Conclusion

Climate change is providing opportunities for agriculture and forestry to serve as suppliers of a global environmental service, i.e., the sequestration of CO_2 from the atmosphere. With the advent of the cap-and-trade mechanism as an efficient means to address environmental challenges such as global warming, we are witnessing transformation opportunities to conserve forests, biodiversity, and their ecosystem assets through environmental markets. The emerging forest carbon markets bring new responsibilities, risks, and trading opportunities for corporations, traders, and land managers. Understanding the forest carbon asset class requires knowledge both of forests as biological systems, as well as their interplay between the environmental and social ecosystems in which they exist. A thorough understanding of these dynamics can assist in unlocking significant value from forest carbon assets.

This chapter focused on expounding on these opportunities. Its focus was to view the forest ecosystem from an investment standpoint and to identify financial risks and opportunities in the space. In order to do so, the chapter explained the important contribution preserving the forest sector makes to mitigating and adapting to climate change and the associated biodiversity and environmental benefits. It described the main drivers of deforestation and degradation. The policy framework surrounding forestry in the global carbon markets was presented along with the major forest program standards. The forest carbon market, buyer's motivations, and private sector participation thus far were elaborated. The chapter highlighted the unique opportunities for biodiversity conservation, ecological services, and socio-cultural attributes that arise out of this sector. The existing marketplace for forest carbon, demand side motivation, and market trends was also discussed.

Clear understanding of the determinants of forest carbon valuation and underlying risks can place market players in an advantaged position extracting value from forest assets. The forest ecosystem as an asset class is unique as it presents a package of environmental attributes, including water, biodiversity, forest carbon etc., all of which may be monetized in the future. Among the multiple options that are available to mitigate greenhouse gases, the forest asset class may possess significant value, i.e., it is an underpriced asset class that provides many social benefits.

We conclude by highlighting that while there exists a huge potential for global forests, the global climate problem cannot be addressed without actively involving forest carbon pools. The global community needs to focus on this sector as a provider of solutions to common environmental challenges we face rather than exclude it based on technological, bureaucratic, or philosophical opposition.

The next chapter extends the scope of environmental markets to sustainable energy. As we have elaborated in previous chapters, a wide variety of sectoral and regional policies have emerged to manage GHGs and other energy and environmental objectives. In addition to reducing GHG emissions, renewable energy facilities have value in creating energy diversity and a cleaner grid. The same is true for energy-efficiency and market incentives for other sustainable and decentralized power production. The next chapter describes some of these related environmental markets that price these attributes.

Chapter 7

CLEAN ENERGY MARKETS
AND ASSOCIATED ASSET CLASSES

The primary policy response to global warming around the world has been the implementation of market-based programs for the reduction of greenhouse gas emissions. Several additional markets and practices, however, have had an impact on climate change and the broader environment. These markets include renewable energy certificates (RECs), renewable identification numbers (RINs), and crediting for energy-efficiency. RECs represent the property rights to the environmental, social, and other non-power qualities of renewable electricity generation.[1] RINs play a role somewhat similar to that of RECs but in the market for transportation fuels. Both markets are in their infancy in terms of trading, but they have the potential to reach reasonable volumes because the underlying values for both are in excess of $1 billion.

Although no traded markets for energy-efficiency truly exist (except in a few states that have included it as part of RECs or alternative energy standards), it represents one of the largest opportunities to save money on energy expenditures and reduce emissions. It is also important because energy-efficiency, even when not directly credited, affects the prices of other markets, including CO_2 and RINs.

---

[1] Renewable Energy Certificates, U.S. Environmental Protection Agency; available online at http://www.epa.gov/greenpower/gpmarket/rec.htm.

RECs developed as an outgrowth of consumer demand for renewable sources of electricity in the late 1990s and requirements that several states put in place to meet targets for renewable energy generation, called "renewable portfolio standards" (RPS). RECs allowed investors to purchase the environmental attributes of renewable energy without having to purchase the actual power. This decoupling made it possible for RECs to, in effect, become a new type of currency for renewable energy projects. One revenue stream could be realized from the sale of the power, and another, from the sale of the RECs. Much like the GHG markets, RECs trade in both voluntary and mandatory markets.

RINs were developed in large part in response to the desire of midwestern states in the United States to help foster growth in agriculture-based renewable transportation fuels. RINs are a product of the U.S. Renewable Fuel Standard (RFS), which requires transportation fuel that is produced and consumed in the United States to contain a percentage of renewable fuels. RINs are effectively a tracking mechanism for the RFS that allows the U.S. EPA to determine whether a company is in compliance with the mandate.

Of all the mechanisms addressing climate change and the broader impacts of energy production on the environment, none is probably more significant than energy-efficiency. The International Energy Agency estimates that implementing energy-efficiency measures in buildings, industrial processes, and transportation could cut global demand by one-third by 2050.

In this chapter, we first describe the REC and RIN markets — in particular, the policy changes that brought these markets into being, general market characteristics, how RECs and RINs are traded and tracked, and opportunities for investors in the REC and RIN markets. Second, we discuss the importance of energy-efficiency.

Renewable Energy Certificates

Currently, in the United States, 29 states and the District of Columbia and Puerto Rico have state-level renewable portfolio standards (RPS).[2] Many large states, including California, Texas, New York, and Illinois, have these standards. Most states use the U.S. Department of Energy (DOE) definition of "renewable," which consists of the following categories of energy generation: wind, concentrated solar thermal, distributed and centralized photovoltaic, biomass, hydro, geothermal, landfill gas, and ocean power. Typically, however, some specialized requirements exist in various state RPSs. For example, the state of New Jersey requires that 20.38% of electricity come from renewables by 2020–2021, with an additional requirement that 4.1% of electricity come from solar sources by 2027–2028.[3]

RECs reflect the "green" attributes of electricity that is generated from renewable energy sources. These certificates are important because they can be a motivating factor for building renewable energy facilities. RECs allow these green attributes to be sold or bought separately from the physical electricity generated from renewable sources. Thus, an owner of a wind farm can have two sources of revenue: from selling electricity and from selling RECs. One REC represents the attributes that are associated with 1 megawatt hour (MWh) of energy from a renewable source. RECs are often assigned a "vintage," usually the year in which the renewable energy is generated.

Renewable Energy Legislation in the United States

The idea of unbundling the attributes of renewable energy from the underlying electricity was first discussed in a design document for the California RPS in 1995–1996.[4] A number of proposals, such as

---

[2] Map of Portfolio Standard Policies, Database of State Incentives for Renewables and Efficiency, North Carolina Solar Center (March 2013); available online at http://www.dsireusa.org/documents/summarymaps/RPS_map.pdf.

[3] New Jersey Incentives/Policies for Renewables & Efficiency, Database of State Incentives for Renewables and Efficiency, North Carolina Solar Center; available online at http://www.dsireusa.org/incentives/incentive.cfm?Incentive_Code=NJ05R.

[4] Much of the information in this section is from the U.S. EPA Green Power Partnership's website on renewable energy certificates; available online at http://www.epa.gov/greenpower/gpmarket/rec.htm.

renewable energy credit trading, were made to the California Public Utilities Commission, but the idea was not adopted.

The same idea came up in 1997 during discussions about implementing environmental disclosure on electricity labels in New England. Stakeholders were concerned with the validity of the fuel mix and emissions level claims of the electricity providers. A potential solution was to separate the electricity itself from various attributes of its generation.

In 1998, electricity markets in California, Massachusetts, and Rhode Island were opened up to retail choice. Automated Power Exchange (APX), which was eventually designated as the regional REC-tracking authority, opened a separate market for green power the day before the California market officially commenced on 1 April 1998. This market was a wholesale market for scheduled electricity deliveries; it was designed to help electricity providers differentiate themselves and their products. The APX Green Power Market traded electricity generated by renewable resource technologies as defined by the California legislation and under its renewable energy programs. One month later, in May 1998, the first retail REC product (called the "Regen") was sold in Massachusetts.[5] One year later, APX began a market for "green tickets." These wholesale products were purchased and "rebundled" with commodity electricity for retail green power sales.

In June 1999, Texas adopted Senate Bill 7, a restructuring law that included a renewable portfolio standard. The law also resulted in the first renewable energy credit trading program in the United States. That December, the Public Utility Commission of Texas adopted the rules required for a credit trading program.

The United States is criss-crossed by various REC tracking systems. These tracking systems closely (although not exactly) mirror the electricity grid of the United States. The lack of a national electric grid creates a variety of complications, not only for delivering power between regions of the grid but also for renewables. Because

---

[5] Retail RECs are those sold to individuals or small businesses.

of the fragmented nature of the grid, exporting renewable power into some states with aggressive renewable energy mandates, such as California, is sometimes difficult. This factor can complicate the development of renewables in states where renewable resources are plentiful (i.e., solar power in Arizona or wind power in South Dakota) because transmission access to states with large demands for renewable power is constrained.

Types of REC Programs

REC markets usually fall into two broad categories: *compliance* RECs that are used to meet state RPS requirements and *voluntary* RECs that consumers and companies buy/sell to match their electricity needs on a voluntary basis. In both markets, RECs can be sold separately or bundled with the sale of commodity electricity. More than 50 actively traded compliance REC markets are in operation; several states have multiple REC markets. The most actively traded markets are PJM Interconnection (New Jersey, in particular), New England Power Pool (NEPOOL) in Connecticut and Massachusetts, and the Electric Reliability Council of Texas.

Compliance market

In 2011, 31 separate RPS markets were in operation.[6] RPS policies collectively required utilities to obtain 133 million MWh from renewable energy sources, roughly 3% of the total megawatt hours produced in the United States.[7] As with the cap-and-trade markets for GHGs and sulfur dioxide, if electric utilities do not meet the mandated levels of renewable energy production, they can purchase RECs in the market. Similarly, if they produce more renewable

---

[6]North Carolina Solar Center at North Carolina State University, Database of State Incentives for Renewables and Efficiency (3 February 2012). The map can be accessed at http://www.eia.gov/todayinenergy/detail.cfm?id=4850.
[7]Platts, "Renewable Energy Certificates." Platts (April 2012); available online at http://www.platts.com/IM.Platts.Content/InsightAnalysis/IndustrySolutionPapers/RECSpecialReport1112.pdf.

energy than their mandates, they can sell their excess RECs in the market.

In compliance markets, REC transfers are performed through such tracking systems as NEPOOL, the PJM Generation Attribute Tracking System, Texas Geographic Information Systems, Western Renewable Energy Generation Information System, and North American Renewables Registry. Currently, the REC compliance markets are most active in Texas, Connecticut, Massachusetts, and Maine.

The multiplicity of rules governing the eligibility of RECs is one of the main reasons the compliance REC market is so fragmented. REC markets are fragmented both within and between states. For example, a wind farm in Illinois may be able to sell RECs into Pennsylvania but the reverse may not be allowed. That same Illinois wind farm may not be able to sell RECs into Ohio, even though Ohio might accept RECs from a wind farm in Pennsylvania.[8] Additionally, state-level rules for specific types of renewables mean that a solar REC in New Jersey may not be fungible with a wind REC from New Jersey.

REC market eligibility depends on the resources available, state of origin, and commercial operation date of the renewable energy source. Other considerations may include specific fuel requirements, vintage, and energy-delivery rules. To promote specific forms of renewable energy, some states adopt "multipliers" and "carve-outs." In multipliers, certain technologies receive more than 1 REC for 1 MWh of energy generated. The result is a financial incentive for energy companies to invest in the form of renewable energy that the state is using the multiplier to promote. But states can also use multipliers as a form of protectionism against out-of-state renewable energy generators, which severely limits interstate REC trading. Similarly, many state programs establish sub-targets — carve-outs

---

[8]Peter Toomey, "REC Markets and Trading 101." 2011 WSPP Spring Operating Committee Meeting, Iberdrola Renewables (21 March 2011); available online at http://www.wspp. org/filestorage/rec_markets_ trading_wspp_oc_mtg_032211.pdf.

or "set-asides" — to promote certain renewable projects. For these sub-targets, in addition to meeting the RPS mandates, energy companies need to prove that they have acquired a specific percentage of their power sales from the technology type required by the state in question. An example of this practice is solar RECs (SRECs). In some cases, multiple technology types are bundled together in "tiers" or "classes."

The complexity of rules governing RECs leads to a number of liquidity issues. Consider the previous case, in which RPS rules in two states were not reciprocal, which is usually the case. The RECs originating from Illinois wind farms are eligible under Pennsylvania's RPS, but Pennsylvania's wind-based RECs are not recognized under Illinois's RPS. Moreover, eligibility rules are often complex and ambiguous and are constantly changing to reflect state demands, a circumstance that can cause abrupt changes in the REC market. So, obviously RECs are not a homogeneous commodity and are subject to the whims of electorates and legislatures.

Voluntary market

The voluntary market for RECs is driven primarily by consumer demand for renewable electricity and corporate commitments to procure green energy. RECs are bought and sold as delivered renewable energy products (bundled with electricity) or bought and sold separately. The bundled product involves a wholesale transaction, whereas separate sales generally entail both wholesale and retail transactions.

The voluntary market is composed of utilities (more than 850 of them, according to the National Renewable Energy Laboratory, or NREL) that offer green power options to their customers, competitive electricity suppliers operating in states with retail competition, and marketers who sell RECs wholesale or retail. In 2009, the NREL estimated that 1.4 million U.S. electricity customers voluntarily bought green power through utilities or competitive suppliers or voluntarily bought RECs from REC marketers. Although

Table 7.1. Summary of Differences between Compliance and Voluntary REC Markets.

Criterion	Compliance market	Voluntary market
Demand driver	RPS, which mandates electricity	Voluntary consumer demand, environmental disclosure, corporate commitments, carbon claims, and so on
	Providers obtain a certain fraction of their electricity from renewable energy sources	
Procurements	Bundled green power (power + RECs)	Bundled green power (power + RECs)
	Unbundled RECs alone	Unbundled RECs alone
Transaction types	Wholesale	Wholesale and retail
Market division	Regional markets (tracking system)	Utility green pricing programs and competitive green power market
	National markets	Voluntary unbundled REC market
Important price factor	Geographical region	Generation type
	Generation type (for specific standard)	Vintage
Price	Higher	Lower
Size of market	133 million MWh	40 million MWh

exact figures are not available, the NREL estimates that approximately 40 million MWh of voluntary RECs were purchased in 2011. The most active voluntary REC markets in terms of total green power sales can be found in California, Illinois, Maryland, Oregon, Texas, and Washington. Table 7.1 summarizes the main differences between the voluntary and compliance REC markets.

Table 7.2 provides a summary of the size, pricing, and notional value of four of the most actively traded REC markets in the United States. The full notional value of the REC market is difficult to

Table 7.2. Examples of State REC Markets.

	2010			2020 estimate		
State	Size (million MWh)	Pricing ($/MWh)	Notional value ($ millions)	Size (million MWh)	Pricing ($/MWh)	Notional value ($ millions)
New Jersey: Class 1	5–10	8–15	40–120	15–20	8–15	120–300
Connecticut: Class 1	4–5	20–30	80–150	8–10	20–30	160–300
Massachusetts: Class 1	3–5	20–30	60–150	8–10	20–30	160–300
California: Tradable RECs	5–15	20–30	100–440	15–25	20–30	300–750

determine because it is largely a brokered market in which prices and volumes traded are not consistently reported. Although the individual states' market sharesare not large, the mandatory market is much larger than the voluntary market in megawatt hour terms.

Market Players in RECs

Compliance RECs are generally bought and sold by utilities and independent power producers to adhere to state mandates for renewable power production. Financial players are also involved in the compliance REC market, both as speculators and as owners of generating assets of renewable and non-renewable power.

In the voluntary market, corporate buyers make up the bulk of REC purchases, often as part of their corporate sustainability efforts. Many of the largest purchasers are some of America's most recognizable corporate brands — for example, Intel, Microsoft, Walmart, Starbucks, and Whole Foods.[9] Individual households and small

---

[9] A full list of the top buyers can be found on the EPA Green Power Partnership site; available online at http://www.epa.gov/greenpower/toplists/top50.htm.

businesses can also purchase voluntary RECs, often through their local utilities.

In both the compliance and voluntary markets, RECs can be directly traded from buyer to seller via exchanges or through third-party marketers, brokers, and asset managers. Many REC market participants are active in both the compliance and voluntary markets. REC marketers typically purchase RECs from renewable energy sources and resell them to utilities or end-users. REC brokers generally do not take ownership of the RECs at any point. Instead, they match sellers with buyers and make a profit on the commission. According to the DOE, 92 commercial and/or wholesale REC marketers, 25 retail marketers, 24 certificate brokers/exchanges, and 19 consumer protection/tracking systems are currently active. Additionally, four exchanges in the United States list REC products: the IntercontinentalExchange (ICE), Flett Exchange, Leaf Exchange, and Environmental Certificate Exchange.[10] ICE is currently the only regulated futures and options exchange offering REC contracts in the United States.

REC Pricing

Factors that affect REC prices in the individual state markets are usually the supply-and-demand dynamic created by the state mandate, generation technology, vintage, volume purchased, generation region, eligibility, and whether the RECs are bought to meet compliance obligations or to serve voluntary retail consumers. Natural gas prices and other forms of conventional generation can affect the cost competitiveness of renewable energy generation, which is reflected in REC prices. To the extent that emission reductions are an attribute of RECs, carbon credit prices may also affect REC prices.

The fragmentation and lack of homogeneity are compounded by opaqueness. REC prices are difficult to obtain except from a broker

---

[10]REC Marketers, the Green Power Network, U.S. Department of Energy; available online at http://apps3.eere.energy.gov/greenpower/markets/certificates.shtml?page=2.

because most transactions are over-the-counter. Some pricing trends for REC classes can be found in sample data from brokers, such as ICAP and Evolution Markets, as well as in periodic disclosures in utility commission proceedings. Using data from these sources, we observed that prices for voluntary RECs are generally much lower than those for compliance RECs. As a result of the multiplicity of REC products, however, no centralized price reporting is publicly accessible, with the exception of products traded on ICE.[11]

Compliance market

State RPS requirements are the chief price determinants in compliance REC markets. The prices for compliance RECs can differ considerably by state and are also affected by resource quality (e.g., wind speed) and regional electricity prices. Currently, more than half of the state-level RPS programs are under threat of being pared back. This phenomenon has increased in recent years as declining natural gas prices have made renewable energy prices comparatively more expensive. Other price determinants include fungibility of RECs between states and the cost of specific renewable energy technologies.

As illustrated in Figure 7.1, REC prices for Massachusetts, New Jersey, and Connecticut have traded from highs of $50/MWh and $60/MWh to lows of less than $10/MWh. These Northeastern states have relatively stringent RPS goals when compared with such states as Pennsylvania and Texas, where RECs consistently trade under $10/MWh. Meanwhile, REC prices remain under $5/MWh in Washington, DC, Delaware, Illinois, Maryland, New Jersey, Ohio, Pennsylvania, and Texas.

State-level carve-outs for specific types of renewable energy can also be a major driver in determining price. For example, SRECs are often priced 6–10 times above RECs generated by wind, biomass, and hydro sources. In fact, SREC prices hovered below $200/MWh

---

[11] *Climate Change Business Journal*, Vol. 4, No. 6/7 (2011); available online at http://www. 3degreesinc.com/sites/default/files/CCBJ_Reprint3DegreesProfile.pdf.

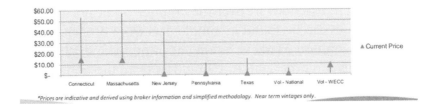

Figure 7.1. Historical OTC Price Ranges in Selected REC Markets.
Note: Prices are indicative and derived from broker information and simplified method-
ology. Near-term vintages only.
Source: Toomey, "REC Markets and Trading 101." *op. cit.*

in 2011, but for such states as Massachusetts and Ohio, prices
have been as high as $400–$550/MWh and, occasionally, higher.
SREC price information is disseminated via two online auction platforms — SRECTrade and Flett Exchange.

One state that presents a case study of not only carve-outs but also
the impact of price signals on behavior is New Jersey. With one of the
most aggressive RPS in the country, New Jersey has become a leading
market in the United States for renewable energy — solar energy, in
particular. New Jersey law requires a minimum of 20.38% of its sold
electricity to come from renewables by the year 2021. It has an additional mandate that solar power contribute 4.1% of the power sold
by 2028. The solar carve-out, established in 2006, has since been
revised upward twice, most recently in 2012. Each of these policy
interventions caused fairly dramatic responses in the market, which
can be seen in Figure 7.2; the increased RPS requirement passed in
2012 caused an increase in prices as well as megawatts installed.

The market response to the solar carve-out in New Jersey illustrates several lessons that can be learned from our study of other
environmental markets, such as those for SO_2 and GHGs. In each
case, the market responded to the price signal far more aggressively
than most analysts expected, resulting in far greater subsequent price
declines than many expected. Much like the installation of scrubbers for SO_2 or the increase in fuel switching and energy-efficiency
in GHG markets, the New Jersey SREC market experienced price

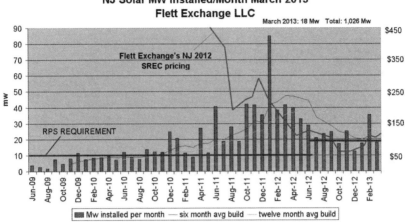

Figure 7.2. Megawatts of Solar Installed in New Jersey by Month, 2009–2013, and Flett Exchange's NJ 2012 SREC Pricing, 2011–2013.

Note: March 2013 = 18 Mw; total = 1,026 Mw (as of March 2013).

Source: Flett Exchange (2013).

declines from a high of roughly $700 to less than $100 in less than two years.

Solar developers responded to the SREC incentive by plowing resources into the state, making it the third-highest generator of solar electricity, behind only California and Arizona, despite its relatively low amount of solar radiation. This price signal attracted the interest of not only utilities but also financial players, who entered the market as independent power producers by financing solar installations.

Voluntary market

Compliance RECs generally must be from sources in a certain region to comply with the RPS in that region. Voluntary RECs are free from geographical constraints, however, and can be sourced nationally. Nevertheless, with some exceptions, most utility green pricing programs and marketers source their RECs from local or regional resources. Nationally sourced voluntary RECs are often demanded by large corporations with facilities in multiple locations nationwide. For voluntary RECs, a premium can be gained if they are competing with compliance RECs or if they come from regions with limited renewable energy resources.

The prices of wholesale RECs used in the voluntary market are considerably different from those in the compliance market. Voluntary REC prices have generally traded in the range of $1/MWh to $10/MWh. The factors that determine the wholesale price differences are also not the same — that is, state-level RPS regulation is not a price driver because there is generally no fungibility between the voluntary and mandatory REC markets. In the voluntary market, more importance is given to the type and location of the renewable resource, the vintage, the volume purchased, and the level of competition created by compliance markets.

For example, Figure 7.3 illustrates the price of western U.S. wind RECs as compared with the price of nationally sourced wind RECS and any other nationwide renewable energy technology. As can be seen, from 2008 to 2012, western wind RECs fetched a premium over the nationally sourced wind RECs. The primary reason for this discrepancy is a strong supply of nationally sourced wind, which brings its REC price down.

Voluntary market retail prices for RECs tend to be higher than wholesale prices to allow marketers to recoup their costs and retain a profit. Because the pricing of retail RECs is less heavily influenced by the location and vintage of the resource, however, the pricing shows more consistency among the states. But price does vary by the type and quality of the renewable resources used to supply the product.

In 2011, the retail sales of renewable energy in voluntary markets exceeded 35 million MWh, which is an 11% increase from 2010. Wind energy continues to dominate the newly built generation capacity in the U.S. renewable energy market and, as a result, dominates the voluntary REC market also. As shown in the breakdown in Figure 7.4, in 2010, wind constituted 83.1% of total green power sales. Although the other categories of REC sales are quite small, some are very important in specific sectors or states in terms

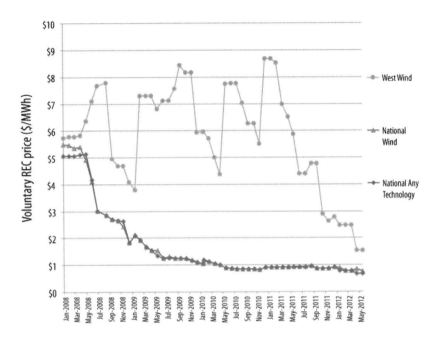

Figure 7.3. Voluntary REC Prices, January 2008–June 2012.
Source: Spectron Group (2012).

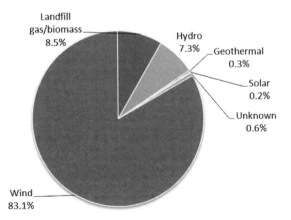

Figure 7.4. Voluntary Market REC Sales Composition.
Source: Jenny Heeter and Lori Bird, "Status and Trends in U.S. Compliance and Voluntary Renewable Energy Certificate Markets (2010 Data)." National Renewable Energy Laboratory (October 2011); available online at http://apps3.eere.energy.gov/greenpower/pdfs/52925.pdf.

of providing an incentive for building new renewable power. The market for SRECs, for example, is still in its infancy in most states. SREC trading is expected to increase from more than 520 Mw in 2011 to nearly 7,300 Mw in 2025.

Investment Opportunities in RECs and Renewable Energy

Investors can purchase RECs directly by accessing one of the regulated or unregulated exchanges or brokers mentioned in the preceding sections. Depending on the type of REC and location, it will be registered at one of the REC registries. Alternatively, investors can invest in companies that generate RECs through the sale of renewable electricity or via the sale of products, such as wind turbines or solar panels. Other, but more limited, opportunities may exist to invest in RECs by taking an ownership stake in exchanges, brokerage firms, and REC registry and tracking companies. Additional and more indirect investment angles may take into account the effects that renewables have on other natural resources. For example, unlike fossil fuels, most renewables use little or no water, so investors may be able to combine investments in renewables with investments in water, which is discussed in the next chapter.

Wind turbine manufacturers — such as Suzlon Energy, Sinovel Wind Group, and Vestas Wind Systems — are companies with market capitalizations in the multibillion-dollar range that operate globally and trade on stock exchanges in Europe, China, and elsewhere. Their exposure to REC markets can be limited, particularly because wind energy has become increasingly less reliant on various subsidies to be competitive with traditional fossil fuel-based generation. Solar companies, although a tiny market overall, are still reliant on forms of subsidies, such as SRECs, to remain competitive. As the price of solar panels has dropped markedly in recent years, however, solar has become less reliant on subsidies than in the past and, in some cases, has become competitive with fossil generation, particularly in countries with demand for off-grid power supply. Companies that operate globally and are considered to be leaders in the field are First Solar, SunPower (NASDAQ:SPWR), and Yingli Green Energy.

Although exchange-traded funds provide little exposure to RECs, a wide variety of ETFs provide exposure to renewable energy. One of the first such ETFs was Power Shares WilderHill Clean Energy (NYSE:PBW). This ETF is based on the WilderHill Clean Energy Index, which lists green energy technology companies and some conventional energy companies. Top holdings as of 2012 were Amyris, Solazyme, and EnerNOC. Assets under management were approximately $133 million.

The Guggenheim Solar ETF (NYSE:TAN) follows the Claymore/MAC Global Solar Energy Index. It includes not only panel manufacturers but also companies that specialize in other links in the solar value chain, such as solar consulting, marketing, and financing firms. Top holdings as of 2012 were GCL-Poly Energy Holdings, First Solar, and GT Advanced Technologies. Assets under management were approximately $71 million.

For wind exposure, several ETFs are available, including First Trust ISE Global Wind Energy Index Fund (NYSE:FAN). The fund's major holdings as of 2012 were EDP Renováveis, Iberdrola, China Longyuan Power Group, and Vestas Wind Systems. Assets under management were approximately $21 million.

Summary

Renewable energy provides environmental benefits beyond simply the electricity it generates. Cleaner air and water, healthier communities, and reduced GHG emissions are all by-products of renewable energy that are not usually priced into the energy itself. Renewable energy certificates provide a way to motivate the use of renewable energy where markets for these beneficial by-products do not readily exist. State and federal renewable energy mandates, together with voluntary RECs, are major drivers in the development of renewable energy in the United States.

REC programs exist in both voluntary and mandatory settings. Some programs emphasize wind generation; others focus on solar or geothermal power. In many cases, RECs can be the difference between a project being built and being shelved. Remember that the energy can be separated from the renewable attributes. Thus, RECs can be bought and sold separately from the power itself, and RECs are often sold in physical locations other than where the power is generated. This aspect provides an opportunity to trade RECs on a regional or even, in some instances, national basis.

Unfortunately, the REC markets are heterogeneous, opaque, illiquid, and fragmented. Because renewable portfolio standards are state-level policies, understanding RECs requires understanding many individual state-based markets. The lack of a national grid system and a national renewable portfolio standard compounds these problems of fragmentation. Thus, a potential investor in RECs must keep abreast of state-level political dynamics that may affect the market.

Renewable Identification Numbers

With the passage of the Energy Policy Act of 2005, the U.S. Congress made the promotion of biofuels a priority. Biofuels are fuels generated from plant matter. The most common type in the United States is ethanol derived from corn.

The centerpiece of the Energy Policy Act is the Renewable Fuel Standard, which began under the 2005 Act and was extended by the Energy Independence and Security Act of 2007. The RFS requires transportation fuel produced and consumed in the United States to contain a percentage of renewable fuel — typically, biofuel. The 2012 requirement for the RFS mandates that 15.2 billion gallons of renewable fuel be used. This percentage amounts to slightly more than 9% of the total volume of gasoline and diesel consumed in the United States in 2012.[12] The current RFS is set to run through 2022. The yearly mandates by fuel type are provided in Figure 7.5.

---

[12] EPA, "EPA Finalizes 2012 Renewable Fuel Standards." EPA Office of Transportation and Air Quality (December 2011); available online at http://www.epa.gov/otaq/fuels/renewablefuels/documents/420f11044.pdf.

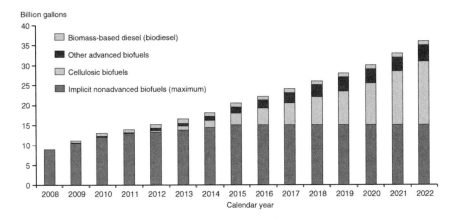

Billion gallons

Legend:
- Biomass-based diesel (biodiesel)
- Other advanced biofuels
- Cellulosic biofuels
- Implicit nonadvanced biofuels (maximum)

Calendar year

Figure 7.5. Renewable Fuel Standard (RFS) Mandates by Type, 2008–2022.

Note: Calendar years.

Source: Lihong McPhail, Paul Westcott and Heather Lutman. USDA ERS, *The Renewable Identification Number System and U.S. Biofuel Mandates*. Outlook No. BIO-03 (November 2011).

To track compliance with the RFS mandates, the EPA created a renewable identification number system. A RIN is a 38-digit number that is assigned to each gallon of renewable fuel produced in or imported into the United States. The numbers are used primarily by fuel refiners for compliance with their RFS requirements. Understanding RINs is important because biofuel use has broad implications for food and fuel prices and because investors may also speculate directly in RINs. Approximately 15 billion RINs were issued last year, and that number will only get larger over time. Their prices generally range from a couple of pennies to a couple of dollars; even at low prices, the underlying value can be significant because of the large quantity issued annually.

Once the traditional fossil fuel — typically, gasoline or diesel — is blended with the renewable fuel — typically, ethanol — the RIN can be separated from the fuel. Thus, a RIN can be traded. So, refiners, rather than blending the renewable fuel themselves, can purchase RINs from another refiner or blender if they find this option economically optimal. Alternatively, RINs can remain with the renewable fuel and be used for compliance by the "obligated party" (as defined under the law) or be held for future compliance. RINs are tracked by the EPA through its Moderated Transaction System. Access to the market is quite simple. Users must register with the EPA and establish an account with the EPA's Central Data Exchange. Transactions are then submitted electronically to the EPA.

Although most RINs are generated from ethanol blending, other types of renewable fuels are also eligible. Cellulosic ethanol and "advanced" biofuels (those not derived from corn) are encouraged under the RFS and have been mandated at increasingly higher levels over time. For instance, compressed or liquefied natural gas for vehicles — despite not being a renewable fuel — can also benefit from the RFS by receiving RINs for avoiding emissions from gasoline- and diesel-fueled vehicles, which generate more pollution than vehicles fueled by compressed or liquefied natural gas. These incentives provide a boost to alternative fuel manufacturers.

Compliance with the RFS mandates is assessed annually. If a refiner or other obligated party does not have a sufficient number of RINs to satisfy its individual mandate, it may carry that deficit into the following year, provided that the previous year's deficit is covered and the next year's obligation is met. If an obligated party has excess RINs, it may sell or bank them into the next year for compliance, provided that no more than 20% of the obligated party's current year's obligation is satisfied with banked RINs. RINs that go unused after a period of two years are retired.

In effect, obligated parties must meet four biofuel compliance targets, or renewable volume obligations. They are:

- Total renewable fuel,
- advanced biofuel,
- biomass-based diesel, and
- cellulosic biofuel.

Each gallon of fuel is weighed on the basis of its energy content relative to the energy content of ethanol and then adjusted for renewable content. In this formula, a gallon of traditional ethanol receives 1 RIN whereas a gallon of biodiesel receives 1.5 RINs, and so on.

The largest players in the RIN market are generally the largest refiners. Thus, Exxon Mobil (NYSE:XOM), BP (NYSE:BP), Chevron (NYSE:CVX), Marathon (NYSE:MRO), Sunoco (NYSE:SUN), and Valero Energy Corporation (NYSE:VLO) make up the list of the largest obligated parties under the RFS. Other important players are the ethanol companies. Although they do not receive RINs from producing ethanol, RINs have an impact on the value of their products. The largest U.S. ethanol companies are Archer Daniels Midland (NYSE:ADM), POET (privately held), Valero, and Green Plains Renewable Energy (NASDAQ:GPRE).

RIN Pricing

RIN pricing is affected by a number of market and policy signals. Among the policy signals outside the RFS itself, which mandates the yearly level of ethanol and biofuel use, are ethanol blender tax credits, import tariffs, and crop subsidies. The Volumetric Ethanol Excise Tax Credit (VEETC) has perhaps the biggest policy-driven impact on RIN prices. The VEETC is available to ethanol blenders in the amount of $0.45 per gallon of ethanol blended with gasoline, an import tariff on ethanol of $0.54 per gallon, and a $1.01 per gallon credit to producers of cellulosic ethanol blended with gasoline. The VEETC was introduced in 2004 and, because of its costs to the U.S. taxpayer, which amounted to $21 billion in 2010, was frequently criticized and allowed to expire at the end of 2011. As a result, many analysts expected RIN prices to increase, which they did.

Among the market factors influencing RIN pricing are corn prices, crude oil prices, soybean prices, natural gas prices, and the prices of other commodities in the agricultural and energy spaces. For example, high corn prices can lead to decreased ethanol production and thus higher RIN prices. Conversely, high oil prices make substitute fuels like ethanol and biofuels more attractive, resulting in increased production and decreased values for RINs. In contrast, natural gas is a primary processing fuel for the ethanol industry. So, increases in the cost of natural gas result in increased production costs for ethanol, decreases in ethanol production, and increased values for RINs. Finally, fuel efficiency standards can have an indirect impact on RINs. As vehicles become more efficient, demand for fuel decreases, thus lowering the demand for RINs.

RINs are traded primarily OTC but are also listed on both the Chicago Mercantile Exchange and ICE. Because RINs are traded primarily OTC, no centralized source for price information on RINs is publicly available. Several private companies, such as Platts, Argus Media, and Oil Price Information Service, provide price histories for subscribers.

Prices vary according to the type of RIN. As can be seen in Figure 7.6, many RINs were trading at historical highs at the time of this writing. Commentators have noted that, although the causes are complex, price increases can be attributed partly to an increased regulatory target for RINs for 2014, which is high relative to current production. As a result of these high prices, the oil industry has increased its efforts to repeal or amend the existing RFS requirements.

Program Design Flaws

Unfortunately, because of a design flaw, the RIN trading program has been the victim of several instances of fraud, mainly in the form of RINs being sold but never actually delivered to the buyer. This fraud is possible because of the lack of a centralized authority for the verification and monitoring of RINs. Although the EPA now maintains the Central Data Exchange, it only tracks RINs and is not responsible for their authentication. This situation has allowed sellers to simply create false RINs and post them for sale. One of the worst episodes of fraud occurred in 2012 when the CEO of Absolute Fuels was arrested for selling more than $50 million in counterfeit

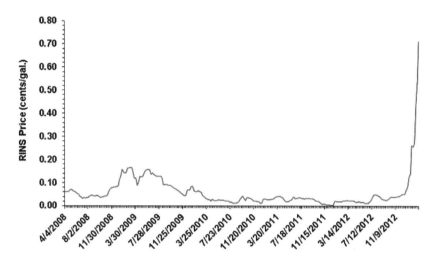

Figure 7.6. Price of RINS in the Secondary Market, 4 April 2008–7 March 2013. *Source*: Scott Irwin and Darrel Good, "Exploding Ethanol RINs Prices: What's the Story?" *Farmdoc Daily*. Department of Agriculture and Consumer Economics, University of Illinois (8 March 2013); available online at http://farmdocdaily.illinois.edu/2013/03/exploding-ethanol-rins-prices.html.

RINs. Several industry-led efforts are under way to correct the problem. These efforts have resulted in the release of proposed rules as part of the 2013 RFS.[13]

The design flaws and instances of fraud demonstrate that markets need to be developed and monitored carefully. The EPA has begun to address this need by approving voluntary "quality assurance programs" that, if used, will make submitting invalid RINs to the EPA far more difficult than in the past.

Investment Opportunities in RINs

At present, the opportunity to invest directly in RINs is limited, primarily because of the risk of purchasing fraudulent RINs. Exchanges

---

[13]EPA proposals can be found here: http://www.epa.gov/otaq/fuels/renewablefuels/regulations.htm.

do, however, offer cash-settled RIN contracts, which provide a safe route for investing in RINs without taking actual ownership. Until the EPA or an outside party that is commonly recognized by the major RIN market participants creates an acceptable verification and registration program, purchasing RINs outright will remain risky.

The stock of listed ethanol, biodiesel, or oil-refining companies is also available for purchase, but these companies provide little exposure to the RIN market.

Summary

Policymakers have engaged in a variety of efforts over the years to limit U.S. dependence on fossil fuels and foreign oil. The RFS and the RIN program are among the more recent efforts. RINs are used by obligated parties — primarily oil refiners — to ensure compliance with the Renewable Fuel Standard, which mandates levels of renewable fuels to be used in transportation. The RFS has come under scrutiny for promoting ethanol production, which is often viewed as uneconomical and a driver of increases in the price of food, including (but not limited to) the corn used to produce ethanol. A rise in corn prices is an especially severe problem in poor countries and communities that depend on corn for a large part of their nutrition. A rise in corn prices also causes increase in the prices of other foodstuffs.

Although the RIN program is in a state of turmoil because of fraudulent RIN transactions, the program can be a success, in the sense that a market has been established, if the EPA is able to establish a reliable verification and registration system, even if the environmental benefits of the RIN program are still up for debate. One reason for this rosy outlook is the long-dated nature of the program's enabling legislation, the RFS. Many environmental markets are plagued by short-term programs or frequent policy disruptions, but the RFS is established through 2022. Therefore, market participants have sufficient time to properly incorporate the impact of the RFS into their decision-making processes.

Energy-Efficiency

Energy-efficiency, defined broadly, is the amount of energy required to provide a good or service, and an improvement in energy efficiency is a decrease in that required amount. Often, people think of energy-efficiency improvements in the context of their own homes — exchanging an incandescent light bulb for a compact fluorescent, adding extra insulation, or simply turning down the thermostat. Although these activities may seem mundane, they actually represent an enormous financial opportunity, not only for individual homeowners but also for companies and portfolio managers. This section reviews various categories of energy-efficiency opportunities, discusses the overall impact that energy-efficiency can have on the U.S. and world economy and the environment, and explores investment opportunities in energy-efficiency.

Energy-efficiency markets are generally not tradable, with the exception of a few states that have incorporated energy-efficiency credits into their renewable portfolio or alternative energy standards or quality assurance programs. Even where energy-efficiency is not directly tradable, however, it does affect other tradable markets by altering the supply-and-demand balance in related markets, such as the carbon dioxide and sulfur dioxide markets. As seen in Chapter 4 on the CO_2 markets, an increase in energy-efficiency can reduce demand for power or transportation fuels. This effect, in turn, decreases demand for the credits associated with power production, such as RECs and SO_2 credits.

Overview and Applications of Energy-Efficiency

A common saying in the energy-efficiency field is that the cheapest form of energy is the energy you never use. Amory Lovins, the environmental scientist who founded the Rocky Mountain Institute and pioneered many ideas related to energy-efficiency, coined the term "negawatt" to express the idea of a unit of energy saved as a result of energy conservation and efficiency.[14] To illustrate the vast scale at which energy-efficiency upgrades can operate, Lovins concluded that the 39% drop in U.S. energy intensity between 1975 and 2000 effectively represented an energy source 1.7 times the size of all U.S. oil consumption. In fact, energy intensity in the United States has been declining steadily since World War II, as illustrated in Figure 7.7. In 2009, McKinsey & Company estimated that the gross energy savings from implementing all of the available

Figure 7.7. U.S. Energy Intensity, 1850–2006.

Source: Lester Lave, "The Potential of Energy Efficiency: An Overview." *The Bridge*, Vol. 39, No. 2 (Summer 2009): 5–14.

---

[14]Amory B. Lovins, "The Negawatt Revolution: Solving the CO_2 Problem." Keynote Address at the Green Energy Conference, Montreal (1989); available online at http://www. ccnr.org/amory.html.

profitable energy-efficiency opportunities would yield gross energy savings worth more than $1.2 trillion.[15]

Energy-efficiency generally takes place in four sectors: the residential, commercial, industrial, and automotive sectors. The following discussion is focused on the first three of these sectors because the topic of energy-efficiency in the automotive sector is widely covered in other publications.[16]

U.S. Residential Sector

With some 115 million residences in the United States, the potential scale of the energy savings opportunities in this sector is huge. According to the DOE, residential buildings consume 22% of the nation's total energy. Some 60% of this energy is used for heating, cooling, refrigeration, and lighting. According to McKinsey & Company, if all residences implemented the energy-efficiency measures with a positive net present value (NPV) for the consumer, the U.S. residential sector would reduce its energy consumption by 28% and save the economy approximately $41 billion annually. (McKinsey estimates the upfront investment of such an effort at $229 billion, yielding a savings of $395 billion in present value terms.[17])

Appliances represent one of the largest areas of improvement in terms of energy-efficiency over the past several decades. Refrigerators, for example, now use about the same amount of electricity per year that they used in 1947, despite the fact that they are now approximately four times larger.

---

[15] McKinsey & Company, "Unlocking Energy Efficiency in the U.S. Economy." McKinsey & Company (July 2009); available online at http://www.mckinsey.com/client_service/electric_power_and_natural_gas/latest_thinking/unlocking_energy_efficiency_in_the_us_economy.

[16] For example, see Amory Lovins, Kyle Datta, Odd-Even Bustnes, Jonathan Koomey and Nate Glasgow, *Winning the Oil Endgame* (Snowmass, Colorado: Rocky Mountain Institute, 2004); available online at http://www.rmi.org/Knowledge-Center/Library/E04-07_WinningTheOilEndgame.

[17] McKinsey, "Unlocking Energy Efficiency in the U.S. Economy." *op. cit.*

Residential energy-efficiency improvement opportunities can be found both inside the home and outside the building "envelope," as it is often called. Improvements to the exterior of the building might include adding insulation, replacing old windows with newer and more efficient models, sealing duct work, and so forth. Interior improvements typically involve technology changes, such as switching to high-efficiency air conditioners, furnaces, and water heaters, improving lighting design, and replacing old appliances with high-efficiency models. A summary of the savings is shown in Figure 7.8.

Although the potential for cost-effective improvements is large, the most important factor in getting them implemented is changing occupants' behavior. Studies show that residents tend to respond

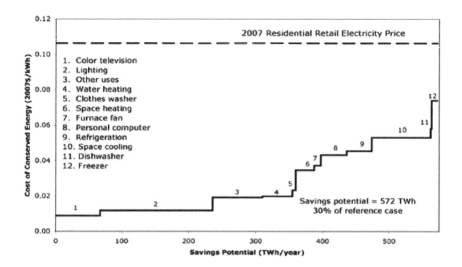

Figure 7.8. Potential for Energy Savings from Residential Products.

Note: kWh = kilowatt-hours; TWh = terawatt-hours.

Source: National Academy of Sciences, National Academy of Engineering and National Research Council, "Real Prospects for Energy Efficiency in the United States." National Academies Press (2009); available online at www.nae.edu/19582/reports/24921.aspx.

to behavior-based energy-efficiency programs. These programs can incorporate data for individual homes that compare residents with their neighbors and provide a goal for energy reduction along with benchmarking. The programs can also be augmented by devices and meters that provide residents with more data about their energy consumption and advice on reducing energy use.

U.S. Commercial and Industrial Sector

The U.S. commercial sector (offices, retail buildings, and so on) consumes almost one-fifth of end-use energy, whereas the industrial sector (light and heavy industry) consumes approximately one-third. McKinsey estimates that if the commercial sector implemented all of the available positive-NPV efficiency improvements, energy consumption in 2020 would be reduced by 29%. The initial investment for these improvements would cost approximately $125 billion and yield a savings of $290 billion.[18]

In some respects, energy-efficiency upgrades in commercial and industrial operations are similar to those in the residential sector. Heating, cooling, and lighting — all play a large role, particularly in the commercial sector. Industrial energy-efficiency improvements, however, often look quite different. Industry uses a wide variety of fuel types, including natural gas; petroleum fuels, such as diesel and fuel oil; and electricity. Although these needs create a more complex energy picture, they provide opportunities for efficient energy generation, such as combined heat and power systems, that often do not exist in commercial or residential settings. Additionally, industry can implement such improvements as converting traditional electric motors, which run at a constant speed, to variable-speed motors that allow for reduced energy use when the full power of the motor is not required.

---

[18] McKinsey, "Unlocking Energy Efficiency." *op. cit.*

Barriers to Implementation and Opportunities for Innovation

If improvement in energy-efficiency is such a large opportunity, why are not more people taking advantage of it? The answer is that there are a lot of barriers to implementation of energy-efficiency.

One barrier to implementation is the uncertainty surrounding the level of actual energy savings to be expected. Many of the gains from energy-efficiency measures are based on estimates. These estimates assume certain usage patterns and other behavior that can fluctuate heavily among users. Actual savings may be above or below the estimates, but the risk of investing the necessary capital to make the improvement and not realizing the anticipated gain from reduced energy consumption makes energy-efficiency a riskier investment than it would otherwise be.

Many states have energy-efficiency mandates. In most cases, these mandates require electric utilities to implement energy-efficiency programs for their customers. The mandates and the programs they require entail a complex set of critical points with many nuances. The discussion here is limited to a short list of the most relevant points.

Given that the primary business and route to profitability for most electric utilities is producing and selling power, requiring electric utilities to implement programs that motivate customers to purchase less power is a less-than-ideal incentive structure. Some states have given utilities greater incentives to invest in customer energy-efficiency by providing, through the regulated rate-making process, a return on the utility's investment in "demand management" (the term of art for exhorting customers to buy less of the utility's product). Perhaps if more policymakers adopted similar policies, or provided incentives directly to consumers instead of penalizing power producers who do not comply with state mandates, a more widespread adoption of energy-efficiency would occur.

Additionally, the structure of electricity purchases is not conducive to promoting energy-efficiency. Electricity bills are normally paid at the end of the month, after the electricity has been used.

Monitoring and displaying power consumption in a more real-time way would probably generate increased interest in saving energy.

Other barriers have less to do with information availability and personal finance and more to do with human behavior and a lack of focus on energy consumption. Old habits are often hard to break. Turning the lights off when you leave the room is easy enough to do. But if you are not focused on energy consumption, you often leave the lights on. This lack of attention paid to energy use exists not only in homes but also in corporate settings. Some companies assume that their energy bills and their level of energy consumption are unavoidable costs of doing business. As energy prices have increased, however, and new companies have formed to help others reduce their energy use, traditional attitudes about energy use have begun to change. Each of these barriers has become an opportunity for the companies that will be listed in the next section.

Investment Opportunities in U.S. Energy-Efficiency

Energy-efficiency presents a wide variety of investment opportunities. To simplify the discussion, we break the opportunities into four primary areas: utility and energy companies, energy-efficiency service providers, equipment vendors, and energy-efficiency financiers.

Utility and energy companies

Among the largest players in the industry are utilities based in states with strong energy-efficiency mandates, including California, Connecticut, and Massachusetts, which have had such mandates for a number of years. Major players include the utilities Sempra Energy (NYSE:SRE), Pacific Gas and Electric (NYSE:PCG), Constellation Energy (NYSE:CEG), and ConEdison (NYSE:ED).

Service providers

Energy-efficiency service providers include engineering firms, consultants, energy-efficiency monitoring companies, energy service companies, and others. Major players are Ameresco (NYSE:AMRC), Johnson Controls (NYSE:JCI), Schneider Electric (EPA:SU), Siemens (NYSE:SI), Honeywell (NYSE:HON), Ener-NOC (NASDAQ:ENOC), and Trane (NYSE:IR).

Equipment vendors

Equipment vendors typically provide parts for building automation and control as well as demand response. Major players include Johnson Controls, Carrier (part of United Technologies, NYSE:UTX), Cisco Systems (NASDAQ:CSCO), KMC Controls (private), Lutron Electronics (private), and Siemens.

Funding sources

Funders can vary from for profit companies (such as banks) to private equity funds, project finance groups, and philanthropic foundations. Major players include Bank of America (NYSE:BAC), GE Capital (NYSE:GE), Johnson Controls, Forsyth Street Advisors (private), Pegasus Capital Advisors (private), and Living Cities.

Tradable Energy-Efficiency Markets

As with the other functioning emissions markets, trading in energy-efficiency requires the creation of property rights. In this case, some form of tradable instrument is needed that verifies that the energy-efficiency goal has been achieved. The integrity of these property rights should be verified by a designated third party, and a registry should be set up to transfer and track the property rights. This section will give a few examples of tradable energy-efficiency markets outside the United States.

India

The Perform, Achieve and Trade program is essentially a cap-and-trade program aimed at reducing energy consumption and improving energy-efficiency in industries across India. The scheme is being

Table 7.3. Energy-Efficiency Commitment in Great Britain, Italy, and France.

United Kingdom (EEC-2, 2005–2008)	Italy	France (planned)
Driver		
Quota system	Quota system	Quota system
• TWh fuel-weighted energy benefits • 2005–2008 • Projects targeted toward domestic consumers only • 50% from "priority group" (low income consumers on social benefits)	• Toe: Ton of oil equivalent • Annual 2005–2009 • Projects targeted at all consumers • 50% from reduction in own energy vector (electricity and gas)	• TWh • 2006–2008 (first period) • Projects targeted at all consumers
Obliged parties		
Electricity and gas suppliers	Electricity and gas distributors	Electricity, gas, liquefied petroleum gas, heat, cold and heating fuel suppliers
Obligation threshold and apportionment criteria		
• Threshold: 50,000 domestic customers served • Reference parameter for apportionment: Number of domestic consumers served • In EEC-1: Progressively tighter for companies with more customers; no longer progressively tighter targets in EEC-2	• Threshold: 100,000 customers served • Reference parameter for apportionment: Electricity/gas distributed (market share) • Linear: Means that the targets get tighter linearly as opposed to some other way (say, exponentially for instance).	• Threshold: 0.4 TWh/year of energy sales • Reference parameter for apportionment: Market shares and energy sales turnover on residential and tertiary sectors
Trading		
• No certificates • Obligations can be traded	• Certificates trade • Spot market sessions • OTC trading	Certificates trade, only bilateral exchanges

(*Continued*)

Table 7.3. (*Continued*)

United Kingdom (EEC-2, 2005–2008)	Italy	France (planned)
• Savings can be traded but only after own obligation has been met • Approval from regulator • No spot market • One-way trade in national emissions trading scheme possible in principle	• Rules approved by the regulator	

Cost recovery

• No fixed cost recovery, suppliers may include costs in the electricity/gas end-user's price; the reason is the competitive nature of supply; suppliers are not constrained by customer or measure type as to how to recover costs	• Only for own energy vector; allowed for customers of another distributor • Determined *ex ante* by the regulator: standard average lump sum (maximum allowed costs)	• Rise in prices and tariffs to be limited to maximum 0.5% of the consumer bill

Penalty

• The regulator can consider whether it is appropriate to set a penalty • No specific guidance on how penalty would be calculated • The penalty can reach up to 10% of the supplier's turnover	• "Proportional and in any case greater than investments needed to compensate for non-compliance" • Fixed by the regulator	• 0.02 euro/kWh

Source: EEA, "Market-Based Instruments for Environmental Policy in Europe." European Environment Agency Technical Report (August 2005).

designed and implemented by the Bureau of Energy-Efficiency in India's Ministry of Power. It is designed to set benchmark efficiency levels for 563 big polluters, such as power plants, steel mills, and cement plants. These emitters account for 54% of the country's energy consumption. Under this program, entities that need to use more energy than mandated will be required to buy tradable energy saving certificates (ESCerts). Similarly, entities that use less energy can sell their ESCerts. The number of ESCerts will depend on the amount of energy saved in a target year. The government estimates that this market will be worth $16 billion in 2014, when trading is to begin.

Europe

As can be seen in Table 7.3, several European countries have already implemented a marketplace for energy-efficiency credits, whereas others are still exploring it. The basic idea is the same in each of the countries presented in the table: Energy savings will be verified by a designated regulator and will be represented by so-called white certificates (tradable certificates for energy savings). In Italy, the certificates are called "energy-efficiency titles," and trading began in 2005.

Conclusion

Energy-efficiency provides many rewarding opportunities associated with environmental markets, in terms of investment as well as energy reduction and environmental gain. The biggest obstacles to large-scale implementation are behavioral and financial. Innovative companies are beginning to address these barriers in interesting ways. Corporations, together with individual homeowners, are beginning to realize the importance of good energy management and the savings potential of energy-efficient upgrades in lighting, heating, cooling, and related activities.

In this chapter, we explored environmental markets that put prices on renewable energy, renewable identification numbers, and energy-efficiency. Given the policy debate regarding climate change and the use of fossil fuels, the emergence of such markets is timely. The use of renewable energy, RINs, and the promotion of energy-efficiencies — all help to lower dependence on fossil fuels.

One other environmental asset that is closely intertwined with energy use and, therefore, part of the equation, is water. And it is the topic of the next two chapters. Water scarcity and quality issues are related topics to energy use and emissions, which has been our focus so far. The water-energy nexus depicts the symbiotic relationship between these two resources. Water is needed to produce energy and energy needed to produce water. Water is a critical input for producing conventional energy because it is used to cool steam turbines. It is also used in refining transportation fuels; extracting some fuels, such as coal and petroleum; and growing biofuel crops. Similarly, the water we use needs energy for its extraction, transportation, and purification. The use of renewable energy and energy-efficient appliances saves both energy and water. Similarly, using renewable energy technologies, such as wind and solar, enables us to eliminate the use of water for electricity production from these sources. Water quantity and quality issues are also deeply impacted by climate change. Climate models have shown increased volatility in precipitation patterns and warming can have significant impact in the snow pack. Climate change could cause droughts, unexpected flooding, and catastrophic events — all of which has dire implications for water supply.

As a resource, water scarcity can have numerous implications including economic, social, and environmental. In the next two chapters, we discuss the challenge of water quantity and quality issues and the use of financial tools and markets to help resolve them. Given the immediate implications of the global water challenge, water markets can provide the same kind of economic and social value as emissions markets have proven in acid rain and global warming.

Chapter 8

WATER MARKETS AND ASSOCIATED ASSET CLASSES

Water promises to be the most important commodity of the 21st century. Global water demand is rising faster than at any other time in human history. Supplies of water, an already scarce resource with no substitute, are declining because of decreasing snow cover and increasing drought. In light of these significant challenges, water must be properly conserved.

The social, economic, and environmental consequences of the water challenge are enormous. Water is an essential ingredient for life sustenance, food production, and energy production. Most manufacturing and production activities have implications for the water supply because they use water both directly as an input and indirectly through energy consumption. Because 22% of global gross domestic product (GDP) comes from regions where water is scarce, the growth-limiting concerns from water scarcity are critical.

From a social standpoint, the estimate is that more than 1 billion people lack access to a safe water supply and close to 2.5 billion people lack access to proper sanitation. In developing countries, 80% of all childhood illnesses and deaths are directly or indirectly caused by unsanitary water.

The purpose of this chapter is to describe how these problems of water shortages and quality are being and can be addressed. Pricing both the rights to use water and the rights to pollute it can achieve social objectives and provide commercial opportunities to the financial and industrial sectors of countries.

Background

Even though we live on a planet whose surface is more than 70% covered with water, little of that water is available for consumption. Only 2.5% of the global water supply is freshwater, and the majority of it is locked away in glaciers, snow cover, and deep underground aquifers. Only 1% of freshwater is readily available for human and animal use.[1] Therefore, much less than 1/10 of 1% of all the water on Earth is readily available for consumption. (For the purposes of this chapter, "freshwater" is defined as water containing minimal amounts of salt — that is, water from rivers, lakes, and aquifers; "clean water" is defined as water suitable for drinking and is a subset of freshwater.[2])

In addition, this available supply is unevenly distributed across the world. North and South America and Europe generally have sufficient quantities of water, whereas parts of China and India, the Middle East, and many parts of Africa are woefully and increasingly short of it. Consider North America versus China. North America has only 8% of the world's population, but it has 15% of the freshwater on Earth. China, in contrast, has 21% of the population but only 7% of the available freshwater.[3] Imbalances such as these, coupled with the fact that many of the world's water basins cross national boundaries, create a recipe for geopolitical conflict and cross-border tension.

---

[1] U.S. Geological Survey, "The World's Water." Water Science School (5 November 2013); available online at http://ga.water.usgs.gov/edu/earthwherewater.html.

[2] U.S. Geological Survey; available online at http://ga.water.usgs.gov/edu/watercycle freshstorage.html.

[3] Deane Dray, Adam Samuelson, Mark Zepf and Ajay Kejriwal, "The Essentials of Investing in the Water Sector, Version 2.0." Goldman Sachs Global Investment Research (24 March 2008); available online at http://www.slideshare.net/Water_Food_Energy_Nexus/goldman-sachs-the-essentials-of-investing-in-the-water-sector.

Like the water supply, the demand for water is uneven across the world. In regions of water abundance, either real or perceived, multiple contributing factors have led to an unsustainable and injudicious use of the resource. For example, the per capita water footprint in the United States is 1,797 gallons per day; in South America, it is 341 gallons per day; and the world average is about 897 gallons per day.[4] On a residential basis, Americans use 100–150 gallons of water per day per person. The average European uses 74 gallons, and the average Chinese person uses 23 gallons.[5]

The per capita water requirement for basic human needs, such as drinking, hygiene, sanitation, and food preparation, is about 15 gallons per day. Some of this demand is triggered by population growth. On a global basis, however, water demand doubles every 20 years, despite a population growth rate of less than half that. Increased water consumption is also driven by increased standards of living. This fact is particularly relevant for such countries as China and India, where millions of people continue to move from rural to urban areas. It is also of interest to the newest group of Asian countries attracting interest from financiers and industrial companies: Malaysia, Indonesia, the Philippines, and Singapore (the MIPS). Like much of the rest of the world, these countries suffer from water imbalances.

The MIPS are exceptionally attractive from an investment standpoint because of their prospects for growth. Singapore, in particular, with its favorable political climate, is uniquely positioned as a financial hub. Because of its geographical location, Singapore is naturally short of water and has been meeting its water needs by importing water from Malaysia, investing in water technology, and building capital-intensive water infrastructure. Malaysia has had abundant water historically but is now facing scarcity as a result of water

---

[4] National Water Footprint Calculator, Water Footprint Network (2012); available online at http://www.waterfootprint.org/?page=cal/waterfootprintcalculator_national.

[5] Peter H. Gleick, "Basic Water Requirements for Human Activities: Meeting Basic Needs." *Water International*, Vol. 21, No. 2 (1996): 83–92.

mismanagement. The two countries are engaged in a long-standing conflict over water supply.

Although Indonesia has access to 21% of the total freshwater available in the Asia-Pacific region, its rapid development and poor infrastructure have led to increasing water scarcity. The country also has undergone significant land use changes, and deforestation and extractive industries have left many areas more vulnerable than in the past to such extreme events as monsoon floods. In 2010, less than half the total population lacked access to safe water and a quarter of the population had access to piped water.[6]

In the Philippines, access to clean water is a serious problem. Waterborne diseases cause 55 deaths a day and $1.56 billion worth of economic losses annually.

The water crisis involves not only quantity but also, and of equal importance, water quality. These two issues are closely related. Nutrients such as nitrogen and phosphorus occur naturally as contaminants in water, soil, and air. Moreover, nitrogen and phosphorus in fertilizer aid the growth of agricultural crops. But the excessive presence of nutrients in watersheds can have harmful consequences. Exposure to excessive levels of nitrate (a form of nitrogen) can reduce oxygen levels in blood, putting infants, children, and adults with lung or cardiovascular disease at increased health risk. Research has also linked long-term consumption of excess nitrates to cancer.

Poor water quality is an issue not only for humans but also for wildlife. High concentrations of phosphorus or ammonia in lakes, streams, and reservoirs are often responsible for fish mortality, foul odors, and excessive aquatic weed growth.

Water pollution sources can be divided into two types. *Point sources* are those that can be attributed to a specific physical location — such as power plants or refineries, which are often located near rivers and lakes for cooling and shipping purposes — and

---

[6]"Indonesia Water Investment Roadmap 2011–2014." World Bank (January 2012); available online at http://water.worldbank.org/sites/water.worldbank.org/files/publication/WATER-Indonesia-Water-Investment-Roadmap-2011-2014.pdf.

nutrient discharges from wastewater treatment plants, industries, or municipalities. *Non-point sources* — the main cause of nutrient pollution — are diffuse sources of pollution; pollution that cannot be attributed to a clearly identified, specific physical location or a defined discharge channel. Such pollution includes the nutrients that run off the ground from any land use — croplands, lawns, parking lots, streets, forests, and so on — and enter waterways. This source also includes nutrients that enter water through air pollution, through groundwater, or from septic systems.

The supply-and-demand imbalance of freshwater is not just a major concern for the health and well-being of the population; it also has massive implications for finance and business. The global water industry is estimated to be valued at $500 billion, an amount that could double by 2030–2035.[7] Annual capital expenditures on water infrastructure alone could grow from their 2010 level of $90 billion to $131 billion in 2016. Global annual investment in wastewater-treatment equipment is expected to rise from $14 billion in 2010 to $22 billion in 2016.[8]

With demand for water outpacing supply by 40%, water scarcity is likely to become as big a policy issue by 2030 as oil scarcity is today. This situation presents a massive opportunity for investors and analysts in the areas of desalination, "smart" water meters, efficient irrigation technologies, wastewater treatment, infrastructure, engineering, and other water-related businesses. The desalination industry alone is projected to be worth as much as $25 billion by 2025. Estimates suggest that annual water investment needs for the Organisation for Economic Co-operation and Development (OECD) countries and the BRICs (Brazil, Russia, India,

---

[7] Sarbjit Nahal, Valery Lucas-Leclin, Julie Dolle and John King, "The Global Water Sector." Bank of America/Merrill Lynch Wealth Management (28 September 2011); available online at http://wealthmanagement.ml.com/publish/content/application/pdf/gwml/global-water-sector.pdf.

[8] Jablanka Uzelac, Ankit Patel and Heather Lang, *Global Water Market 2011: Financing the World's Water Needs until 2016* (Oxford, UK: Media Analytics, 2010).

and China) will rise to more than \$770 billion by 2015.[9] Without investment in water-related products, services, and infrastructure, 45% of projected global GDP in 2050 could be at risk. (This percentage amounts to \$63 trillion in 2000 prices.) The economic sectors most affected are likely to be those that rely heavily on water: utilities, oil and gas, mining, food and beverages, and cosmetics.[10]

Growing Demand for a Finite Resource

Demand for water is being driven by population growth, rising agricultural needs, urbanization, and growing energy demand.

Agriculture

The challenges agriculture faces, even without taking into account issues of water scarcity, are daunting. The OECD estimates that the world will need to produce almost 50% more food than is produced today by 2030 to meet increased demand and population growth.[11]

The imbalance between water supply and demand in agriculture stems from two factors: (1) waste, primarily through irrigation losses, and (2) subsidies and the lack of proper water pricing. Agriculture consumes about 70% of the world's freshwater *withdrawals* (that is, extractions from a freshwater resource, such as a river, lake, or aquifer), and agriculture is also one of the primary causes of non-point source pollution and water contamination. Moreover, most of the water withdrawn is *consumed*; little is returned to its source.

In the United States, for example, water used for irrigation and livestock makes up about 31% of water withdrawals, and because so little agricultural water is returned to its source (unlike water

---

[9]The OECD consists of 34 mostly developed countries and was founded in 1961 to stimulate economic progress and world trade.

[10]Nahal *et al.*, "The Global Water Sector." *op. cit.*

[11]Water Law Research Guide, Georgetown Law Library; available online at http://www.law.georgetown.edu/library/research/guides/waterlaw.cfm.

for electricity generation), agriculture makes up 85% of U.S. water consumption. This circumstance presents a massive opportunity for companies working on reducing losses in irrigation and other agricultural uses. By reducing just 15–20% of the water consumed by irrigated agriculture, we could largely alleviate water scarcity globally.[12] We will discuss specific opportunities later in this chapter.

Additionally, property rights for water are often allocated in ways that introduce inefficiencies into the market. In the western United States, agricultural users have senior rights, even though they may add less value per unit of water than other users. Thus, an opportunity for gains from trade in water rights exists.

Water's role as the primary non-point source of pollution and a leading source of water contamination comes from the excess application of pesticides, poor management of animal feeding and grazing operations, excessive plowing, and improper irrigation techniques. All of these practices contribute to non-point source pollution through excess nutrients in surface and groundwater bodies, sediment runoff, the buildup of metals and salts, and the introduction of pathogens.

Some insight into agriculture's impact on water use can be gained by considering the volume of water embedded in the food we consume.[13] A pound of corn requires 55 gallons of water. Similarly, a pound of wheat requires 156 gallons of water. These quantities may not seem like a lot, but remember that most of the corn produced is eventually fed to beef cattle. For this reason, increased meat consumption is a primary driver of the growing demand for water from agriculture. Beef, in particular, requires a large amount of water to produce. Producing a pound of beef is estimated to require 1,857 gallons of water.

A gallon of milk requires 880 gallons of water, and a pound of pork requires 756 gallons. Contrast these requirements with what

---

[12]Brian Richter, "Tapped Out: How Can Cities Secure Their Water Future?" *Water Policy*, Vol. 15, No. 3: 335–363.

[13]The source of these data is the Water Footprint Network; available online at www.water footprint.org.

fruits and vegetables require: A pound of oranges requires only 55 gallons of water.

This difference is one reason water use tends to increase as incomes increase — rising incomes generally lead to increases in meat consumption. Diet upgrades in developing countries, therefore — if those consumers follow the same diet patterns observed in the United States and Europe — have the potential to dramatically increase water demand.

Urbanization

According to the United Nations, urban areas will house approximately 60% of the global population by 2030.[14] In 2007, the world for the first time in its history had more urban dwellers than rural. Unfortunately, many of these urban dwellers, particularly the poor, lack access to safe drinking water and sanitation. As a result, such diseases as diarrhea, malaria, and cholera are common in some urban areas. The estimate is that urbanization leads to a fivefold increase in water demand beyond the basic requirements of drinking, cleaning, and sanitation.

Energy

Production of energy requires a significant quantity of water and also has an impact on water quality. Water is an important ingredient for cooling steam electric power plants and is required to generate hydropower. Water is also used in extracting, refining, and producing petroleum fuels; growing biofuel crops; and hydraulic fracking for natural gas. Similarly, a lot of energy is consumed in treating

---

[14] Information in this paragraph comes largely from "Global Themes Strategy: Thirsty Cities — Urbanization to Drive Water Demand." Citi Thematic Investing Research (20 July 2011); available online at http://fa.smithbarney.com/public/projectfiles/f8e732d5-6162-4cd9-8b1d-7b7317360163.pdf.

and transporting water for consumption and for industrial and irrigation purposes. Given the strength of this water-energy nexus, one can infer that a water shortage can inhibit energy production — a problem that may be exacerbated by an increased demand for electricity.

According to the International Energy Agency (IEA), the amount of freshwater consumed for energy production may double in the next 25 years (from 66 billion cubic meters [bcm] annually today to 135 bcm).[15] In the United States, power plants withdraw 143 billion gallons of freshwater daily, more than the amount withdrawn for irrigation and three times as much as is used for public water supplies. Unlike most other water withdrawals, however, the vast majority of water withdrawals for power production and urban use are returned to the source after use.

Decreasing Supply

Whether or not climate change is anthropogenic, the effects of a changing climate and water stress are clearly now marching forward hand in hand. With extreme weather events and patterns being observed with increasing frequency, questions regarding the impact of the changing climate on the water supply are becoming commonplace. The United Nations Convention to Combat Desertification estimates that roughly a third of the land surface of the planet is now turning to desert land and that the affected area is growing by more than five million hectares annually.[16] Much like the distribution of water, the impact of climate change on the water supply varies significantly by location. Australia and parts of the United States are experiencing record droughts and diminished snow pack,

---

[15] Data in this paragraph come from International Energy Agency, "World Energy Outlook 2012"; available online at http://www.worldenergyoutlook.org/publications/weo-2012/.
[16] 1 square mile is roughly 259 hectares.

whereas some tropical regions are experiencing large increases in rainfall, mudslides, and runoff.

Water Pricing and Subsidies

Among the many reasons the world has arrived at its current water crisis, perhaps none is more important than the lack of a proper price for water itself. The mispricing of scarce resources has been shown, time and again, to result in suboptimal allocation of those resources. Prices for the delivery of water in Chicago and New York are roughly $0.002 and $0.004 per gallon, respectively.[17] The price of water in New Delhi is only a fifth of the cost of delivering it.[18] These prices do not even take into account the cost of the water itself, which is essentially viewed as a free and unlimited resource. The U.S. government subsidizes more than half the cost of water and wastewater systems. Researchers also estimate that U.S. farmers would pay roughly 25% more if water for agricultural use were unsubsidized. Unfortunately, such mispricing of water is not uncommon, and it leads to increased demand and misallocation of resources.

Budget constraints do, however, put pressure on politicians to reduce water subsidies. This confluence of factors is likely to become increasingly relevant for investors and analysts. As subsidies diminish, changes in consumption are sure to follow on both the industrial and residential levels. These changes may mean new opportunities for smart water meters; advanced leak detection equipment; changes in practices at water-intensive industries, such as semiconductor manufacturing; and of course, changes in agriculture.[19]

---

[17]The source for Chicago prices is Whet Moser, "Chicago's Proposed Water Rate Hike: At What Cost?" *Chicagomag.com* (14 October 2011); available online at http://www.chicagomag.com/Chicago-Magazine/The-312/October-2011/Chicagos-Proposed-Water-Rate-Hike-At-What-Cost. The source for New York City comes from the rate schedule effective 1 July 2012, NYC Water Board.

[18]Nahal *et al.*, "The Global Water Sector." *op. cit.*

[19]Dray *et al.*, "The Essentials of Investing in the Water Sector." *op. cit.*

It is important to emphasize that this discussion of pricing only applies to water consumption above and beyond the amount needed for basic hydration and hygiene purposes.

Solutions to the Supply–Demand Imbalance: The Role of Trading

Driven by economic growth and increasing agricultural withdrawals, global water demand is expected to grow from about 4,500 bcm to 6,900 bcm by 2030. The historical solution for meeting water demand has been to increase supply though large infrastructure projects and technological solutions. They include more inventory and delivery infrastructure, such as dams and canals, and increased technology supply, such as desalination plants. Such large-scale projects are usually expensive, time intensive, and disruptive to the ecosystem and local communities. With water pricing and defined resource rights, however, a number of measures that enhance efficient use of water become viable, can be deployed quickly, and may be cheaper than the traditional technological solutions. Such measures as irrigation scheduling, wastewater reuse, and enhanced efficiency of industrial water use can be "low-hanging fruit" solutions that merit attention.

A water trading program that facilitates pricing and transferability of water rights provides the incentives to initiate such low-cost measures. In addition, water pricing can drive consumers to put water to its most valuable and highest use.

Because water is a local or regional resource, local availability, supply-and-demand characteristics, and environmental stress will play important roles in determining which strategies are best. Trading can expand the options available beyond purely local ones, however, as can be seen historically with acid rain pollutants and carbon dioxide. For example, desalination technology, a much-talked-about technological solution to meeting freshwater demands, costs on average $650–$2,200 per acre-foot (the volume of 1 acre of surface area to the depth of 1 foot, or about 326,000 gallons). In comparison, optimal irrigation scheduling can provide net savings of $24–$148 per acre-foot and such industrial measures as changing to paste tailing in mining can provide net savings of $370–$740 per acre-foot.[20] Whenever diverse options with varying abatement costs exist, trading mechanisms like those described in this book provide the lowest-cost solutions and, therefore, highest social gains.

One example involves the investment decision facing the city of Adelaide in South Australia. The Adelaide government faced the task of meeting city water demand. The decision involved building desalination capacity of 100 gigaliters (GL) per year versus purchasing an equivalent amount of high-reliability Victorian Murray (VM) entitlements.[21] The project involved capital expenditures of AU$1.83 billion and operating costs at full capacity of $130 million annually, or $0.005 per gallon. The trading alternative involving the high-reliability VM entitlements would cost $190 million, with operating costs between $0.0008 and $0.0010 per gallon.[22] Clearly, the trading option was cheaper from the standpoints of capital expenditures and operating costs. In addition, the trading option ensured flexibility because in good years, any unused entitlements could be sold to other market participants.

Another example involves meeting water demand for the southern Indian city of Chennai.[23] The city faced chronic water shortages that forced rationing of water for residents and closed factories because of lack of water. Aided by a lack of regulation governing groundwater, the common technological solution involved sinking deep tube wells (in which 100–200 mm [5–8 inch] wide stainless steel tubes or pipes are bored into an underground aquifer). This solution soon becomes futile, however, because groundwater levels

---

[20]Tailings are the materials left over after the valuable parts have been separated from the uneconomic parts of an ore. Paste tailings are tailings that have been significantly dewatered.

[21]One gigaliter is 810.7 acre-feet. The Victorian Murray catchment is the basin of the Murray River in the state of Victoria. The term "high reliability" is explained later in this chapter.

[22]Based on the February 2011 average price, tendered from Australia's government environmental purchasing program.

[23]*India's Water Economy: Bracing for a Turbulent Future* (Washington, DC: World Bank, 2005); available online at https://openknowledge.worldbank.org/handle/10986/8413.

Table 8.1. Comparative Costs and Quantities of Supplying Water to Chennai.

Method	Capacity (gallons per day)	Cost ($ per gallon)
Recycled industrial sewage	6,075,956	0.0038
AK aquifer water entitlements	59,967,044	0.0001
Veeranam Project	11,887,740	0.0009
Desalination unit	26,417,200	0.0034

Note: This analysis assumes an exchange rate of 55 Indian rupees per U.S. dollar. Recycled industrial sewage costs per gallon are high because of local environmental regulations.

drop and sea saltwater intrudes on the aquifer. The local government, together with the World Bank, conducted a feasibility study in 1996 to weigh other solutions. The technological alternative, the Veeranam project, involved piping water 155 miles to the city and included a desalination plant. The trading alternative involved buying water entitlements from rice farmers in the Araniar-Kortalaiyar (AK) aquifer, which was close to the city. The aquifer was shown to have a sustainable water yield sufficient to meet the city's water demands. As shown in Table 8.1, the water trading option was by far the cheapest option.

City policymakers were not keen on the entitlement option because they feared it would anger the farmers. They believed AK aquifer water was considered an inalienable right by the farmers and that any attempt to export the water to the city would be seen as politically unfavorable. However, the option was reluctantly adopted. In 2003, 70% of the city's water came from buying water entitlements sold by farmers.

In fact, the farmers *were* upset, but not because their "inalienable right" was being taken away. They were upset because they could not sell all that they wanted to the local water utility.

This story demonstrates that when transferable property rights are properly assigned and price is established, rational actors will optimize the use of a resource. In this case, rice farmers found it more profitable to generate revenues by selling water rights than it would have been to use the water for farming.

Virtual Water: Synthetic Trading

The concept of virtual water is a recent one, but its underlying principle has existed for millennia. Virtual water is a way of expressing the quantity of water embedded in food or other goods that are traded around the globe. The notion of virtual water came about as a way to express the idea that countries with relatively few freshwater resources would be better off outsourcing water-intensive activities to countries with greater freshwater resources. In the absence of functioning markets for water, there is a surrogate for water trading: The global grain trade is, in effect, a virtual water trade, although it is not often referred to as such.

Today, many countries engage in crop production or other water-intensive activities in other countries that have relatively abundant water resources. China, for example, has invested in more than 6 million acres of rice, sugar, maize, and biofuel production in several African countries and the Philippines. Saudi Arabia has invested in more than 5 million acres of rice, wheat, vegetables, and other agricultural production in Sudan, Tanzania, Indonesia, and other countries with available freshwater resources. The United Nations Environment Programme estimates the trade of virtual water to be roughly 612 trillion gallons (2,320 bcm) per year, with the biggest net importers being the Middle East, North Africa, Mexico, Europe, Japan, and South Korea. The estimate is that without this virtual water trade, the world would have used an additional 92 trillion gallons (352 bcm) annually between 1997 and 2001.[24] Using Chicago's water delivery cost of $0.002 cents per gallon and the estimated savings of 92 trillion gallons per year, the world saves an estimated $186 billion annually through the virtual water trade.

---

[24]Mesfin M. Mekonnen and Arjen Y. Hoekstra, "National Water Footprints Accounts: The Green, Blue and Grey Water Footprint of Production and Consumption." Value of Water Research Report Series No. 50, UNESCO-IHE (May 2011); available online at http://www.waterfootprint.org/Reports/Report50-NationalWaterfootprints-Vol1.pdf.

Water Quality and Quantity Trading

Recall the difference between rights to *pollute* and rights to *use*. Sulfur dioxide, nitrous oxide, carbon dioxide, and greenhouse gas allowances are all rights to pollute. Water quantity trading is the first example in this book of rights to use; it constitutes the right to use a pre-specified amount of a natural resource — in this case, water.

Although some impediments to trading water exist, they are not insurmountable and can be overcome with good contract and market design. Some of the characteristics unique to water as a commodity, to differentiate it from the other environmental assets, are as follows:

- Water is a regional product. It is bulky and costly to move in the volumes typically required for production, so it can be transferred only between neighboring river basins up to about 500 kilometers, or about 0.621 miles (or even shorter distances if it needs to be pumped uphill). Because of this characteristic and the flow of water from upstream to downstream users, risks and responses must be understood on the basis of a river basin, not on a global scale as can be done for carbon.
- Water availability is variable in time and space, and therefore, its short- and long-term future availability is uncertain.
- Water is a finite but renewable resource, the availability of which is physically constrained by the infrastructure in place and legally constrained in many locations by complex historical water rights systems.
- Water is non-substitutable in most domestic and productive activities, although it may be more efficiently used.

Despite these unique characteristics, water markets are like all other markets in that they can thrive only in an environment of unambiguous property rights. Much like the institutions that were created for SO_2 and CO_2, a market infrastructure is needed for water markets to exist and thrive. Monitoring, verification, product standards, and so forth, are necessary, but the foundation upon which the market framework is built is unambiguous property rights.

The structural changes necessary for the establishment of an organized water market are already under way in many parts of the world. Such design elements as standardization, grading and quantification guidelines, a legal framework that recognizes property rights, proper monitoring and verification procedures, ability to track transfers, and so forth, are all being developed as water markets begin to take shape. Although many of the markets are still in the early stages of development, they provide important proof-of-concept lessons for others considering the use of markets to efficiently manage water quality and quantity.

Water pollutants trading

The fundamentals of water trading are quite simple. On the quality side, a cap is typically placed on the amount of pollutant entering the watershed. Much like a cap-and-trade program for GHGs or other environmental commodities, a reduction goal is then established for the pollutant and permits are allocated to the participating (i.e., capped) sources. Once the capped sources have been allocated their permits, they are motivated to reduce their pollutant discharges beyond their reduction targets because they can sell any excess permits that may result. This buying and selling of permits allows the capped sources to take advantage of the lowest-cost opportunities to reduce their levels of pollution.[25]

To give an example, the nitrogen and phosphorus discharges from factories and farms were polluting the Chesapeake Bay in the United States by reducing the oxygen level of the water. The result was harmful to the marine ecosystem and human health. In 2005, a nutrient cap-and-trade program was initiated that limited the amount of nutrients flowing into the rivers by issuing "water

---

[25] The World Resources Institute has written extensively on water quality trading; available online at http://pdf.wri.org/water_trading_quality_programs_international_overview.pdf.

quality credits" to polluting entities. Various legislative proposals are calling for the system to be expanded. The program could eventually be extended to include fishermen, based on the idea that catches will increase if the bay has fewer "dead zones" caused by oxygen depletion. A 2012 report by the Chesapeake Bay Commission concluded that implementing a watershed-wide cap-and-trade system could result in a cost savings of approximately $1.2 billion annually for entities that are subject to the Environmental Protection Agency's water pollutant regulations.[26]

Water temperature trading

Water quality trading can also be based on water temperature, which matters because the aquatic ecosystem — specifically, certain species of fish — can be especially sensitive to sudden changes in water temperature. Thus, water temperature credits were developed to mitigate incidents when factories, power plants, or wastewater-treatment systems release a large amount of warm water into a lake or river. Instead of mandating the installation of expensive water-cooling systems, regulators allow farmers and other landowners to plant trees and other stream bank vegetation to shade streams to cool them down naturally. This practice also improves the animal habitat and provides other environmental benefits. Credits are then issued for cooling the streams and can be sold to regulated entities, such as wastewater treatment authorities.

The development of creative regional markets regulating riparian water temperature in the western United States to protect local fishery resources serves as a reminder that many environmental outcomes can be achieved through properly designed markets.[27] In 2006, the Oregon Department of Environmental Quality (DEQ)

---

[26]Erich Hiner, "Could Cap and Trade Cut Costs for Water Polluters?" *American Water Intelligence*, Vol. 3, No. 6 (June 2012); available online at http://ehiner.wordpress.com/2012/07/29/could-cap-and-trade-cut-costs-for-water-polluters/.

[27]The term "riparian" means of, on, or relating to the banks of a natural course of water.

finalized the Willamette River temperature requirements to protect salmon during the spring and autumn when they are spawning and during the summer when they are reaching adulthood and
migrating.

The development of water temperature trading illustrates that
markets can help by addressing issues of nutrient loads as well as by
playing a role in water quality attributes, such as temperature. This
trading may also be important for investors or analysts looking at real
estate and agricultural land with surface streams and rivers. Moreover, the re-establishment of stream banks may be a new income
source in areas where these markets are in place.[28]

Water quantity trading

Water quantity trading is a system whereby the rights to use water
are traded. The most mature of these markets are in Australia, which
began to establish them in the 1990s because the authorities were
worried that farmers were depleting the country's reserves. In 1994,
water reforms by the Council of Australian Governments (COAG)
enabled the separation of water rights from the land rights.[29] This
reform also sought to open up interstate water trading. In 2010, the
Australian water market was estimated to be valued at approximately
AU\$3.1 billion. Similarly, water trading of some kind exists in many
states of the western United States as well as in Alberta, Canada.
Water exchange systems also exist in South Africa and Chile.

Because the Australian system is the longest-running and most
advanced system, we discuss it in detail in this chapter to illustrate
the benefits of water quantity trading.

---

[28]Department of Environmental Quality, "Water Quality Trading in NPDES Permits
Internal Management Directive." Oregon Department of Environmental Quality Internal
Management Directive (December 2009); available online at www.deq.state.or.us/wq/pubs/
imds/wqtrading.pdf. NPDES is the National Pollutant Discharge Elimination System.

[29]The COAG comprises the Prime Minister, State Premiers, Territory Chief Ministers, and the
President of the Australian Local Government Association. The role of the COAG is to initiate,
develop, and monitor the implementation of policy reforms that are of national significance and
that require cooperative action by Australian governments.

Australian Water Markets

Australia is an arid country. Scarcity is naturally a key concern in many parts of Australia, where long periods of drought threaten the availability of water for agricultural irrigation and the long-term secure drinking supply. Rainfall distribution is geographically uneven and highly seasonal.

Prior to 1970, water rights in Australia were tied to the land. Available water was allocated on a first-come/first-served basis, and the charge (or marginal cost) to users was close to zero. Increases in demand were met through government-funded increases in infrastructure investment, which often were motivated more by politics than by a formal cost–benefit assessment. During droughts, a variety of quantitative regulations were used to ration supplies. These allocation procedures applied for cities and countryside and for surface and underground water. Competition among farmers (and, to a lesser extent, among irrigators and other users) for limited water was accompanied by the perception that some potential new users placed higher marginal values on water than did existing users. This view was later supported by formal analysis.

The movement toward a nationally uniform system of tradable water rights began in 1994 with the adoption by the COAG of a strategic framework for reform of the Australian water industry.

Enabling Legislation

The COAG plan called for the institution of trading arrangements in water entitlements. In June 2004, COAG negotiations culminated in an agreement to establish a new national market to trade water rights — the National Water Initiative. The initiative marked a significant development in transboundary water regulation in Australia because it represented an acceptance of the incorporation of price and trading criteria into water management on a large scale.

In most Australian states, a licensing system now regulates water access and distribution. The licenses are often equated with water "ownership," but water in Australia remains a public good in legal terms. Licenses simply give the license holder the right to use an amount of water at a particular time and place.

Water trade in Australia involves trade in both water entitlements and seasonal water allocations. The difference is analogous to buying versus renting a home. One is viewed as temporary; the other, as permanent.

- Trade in water entitlements (sometimes referred to as "permanent trade") involves transferring the ongoing right to access water for the term of the entitlement. The two types of permanent entitlements are high security and general security. *High-security* entitlements receive allocations close to the full volume of entitlement, whereas *general-security* entitlements receive highly variable allocations of water ranging from 0% to 100%. High-security entitlements are valued far more highly than general-security entitlements.
- Trade in seasonal water allocations (sometimes called "temporary trade") involves transferring some or all of the water allocated to the entitlement to another party for the current irrigation season or an agreed number of seasons.

The water trading program sets a cap on current water use and allows trading of current allocation licenses. Such trading enables new users to obtain water supply and allows current license holders who do not use their full allocations to sell excess water entitlements. In addition to providing a cap on water use, Australia's water trading programs regulate different types of water use through the establishment of different water-access license types. Water licenses are given a priority rating, so in times of scarcity, those with less "secure" licenses are the first to lose entitlements and the permanent security license holders (such as drinking water providers and year-round irrigators — e.g., rice farmers) are protected. In New South Wales, for example, because rights are organized on a priority basis, if scarcity increases, the access entitlements are reduced, beginning with the lowest-priority license holders.[30]

States and territories have a legal responsibility to record water-access entitlement, ownership, and other trade details in a registry. As a result, regional variations can be found in registries in terms of information recorded, compatibility, and accessibility. The National Water Market System is undertaking work to improve efficiency, effectiveness, and compatibility of registers.

Entitlement-trading volume in 2011–2012 was 380 billion gallons (1,437 GL), and allocation trading was 1.1 trillion gallons (4,297 GL). In terms of market value, the overall turnover in Australia's water markets in 2011–2012 was estimated at $1.66 billion. This volume represents a 12% increase over the previous year.[31]

Case of the Murray–Darling Basin

The Murray–Darling Basin (which gets its name from the two major rivers in the basin, the Murray and the Darling) is by far the most active of the regional water trading systems in Australia. It represents 70–80% of all water traded in Australia (by volume). The basin is located in Southeastern Australia and makes up the majority of Australia's prime agricultural land. The Murray–Darling Basin receives little rainfall; it gets most of its water for agricultural use from surface water. Nevertheless, the basin has a history of growing water-intensive crops, including cotton and rice, which are generally heavily irrigated.[32]

---

[30]The source of this information and the report mentioned throughout this discussion is "Australian Water Markets Report 2011–2012." Australian Government National Water Commission (2013); available online at http://www.nwc.gov.au/_data/assets/pdf_file/0008/29186/Introduction.pdf.

[31]Because 1 gigaliter is 810.7 acre-feet, in this example, entitlement trading is about 1,164,976 acre-feet and allocation trading is 3,483,578 acre-feet.

[32]A map of Australia showing areas discussed in this section is available online at http://www.murrayriver.com.au/river-management/murray-darling-basin-commission/.

Prices for entitlements and allotments vary greatly, depending on geography, water availability, and other factors. The National Water Commission reports that water entitlements generally trade at higher prices than allotments. This case is intuitive because entitlements are permanent transfers and allotments are temporary. The prices of both entitlements and allotments appear to be driven also by basic supply-and-demand factors: Prices tend to be higher in areas where demand is greatest and water is scarce.

To demonstrate how price varies with geography, Figure 8.1 provides entitlement prices for various geographical subdivisions of the Murray–Darling water trading system. As the figure shows, although a good bit of consistency characterizes high-reliability allotments, low-reliability allotments show a wide range of prices, depending on their location.

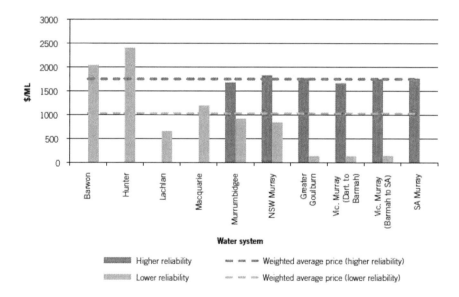

Figure 8.1. Entitlement Prices Across Water Systems in 2011–2012.
Notes: ML = megalitre; NSW = New South Wales; Vic Murray refers to the area of Victoria and the Murray River; Dart. = Dartmouth; SA = South Australia.
Source: "Australian Water Markets Report 2011–2012." *op. cit.*

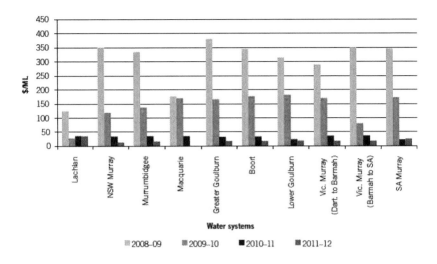

Figure 8.2. Allocation Prices Across Water Systems, 2008–2012.
Source: "Australian Water Markets Report 2011–2012." *op. cit.*

Figure 8.2 illustrates price variability across time in the various water systems within the Murray–Darling trading program. According to Figure 8.2, prices have declined drastically in all of the affected water systems. The National Water Commission reports that the lower prices are generally the result of increased rainfall in recent years relative to earlier years. Although these price declines follow a pattern similar to those in other markets, such as the SO_2 market, it is probably too early to draw many parallels, particularly because the Murray–Darling markets seem to respond mainly to water availability. Nonetheless, these price declines are reminiscent of the price declines in the emissions markets.

Figure 8.3 shows permit prices for the Murrumbidgee high-security market in the Murray–Darling Basin. The Murrumbidgee is one of more than 15 separate active markets within the basin.

Effects of Water Trading in Australia

Water trading has many effects in Australia. In this section, we focus on one particular effect in the agriculture sector to illustrate the

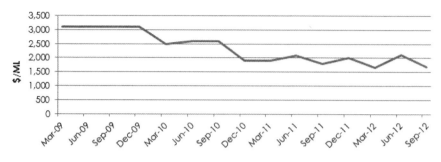

Figure 8.3. Quarterly Volume-Weighted Average Price for Murrumbidgee High-Security Market.

Note: Prices in this figure are in Australian dollars.

impact of water markets on agribusiness, investment, the environment, and — perhaps most importantly — the people participating in the market.

The implementation of the water market in the Murray–Darling Basin has brought about important changes in the way water is used there. Surveys conducted by the Australian Department of Agriculture, Fisheries and Forestry show that water trading is providing irrigated agribusinesses with an increased suite of options for optimizing water management on the farm. Some irrigators have reduced water use while others have expanded it, and those who reduce are able to sell water permits to those who expand.

Water trading has also allowed farmers to adjust their operations on the basis of water availability in a particular year. Research has shown that during a recent drought, some irrigators chose to actually reduce water consumption and sell water credits rather than attempt to further irrigate crops in such dry conditions. Additionally, water trading allows farmers who require fairly consistent levels of irrigation, such as those who grow tree-based crops, to purchase water credits from farmers who are able to adjust their crops on an annual basis. Surveys also show that water application rates went down in the 2006–2010 period as farmers reacted to reduced water allocations by modifying their irrigation practices. As a result, the region has gradually seen a shift in production from low-water-value agricultural commodities to those of higher value, such as horticulture, vegetables, and fruit.

The Australian water market, one of the world's first large-scale experiments in water rights trading, has been successful in providing important price signals for market participants. Like other emissions rights markets, the Australian market incorporated important design steps. Its framers clearly identified and assigned the property rights, established clear limits for the use of the traded commodity, provided for transferability through a registry mechanism, and emphasized water management and monitoring. Other positive elements involve natural characteristics: Rainfall in Australia is highly variable, making water supply also quite variable; most of the water in the system can be traded from one zone to the other, resulting in a more fungible commodity than within zone trading only; and water can be held in reservoirs from one season to another, which makes supply adjustments possible. The Australian water authorities have also been active in the dissemination of economic research and data to market participants, important conditions for any successful market.

Technical Solutions to Water Scarcity

For the world, trading in the rights to use water may have a positive impact on the supply of freshwater in the coming years. Future water demand estimates based on current projections of population and economic growth suggest that by 2030, water requirements will be 40% greater than current supply. One-third of the world's population, mostly in the developing world, will live in basins that have water deficits larger than 50%.

Solutions to water scarcity problems abound, but without knowing the true price of water, determining the *optimal* solution is difficult. Unfortunately, as a result of the lack of organized water markets, we are often left to guess which solution may be the best. Prices not only help inform us about which solutions are optimal but also encourage the development of the solutions themselves.

As seen in the SO_2, CO_2, and other environmental markets, inventors of solutions are often driven by a market price. Command-and-control regulatory approaches to water scarcity, which is what we generally have in most countries today, are unable to provide the incentives found in markets. Although regulation and associated penalties are effective as a stick (i.e., punishment), they have a mixed record when it comes to carrots (i.e., motivating agent). For this reason, we believe pricing and markets to be the better solution (pricing should apply only to the amount of water that exceeds the amount needed for health, hydration, and hygiene). For water markets to function properly, an effective regulatory regime must be in place to define property rights and to provide effective monitoring and enforcement. In the following sections, we discuss some of the technical solutions to water scarcity that exist today.

Water Infrastructure

Upgrading water infrastructure by fixing leaky pipes and valves represents one of the largest opportunities developed societies have to decrease water loss and, in effect, increase our water supply. Despite the fact that the United States is considered one of the global leaders in water infrastructure, the American Society of Civil Engineers reports that water leaks resulting from aging infrastructure cost the United States two trillion gallons and $3 billion annually. In the United States, up to 20% of water is lost to leaks. The estimate is that replacing the U.S. water infrastructure would cost between $300 billion and $1 trillion. Unfortunately, water infrastructure investment in the United States and in most developed countries is chronically underfunded. Remedying this problem presents both significant challenges and significant investment opportunities. For-profit water management companies and public–private partnerships are likely to be key in bridging the gap in funding.

Among those companies working to fill the need for new and improved water infrastructure are Pentair (NYSE:PNR), which makes pumps, valves, and controls for the water industry; Mueller

Water Products (NYSE:MWA), which focuses on water transmission and delivery; and Watts Water Technologies (NYSE:WTS), which focuses on valves and related products for the water industry.

Measurement, Monitoring, and Verification

An often-repeated saying is that what gets measured gets managed. Water is no exception. Unfortunately, little water gets measured and even less is properly managed. Much as increased energy-efficiency often provides the best return on investment for companies and individuals hoping to reduce their energy bills, increased water efficiency through proper measurement and monitoring may be the most cost-efficient way to decrease exposure to water-supply risks. Proper water management requires intelligent instruments that allow for automated collection of information in real time. This information is necessary to make informed decisions about how to manage water resources. The information and decisions are important for investors and analysts, particularly in regions where water prices are on the rise and thus efficient use of water is most financially beneficial. In other words, as prices for water increase, the demand for measurement, monitoring, and verification products and services related to water use should also increase.

IBM (NYSE:IBM) is one of the companies at the forefront of water use monitoring, and it has provided positive results in pilot programs focusing on the implementation of water use monitoring technology. In one case, real-time monitors providing water consumption data every 15 minutes were used in households in Dubuque, Iowa. The information was sent to the households to alert them to potential leaks and anomalies in water use. The city saw a decrease in water use of 6.6% during the pilot program, an amount projected to translate into 64.9 million gallons a year in savings.

Other companies working on water use monitoring and measurement include Pure Technologies (TSE:PUR), which provides monitoring and surveillance for physical water infrastructure, and TaKaDu, an Israeli company that provides software to utilities for monitoring water networks.

Advances in Irrigation and Crop Science

Irrigation is one of the largest and most inefficient uses of water today. According to the U.S. Department of the Interior, irrigation accounts for 34% of water demand in the United States. The United Nations estimates that 70% of all water withdrawals globally are for agriculture and expects this number to rise because of the increasing amount of land allocated to agriculture. Although many users of water, such as electric utilities and industrial users, return much of the water they take, irrigation water is almost never returned to its source. To make matters worse, more than half of all water used in irrigation is lost in the process of irrigating, either through evaporation or from leaks in irrigation systems. For these and other reasons, efficiencies in irrigation would represent a significant opportunity to save water, particularly in developing countries.

Much of the developing world continues to use flood irrigation, often losing nearly half of the water before it reaches the plant being irrigated. Micro and drip irrigation systems, bringing more than 90% of their water to the root zone of the plant, represent significant advances over flood irrigation. Even conventional sprinkler-based systems, which bring 50–70% of their water to the root zone of the plant, are an improvement over flood irrigation. Among the companies providing advanced irrigation equipment are Toro Company (NYSE:TTC), Jain Irrigation Systems in India (BOM:500219), and John Deere (NYSE:DE).

Additionally, drought-tolerant seed varieties are likely to be in greater demand as rainfall levels decrease in some areas of the world. Many of the world's large crop-science companies provide seeds and other products to aid in drought tolerance; some are DuPont (NYSE:DD), Monsanto (NYSE:MON), and Syngenta AG (VX:SYNN).[33]

---

[33]VX is the SIX Swiss Exchange.

Water Treatment and Filtration

In 2008, Goldman Sachs estimated that the annual global sales of water- and wastewater treatment products and services were \$164 billion.[34] The type of treatment used for water depends on its desired end-use. Typically, water undergoes physical filtration processes that separate out the solids and is then treated chemically through disinfection or similar processes. Increasingly, residential water systems are being exposed to contaminants that were not on the radar when the water-treatment systems were designed and built. Runoff from agricultural operations, pharmaceutical by-products, and other household contaminants are driving a need for advanced cleanup technologies. Chemical treatment has been the preferred method of dealing with these contaminants, but new filtration and ultrafiltration methods are becoming common.

In addition to treatment methods, water conservation and recycling are playing increasingly important roles, particularly in the use of lightly treated wastewater for landscaping irrigation or to recharge groundwater aquifers.

Investment opportunities in water treatment and filtration include a wide variety of companies, such as Veolia Environnement in France (NYSE:VE), Sabesp in Brazil (NYSE:SBS), Aqua America (NYSE:WTR), Tianjin Capital Environmental Protection in China (SHA:600874), and Severn Trent Water in the United Kingdom (LON:SVT).

Desalination

Given the scarcity of freshwater we have described, desalination systems have attracted a great deal of interest. Desalination is the removal of salt and other minerals from seawater. According to the International Desalination Association, more than 14,000 desalination plants were in operation worldwide as of 2009 and the market for desalination systems is experiencing growth of around 12% annually. These plants provide only a small amount of the global

---

[34]Dray *et al.*, "The Essentials of Investing in the Water Sector." *op. cit.*

water supply but are particularly prevalent in the Middle East, where energy costs are relatively low and the water shortage is often acute.

Traditionally, desalination systems have been hindered by high energy requirements for producing potable water. Approximately 60% of the operation and maintenance cost for a desalination plant can be attributed to the cost of energy. The conventional treatment of surface water uses 0.2–0.4 kWh of energy per cubic meter (roughly 264 gallons) of water treated.[35] In comparison, desalination uses 2.6–3.7 kWh of energy.

Advances in the efficiency of desalination plants — in particular, in membrane technology — are beginning to make them cost competitive with more conventional sources of clean water. Currently, however, even with these efficiencies, the cost of desalination is prohibitive in much of the world. The Los Angeles County Economic Development Corporation estimates that over the life of the treatment facility, it costs at least $1,000 to treat each acre-foot of water.

With projected double-digit annual growth for desalination companies, however, many investors in recent years have found them an attractive investment. A difficulty facing average investors is that many of these companies receive only a fraction of their revenues from desalination activities. Such companies as Dow Chemical Company (NYSE:DOW), GE, ACCIONA in Spain (MC:ANA), Veolia Environnement, and Hyflux Ltd. (SI:HYFL) are leaders in desalination, although much of their revenues come from other business activities.[36] A few companies, however, do focus primarily, if not entirely, on desalination. IDE Technologies is a private Israeli company focused on desalination, and Consolidated Water (NASDAQ:CWCO) develops and operates desalination plants in the Caribbean.

---

[35] Leaving ten 100-watt light bulbs on for an hour consumes 1 kWh of energy.

[36] MC is the Barcelona Stock Exchange, and SI is the Singapore Stock Exchange.

An interesting aspect is that the cheapest water entitlements in the Australian market are priced at around \$147/megaliter (ML) whereas one of the most efficient desalination plants in the world, located in Israel, produces freshwater at \$510/ML (or 0.51 cents/kiloliter). Some economists believe that markets help drive down water prices and that trading may be cheaper than high-capital-expenditure water projects.

Related Investment Opportunities in Water

Investment opportunities related to water include equity investments, exchange-traded funds, and water funds and indices.

Water Equities

Opportunities in water stocks exist in filtration, infrastructure, desalination, engineering, treatment, testing, and other aspects of the water value chain. These areas can be broadly categorized into three groups: Treatment, management, and infrastructure.

Many of the large banks and investment management firms publish lists of stocks that provide exposure to water, often broken down by market segment. Many dozens, if not hundreds, of companies are available for investors to consider. Many of the world's largest companies — including GE, Dow, United Technologies, and others — are active in water. As noted, many of these large corporations receive only a small percentage of their revenues directly from water-related business. Among the large corporations that do receive a large percentage of their revenues from water are two French companies, Veolia Environnement and Suez Environnement (SEV:EN). Smaller companies that receive the majority of their revenues from water include Pentair, Kurita Water Industries (TYO:6370), Aqua America, and Christ Water Technology (VI:CWTE).

Exchange-Traded Funds

ETFs have become increasingly popular with investors seeking exposure to a commodity or asset class that may otherwise be difficult to access. Water ETFs are no different in this regard. As interest in water-related investments has increased in recent years, so has the number of ETFs providing investors with exposure to the water market. Among these funds are the following:

- PowerShares Water Resources Portfolio (PHO) is among the most popular water ETFs. All of the assets are based in the United States, and the fund focuses heavily on industrial water companies rather than utilities. It is made up primarily of mid- and small-cap companies that focus on water conservation and purification. Among the top holdings are American Water Works Company, Flowserve Corporation, and Toro Company.
- PowerShares Global Water Portfolio (PIO) is split about 60/40 between industrial stocks and water utilities. Two of the larger holdings are Pentair and Flowserve. It is quite similar to PHO but is more global, although with significant allocations in the United States.
- The S&P Global Water Index is split evenly between water utilities and services, such as equipment and materials. It provides both U.S. and international exposure.
- The First Trust ISE Water Index Fund is primarily a U.S. equity ETF focusing on wastewater treatment and the potable water industry. Among the top holdings are Veolia Environnement and Mueller Water Products.

Water Funds and Indices

A handful of water-focused mutual funds has emerged in the past several years. Among the most popular are the following:

- Calvert Global Water Fund holds about 100 companies focused on water utilities, water technologies, and water infrastructure. Most of its holdings are small- to mid-cap companies. The fund has total assets of more than $98 million and a three-year annualized return of +12.99%.

- Allianz RCM Global Water Fund (AWTAX) invests primarily in companies in the S&P Global Water Index and the Palisades Water Index. It invests in companies involved with both water quality and water quantity. AWTAX holds 20–50 stocks. The fund has total assets of $126 million and a three-year return of +14.29%.
- The Palisades Water Index tracks the performance of companies involved in a wide range of activities along the water value chain. The sectors covered by the index include utilities, water treatment, analytical infrastructure, resource management, and multibusiness.
- The Dow Jones U.S. Water Index is composed of international and domestic companies that are affiliated with the water business. Companies are required to have a minimum market capitalization of $150 million.
- The S&P 1500 Water Utilities Index is a subset of the S&P Composite 1500 Utilities Index. It includes 50 companies that are in water-related businesses. The 50 companies are distributed equally between water utilities and infrastructure, on the one hand, and water equipment and materials, on the other hand.

Conclusion

The next chapter focuses on the topic of water quality. Water quality issues are as important as water quantity issues and the two are closely related. Water quality issues have deep social implications. One out of every six people lives without access to safe drinking water.[37] Twice that number live without access to proper sanitation. Alarmingly, 80% of childhood deaths in the developing world are

---

[37]United Nations Development Programme, "Human Development Report 2006, Beyond Scarcity: Power, Poverty and the Global Water Crisis." (2006); available online at http://hdr.undp.org/sites/default/files/reports/267/hdr06-complete.pdf.

linked to unsanitary water conditions.[38] Agriculture and industrial activities frequently degrade the quality of water consumed. The recent concerns on the hydraulic fracking industry also highlight the close relationship between water quality and energy production. The next chapter explores what role markets can have in solving water quality issues.

[38] Peter H. Gleick, *The World's Water 1998–1999: The Biennial Report On Freshwater Resources* (Wahsington, DC: Island Press, 1998).

Chapter 9

WATER QUALITY TRADING AND ITS ASSOCIATED ASSET CLASSES

The previous chapter dealt with water quantity and the demands for water by an ever growing and thirsty population. It is important to note however that the water crisis involves not just quantity, but water quality as well. In many ways, water quantity and quality are closely related. Nutrients, such as nitrogen and phosphorus are substances that occur naturally in water, soil, and air. Nitrogen and phosphorus in fertilizer aid the growth of agricultural crops, but excessive presence of nutrients in watersheds can have harmful consequences. Exposure to excessive levels of nitrate (a form of nitrogen) can reduce oxygen levels in blood, putting infants, children, and adults with lung or cardiovascular disease at increased health risk. There has also been research linking long-term consumption of excess nitrates to cancer. Poor water quality is not only an issue for humans but wildlife as well. High concentrations of phosphorus or ammonia in lakes, streams, and reservoirs are often responsible for fish mortality, foul odors, and excessive aquatic weed growth.

The purpose of this chapter is to describe how these problems of water quality are and can be addressed. Its interest to policymakers is self-evident. Once again pricing water pollution can achieve social objectives and provide commercial opportunities to the financial and industrial sectors.

The chapter is divided into six sections: (1) Introduction; (2) background on water quality trading; (3) sources of water pollution; (4) barriers to implementation and necessary conditions for successful trading programs; (5) active water quality trading programs; and (6) conclusion.

Background

The fundamentals of water quality trading are quite simple. A cap is typically placed on the amount of pollutant entering the watershed. Much like a cap-and-trade program for GHGs or other environmental commodities, a reduction goal is then established for the pollutant and permits are allocated to the participating (also known as "capped") sources. Once the capped sources have been allocated their permits, they are incentivized to reduce their pollutant discharge beyond their reduction target in an effort to sell any excess permits that may result. This buying and selling of permits allows the capped sources to take advantage of the lowest cost opportunities to reduce their levels of pollution.[1]

To give an example, the nitrogen and phosphorus discharges from factories and farms were polluting the Chesapeake Bay in the United States by reducing the oxygen level of the water. This was harmful to the marine ecosystem and human health. In 2005, a nutrient cap-and-trade program was initiated that limited the amount of nutrients flowing into the rivers by issuing water quality credits to polluting entities.[2] Various legislative proposals are calling for the system to be expanded. The program could eventually be extended to include fishermen, based on the idea that catches will increase if there are fewer dead zones caused by oxygen depletion. A 2012 report by the Chesapeake Bay Commission concluded that implementing a watershed-wide cap-and-trade system could result

---

[1] The World Resources Institute has written extensively on water quality trading markets; available online at http://www.wri.org/publications/4131.

[2] Chicago Climate Exchange. Outline for Pennvest's Role as Nutrient Credit Clearinghouse in Pennsylvania's Water Quality Nutrient Credit Market (November 2009).

in a cost saving of approximately $1.2 billion annually for entities that are subject to EPA's water pollutant regulations.[3]

Unfortunately, water quality impairment is all too common. EPA estimated in a 2006 survey that 48% of U.S. rivers and streams and 60% of lakes, reservoirs, and ponds were impaired or threatened for their designated uses. On a global basis, 532 coastal areas experience eutrophication or excess nutrients. The formation of hypoxic (areas of water without sufficient oxygen) areas have created so called dead zones in the Gulf of Mexico, Chesapeake Bay, and in other areas around the world. [4]

Sources of Water Pollution

Water pollution sources can be divided into two types: point and non-point. Point sources can be attributed to a specific physical location such as power plants and refineries, which are often located near rivers and lakes for cooling and shipping purposes, as well as nutrient discharges from waste-water treatment plants, industries, or municipalities. Non-point sources — the main cause of nutrient pollution — are diffuse sources of pollution that cannot be attributed to a clearly identified, specific physical location or a defined discharge channel. This includes the nutrients that run off the ground from any land use — croplands, lawns, parking lots, streets, forests, etc. — and enter waterways. It also includes nutrients that enter through air pollution, through groundwater or from septic systems.

Barriers to Implementation and Necessary Conditions for Successful Trading Programs

While there are impediments to trading water, they are not insurmountable and can be overcome with good contract and

---

[3]Chesapeake Bay Commission, "Nutrient Credit Trading for the Chesapeake Bay: An Economic Study." (May 2012); available online at www.chesbay.us/Publications/nutrient-trading-2012.pdf.

[4]Mindy Salmon, Evan Branosky and Cy Jones, Water Quality Trading Programs: An International Overview. World Resources Institute Issue Brief No. 1 (March 2009).

market design. This section presents a discussion on how water quality markets work, addresses common elements of successful programs, and looks at some of the characteristics unique to water as a commodity in order to differentiate from the other environmental assets.

Despite these unique characters, water markets, like all other markets, can only thrive in an environment of unambiguous property rights. While monitoring, verification, product standards, etc. are also necessary, unambiguous property rights are the foundation upon which the market framework is built. Much like the institutions that were created for SO_2 and CO_2, a proper infrastructure is needed for water markets to exist and thrive. It is only then that a cap on use can be put in place and trading commence.

The structural changes necessary for the establishment of an organized water market are already in motion in many parts of the world. Design elements such as standardization, grading and quantification guidelines, a legal framework which recognizes property rights, proper monitoring and verification procedures, ability to track transfers, etc. are all being developed as water markets begin to take shape. While many of these markets are still in the early stages of their development, they provide important proof of concept lessons for others considering the use of markets for water quality and quantity. Below is a summary of the elements necessary for the successful implementation of a water quality trading program.

Regulatory or Legislative Mandate for Action

Similar to other environmental markets, the primary driver for creation of a water quality trading market is nearly always a policy response to environmental degradation. In the case of water quality markets in the U.S., this driver is typically the Clean Water Act (CWA). The CWA requires each state to adopt limits on what can be released by point sources into water bodies. In cases where point source polluters violate these standards, they can be subject to fines or further legal action. If a water body does not meet the standards established under the CWA, the state must establish a total maximum daily load (TMDL) which is a calculation of the maximum amount of pollution that a water body can receive and still meet established water quality standards. Establishing a TMDL involves allocating a pollutant limit to all the various sources of pollution in the watershed. These sources can be non-point sources like farms or point sources like power plants. It is the establishment of TMDLs that allow for the establishment of many water quality trading programs.

Establishment of a Cap on Water Pollution

Caps on point sources

Most caps placed on pollutants are a limit of a specific pollutant over a specific time period and an annual facility flow volume. For instance, a cap for a wastewater treatment facility may allow the plant to discharge no more than 300,000 pounds of nitrogen each year. To arrive at this number the regulator will look at the design capacity of the plant which, for example, could be 10 million gallons of water processed per day and assign a limit on the amount of nitrogen allowed per gallon released, for example, 6 milligrams per liter. Assuming that this wastewater treatment plant is operating at or under capacity, it is unlikely to have great difficulty staying under the cap. However, in many areas of the U.S., growth in urban and suburban areas has led to increases in the amount of water needed to be processed at such plants. This is one of the primary reasons for wastewater treatment plants exceeding their cap — there is more water to process than they were designed to handle.

Caps on non-point sources

Most water quality trading programs do not place caps on non-point sources similar to those on point sources. Because there are often so many non-point sources, such as farms, it is difficult and sometimes impractical to administer a program whereby every farm receives a cap. Measurement, verification, and monitoring of effluent levels at individual farms would make most water quality trading programs impossible.

However, because non-point sources cause the majority of water pollution in many watersheds they clearly must be incorporated into the trading program. Typically, non-point sources are incorporated by establishing a baseline set of management practices that must be put into place prior to receiving credits for additional practices that may be deemed worth of water quality offset credits under a trading program. Often the baseline practices may include so called best management practices such as planting buffers of vegetation along stream banks, using cover crops to reduce erosion, etc. Additional activities such as no-till agriculture or installing fencing to keep animals out of waterways may then be eligible for offset credits which can then be sold in the trading program.

Other methods for incorporating non-point sources include establishing a firm date after which a set list of management activities similar to those listed above would be eligible for crediting. Activities conducted prior to the cut-off date would not be eligible. While the cut-off date can be seen as arbitrary, it does provide for a more easily administered program.

Measurement, Monitoring, and Verification

For point sources, measurement, monitoring, and verification of adherence to program rules is relatively straightforward. Most point source entities require permits to operate and must provide evidence of adherence to permitting requirements to the EPA or other authorities. For non-point sources however, measurement, monitoring, and verification can be far more difficult. They can be done directly by on-site sampling, through site specific estimates, or through performance criteria that establish pre-determined reductions for implementing specific management practices.

Active Water Quality Trading Programs

A recent study[5] estimated that there are 21 active water quality trading programs operating globally (see Table 9.1). Table 9.1 categorizes the programs into trading and offset programs. Offset programs involve a single buyer with one or more sellers while trading programs have multiple buyers and sellers. Most of these 21 programs are quite small. Highlighted below is one trading program and one offset program.

Hunter River Salinity Program (Trading Program)[6]

Prior to the introduction of the Hunter River salinity trading program, the river at times became so salty that it could no longer be used for irrigation of crops. As the primary cause of this increase in salinity was effluent from nearby industrial sources, this created considerable tension between the industrial and agricultural communities that operate along the river.

The Hunter River of New South Wales Australia drains a coastal catchment covering roughly 22,000 kilometers (see Figure 9.1). Agricultural operations along the river include wineries, dairy, vegetables, fodder, beef, and horse breeding. The river also has 20 of the world's largest coal mines nearby as well as several power plants including Australia's largest.

While some of the salt in the river and soils occurs naturally, the salinity of the river is raised by coal mining and power plant operations. This is particularly problematic at times of low flow, when

---

[5] K. Fisher-Vanden and Sheila Olmstread, "Moving Pollution Trading from Air to Water: Potential, Problems, and Prognosis." *Journal of Economic Perspectives*, Volume 27, Number 1 (Winter 2013): 147–172.

[6] Information on the Hunter River Salinity Program was obtained from the Department of Environment and Conservation of New South Wales, Australia; available online at http://www.epa.nsw.gov.au/licensing/hrsts/ and here http://www.epa.nsw.gov.au/resources/licensing/hrsts/hrsts.pdf.

Table 9.1. Active Water Quality Trading and Offset Programs.

Program name	Year est.	Location	Types of trades/offsets	Pollutants	Trading or offset structure
Trading programs					
Tar-Pamlico Nutrient Trading	1990	NC, U.S.	PS-PS/NPS	N/P	Bilateral/Clearinghouse
South Creek Bubble Licensing	1996	NSW, Austr.	PS-PS	N/P	Bilateral
Cherry Creek Reservoir Watershed Phosphorus Trading	1997	CO, U.S.	PS-PS/NPS	P	Clearinghouse
Chatfield Reservoir Trading	1999	CO, U.S.	PS-PS/NPS	P	Bilateral/Clearinghouse
South Nation River Watershed Trading	2000	ONT, Can.	PS-NPS	P	Clearinghouse
Long Island Sound Nitrogen Credit Exchange	2002	CT, U.S.	PS-PS	N	Clearinghouse
Neuse River Basin Total Nitrogen Trading	2002	NC, U.S.	PS-PS/NPS	N	Bilateral/Clearinghouse
Hunter River Salinity Trading	2004	NSW, Austr.	PS-PS	Salinity	Exchange market
Great Miami River Watershed Trading Pilot	2006	OH, U.S.	PS-NPS	N/P	Clearinghouse
Minnesota River Basin Trading	2006	MN, U.S.	PS-PS	P	Bilateral
Maryland Water Quality Trading	2008	MD, U.S.	PS-PS/NPS	N/P/sediment	Exchange Market/Bilateral
Pennsylvania Nutrient Credit Trading	2010	PA, U.S.	PS-PS/NPS	N/P/sediment	Exchange Market/Bilateral
Chesapeake Bay Watershed Nutrient Credit Exchange	2011	VA, U.S.	PS-PS/NPS	N/P	Clearinghouse/Bilateral

(Continued)

Table 9.1. (*Continued*)

Program name	Year est.	Location	Types of trades/offsets	Pollutants	Trading or offset structure
Offset programs					
Rahr Malting	1997	MN, U.S.	PS-NPS	CBOD5	Bilateral
Pinnacle Foods	1998	DE, U.S.	PS-NPS	N, P	Bilateral
Southern Minnesota Beet Sugar Cooperative	1999	MN, U.S.	PS-NPS	P	Clearinghouse
Bear Creek	2001	CO, U.S.	PS-PS	P	Bilateral
Piasa Creek Watershed Project	2001	IL, U.S.	PS-NPS	Sediment	Bilateral
Clean Water Services/Tualatin River	2005	OR, U.S.	PS-PS/NPS	BOD/NH4/temp.	Bilateral
Red Cedar River Nutrient Trading Pilot	2007	WI, U.S.	PS-NPS	P	Bilateral
Alpine Cheese Company/Sugar Creek	2008	OH, U.S.	PS-NPS	P	Bilateral

Notes: Abbreviations in column 4 refer to point sources (PS) and non-point sources (NPS). In column 5, abbreviations refer to nitrogen (N), phosphorus (P), biochemical oxygen demand (BOD), 5-day carbonaceous biochemical oxygen demand (CBOD5), ammonia (NH4), and temperature (temp.).

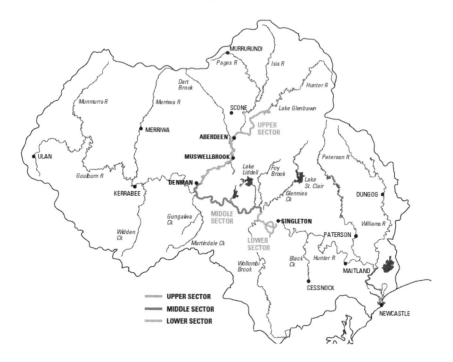

Figure 9.1. Map of Hunter River Catchment.

a discharge of highly saline water can have an especially negative impact on the river. Thus, one solution is to discharge salty water into the Hunter River only at times when there is plenty of low-salt, fresh water to dilute it.

In order to implement the trading system, monitoring points were established along the river to measure the flow rate. When the river is low, no discharges are allowed. When the river is high, limited discharges are allowed and are controlled by a salinity trading permit system (see Figure 9.2, Hunter River Flow Categories). When the river is at flood stage, unlimited discharges are allowed provided that the salt concentration does not exceed an upper bound limit. The program is administered such that each member coordinates their discharges so that the upper bound limit is not breached.

There are a total of 23 permit holders in the system with a total of 1,000 permits among them (see Table 9.2). Each permit

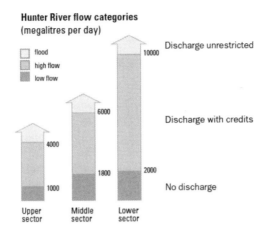

Figure 9.2. Hunter River Flow Categories.

holder was allocated an initial number of permits at the beginning of the program with each permit allowing them to discharge 0.1% of the total amount of saline water.

Trading of permits takes place via an online electronic platform. Trades can be executed for a single day or multiple days and negotiations on prices take place between the members involved. Each permit is assigned to a particular section of the river (upper, middle, or high) and is for a specific period of time. A registry tracks the transfer of permits and is publically available. A snapshot of the registry is provided in Figure 9.3.

The success of the program can be seen in the electrical conductivity of the river. As saltier water conducts electricity better, electrical conductivity is measured to estimate the salinity of the river. As can be seen in Figure 9.4, the salinity of the river as measured in electrical conductivity has increased steadily since the initial program trials commenced in 1994.

Oregon Temperature Program (Offsets Program)

Water quality trading can also be based on water temperature since the aquatic ecosystem, specifically certain species of fish, can be

Table 9.2. License Holders and Credit Allocations at Commencement of Regulation.

Credit holder	Licence number (if applicable)	Premises name (if applicable)	No. of credits
Bengalla Mining Company Pty Ltd	6538	Bengalla Mine	35
Bulga Coal Management Pty Ltd	563	Saxonvale Colliery Holding	40
Camberwell Coal Pty Ltd	3390	Camberwell Coal Mine Colliery Holding	15
Coal and Allied Industries Ltd	640	Hunter Valley Operations	120
Coal and Allied Industries Ltd	1976	Mt Thorley Colliery Holding	0
Cumnock No 1 Colliery Pty Ltd	37	Cumnock No 1 Colliery	15
Dartbrook Coal Pty Ltd	4885	Dartbrook Coal Mine	15
Drayton Coal Pty Ltd	1323	Drayton Coal Mine Colliery Holding	25
Hunter Valley Coal Corporation Pty Ltd	4460	Mt Owen Coal Mine	15
Lemington Coal Mines Ltd	1497	Lemington Coal Mine Colliery Holding	40
Liddell Coal Operations Pty Ltd	2094	Liddell Colliery Holding	55
Macquarie Generation	779	Bayswater Power Station	230
Mt Arthur Coal Company Ltd	113	Bayswater Colliery	25
Muswellbrook Coal Company Ltd	656	Muswellbrook No 2 Open Cut Coal Mine	10
Nardell Coal Corporation Pty Ltd	10337	Nardell Coal Corporation Pty Ltd	30
Ravensworth Operations Pty Ltd	10860	Ravensworth East Mine	0
Ravensworth Operations Pty Ltd	2652	Ravensworth Operations Narama Mine	100
Redbank Project Pty Ltd	11262	Redbank Power Station	35
Rix's Creek Pty Ltd	3391	Rix's Creek Colliery	25

(*Continued*)

Table 9.2. (*Continued*)

Credit holder	Licence number (if applicable)	Premises name (if applicable)	No. of credits
United Collieries Pty Ltd	3141	United Colliery	10
Wambo Mining Corporation Pty Ltd	529	Wambo Mining Corporation	35
Warkworth Mining Ltd	1376	Warkworth Colliery Holding	40
New South Wales Environment Proection Authority	NA	NA	85
Total credits			**1,000**

Notes:

- Initial credit holders are shown in the table, however, credit holders may vary from time to time. Details of current holders can be found on the DEC website (www.environment. nsw.gov.au/hrsts/).

- Although some of the participants referred to above were not initially issued with credits, they will be able to participate in trading.

- Some credits were initially kept by the EPA as a transitional mechanism. All residual credits were allocated during 2003, so all 1,000 credits are held by participants.

especially sensitive to the sudden changes in water temperature. Thus water temperature credits were developed to mitigate incidents whereby factories, power plants, or wastewater treatment systems release a large amount of warm water into a lake or river. Instead of mandating the installation of expensive water cooling systems, regulators have allowed farmers and other landowners to establish trees and other stream bank vegetation to shade streams in order to cool them down naturally. This also provides increased animal habitat and other environmental benefits. Credits are then issued for cooling the streams and can be sold to regulated entities like wastewater treatment authorities which use them to comply with temperature requirements.

Water temperature trading is a relatively new phenomenon in environmental markets. In 2006, the Oregon Department of

River Register			
Block Number 2003-56(4) Fixed	Total Allowable Discharge: 847 Tonnes (not applicable if in flood)		DATE WHEN BLOCK PASSES SINGLETON 25/02/2003

Credit Holder	Site Discharge Period Discharge Start	Discharge Stop	Sector
Dartbrook	24-02-2003 05:00	25-02-2003 05:00	UPPER
Muswellbrook No. 2	23-02-2003 11:00	24-02-2003 11:00	Block Classification: High
Bengalla	24-02-2003 07:00	25-02-2003 07:00	Sector Credit Discount Factor : 1
Hunter Valley Operations West	24-02-2003 03:00	25-02-2003 03:00	MIDDLE
Hunter Valley Operations North	24-02-2003 18:00	25-02-2003 18:00	Block Classification: High
Liddell Coal	24-02-2003 08:00	25-02-2003 08:00	Sector Credit Discount Factor : 1
Bayswater Power Station	24-02-2003 03:00	25-02-2003 03:00	
Mount Owen	24-02-2003 13:00	25-02-2003 13:00	
Ravensworth/Narama	24-02-2003 18:00	25-02-2003 18:00	
Lemmington	25-02-2003 00:00	26-02-2003 00:00	LOWER
Wambo	24-02-2003 16:00	25-02-2003 16:00	Block Classification: High
Redbank	24-02-2003 18:00	25-02-2003 18:00	Sector Credit Discount Factor : 1
Bulga/Saxonvale	24-02-2003 09:00	25-02-2003 09:00	
Warkworth	24-02-2003 18:00	25-02-2003 18:00	
Mt. Thorley Operations	24-02-2003 18:00	25-02-2003 18:00	

DATE AND TIME OF ISSUE: 25/02/2003 08:51:58 EASTERN STANDARD TIME
Start and stop times are from discharge points.

Figure 9.3. Hunter River Salinity Trading Scheme Registry.

Environmental Quality finalized the Willamette River temperature requirements in order to protect salmon during the spring and fall when they are spawning, and during the summer when they are rearing and migrating. This marked the first formal attempt in the U.S. at reducing water temperature through an environmental market. The model may prove to be important for streams outside of Oregon as well. EPA estimates that Oregon, Washington, and Idaho have over 35,000 miles of streams where temperatures are too high for salmon. The Oregon Department of Environmental Quality has developed a tool to calculate how much shade is needed to reduce the water temperature to its desired level. This tool tells those conducting the shade producing restoration how many trees or other vegetation to plant in order to make the required reductions in temperature. It also provides the metrics necessary for outside verifiers

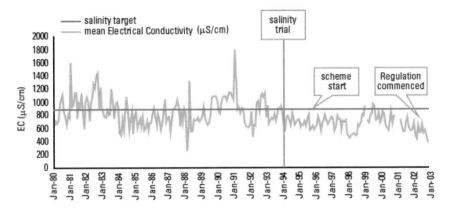

Figure 9.4. Electrical Conductivity at Singleton 1980 to 2002 (Monthly Means).

or monitors to check that the appropriate amount of temperature mitigating action has been taken.[7]

In the first such trade of its kind, the city of Medford Oregon's wastewater treatment facility was under mandate to cool the temperature of its effluent. The plant releases about 20 million gallons of water per day into the Rogue River at a temperature slightly above the natural temperature of the river. Although the temperature change is slight, the warmer water causes salmon eggs to hatch too early in the year, before there is adequate food for them to eat.

Instead of installing expensive water chilling equipment, Medford received approval to purchase temperature credits from landowners along a 40 mile stretch of the Rogue River. The trade was coordinated by the Freshwater Trust, who worked with landowners to plant the vegetation necessary to cool the waterway. Each landowner agrees to sell a 20-year easement on the land being restored to allow for the restoration, monitoring, and verification to take place.[8]

---

[7] Oregon Department of Environmental Quality, Water Quality Trading in NPDES Permits Internal Management Directive (December 2009).

[8] Mark Freeman, City of Medford Partners with Landowners to Help Shade Rogue River. *Mail Tribune* (14 July 2013).

In order to meet the demands the Department of Environmental Quality has placed on the water treatment facility the restoration efforts must take place according to a strict schedule expected to conclude in 2022. Each of the restoration projects along the river will be audited by a third party until 2032 to ensure the legitimacy of the credits issued to the landowners, who typically receive around $100 to $300 per acre of restored land. In addition to the third-party audit, the rules of the program require that the wastewater treatment plant purchase twice the amount of credits needed to offset the temperature increase of the wastewater treatment plant. This is done to ensure that the program as a whole is conservative in its crediting and achieves at least the amount of environmental gain necessary to offset the temperature increase caused by the wastewater treatment plant. Even with conservative program rules, the wastewater treatment facility estimates that it will be able to achieve the temperature reductions at roughly half the cost of traditional technology driven temperature reductions, saving the city's tax payers approximately $8 million.[9]

The development of creative regional markets regulating riparian water temperature in the Western United States to protect local fishery resources serve as a reminder that many environmental outcomes can be achieved through properly designed markets. The development of water temperature trading illustrates that markets cannot only help in addressing issues of quantity or nutrient loads but can also play a role in other water quantity attributes like temperature. It may also be important for investors or analysts looking at real estate and agriculture with surface streams and rivers. The re-establishment of stream banks may be a new income source in areas where these markets are in place. While it is difficult to determine the potential size of these markets at this early stage, it is

---

[9] *Ibid.*

estimated that the Oregon market alone could be worth more than $100 million annually.[10]

Conclusion

Water is one of the few commodities on Earth we cannot live without. It is essential to our very existence and has a profound effect on the way we conduct our daily lives. Given the scale of the water problems before us, ranging from agricultural runoff to aging infrastructure and a growing population, real changes are going to be required in the way we interact with and manage our water supply if we are to prosper as a species in the long run. Significant changes in the global water industry are both unavoidable and desirable. This chapter discussed how these changes will provide opportunities as new markets, technologies, and policies develop to deal with the increasing demand and diminishing supply of freshwater. Prominent criticisms of water markets, including the claim that people should have free and unlimited access to water, are understandable given the importance of water in our daily lives. The authors believe that markets must play a role in water above the amount needed for health and hygiene. Water markets are in their infancy and the authors see ways to improve upon these early efforts to establish markets. It is important that we continue to improve and expand the role of markets for water.

Markets can and are being utilized to reduce air pollution, and to address water quality and quantity problems. These are all key sustainability issues that are closely interrelated. Together, the dynamic interaction between marine, terrestrial, and atmosphere ecosystems have tremendous impacts on the quality of life. For example, global

---

[10]Freshwater Trust. Water Quality Trading: Program Overview; available online at http://www.thefreshwatertrust.org/main/wp-content/uploads/2013/09/WQT_Program-licensing/Overview_WEB_General.pdf.

climate change and water scarcity can impact our ability to provide food — both from land and oceans. The state of the oceans and land resources impact the quantity and quality of food that we can produce. Growing population, environmental pollution, and economic prosperity impact the quantity and type of food demanded. This has put tremendous pressure on land and ocean. The next chapter discusses these dynamics in the context of fish resources. Here again, economic instruments and markets can play a role to promote sustainable utilization of fishing resources.

Chapter 10

SUSTAINABLE FISHERIES MANAGEMENT AND ITS ASSOCIATED ASSET CLASSES

Fish stocks around the globe are declining rapidly. Catches are at, or close to, their maximum sustainable yields in over half of all fish stocks. While this is in part the result of an ever growing population demanding increasing amounts of fish, it is also a function of poor fisheries management. Poor management not only results in declining fish stocks but also takes a heavy toll on the greater marine environment and results in poor economic performance for those involved in the capture and processing of fish.

The purpose of this chapter is to describe how the decline in global fisheries and the resulting economic impacts are and can be addressed. This chapter will address the economic and environmental benefits of sustainable, market-based fisheries management with a focus on U.S. and New Zealand fisheries. The chapter will explain how pricing the rights to a share of the total fish catch can achieve social and environmental objectives while providing improved commercial opportunities for fishermen, processors, and related industries.

The chapter is divided into five sections: (1) Causes of the decline of global fisheries; (2) impacts of the decline of global fisheries; (3) solutions to the problem; (4) an example of success — Gulf of Mexico red snapper; and (5) conclusion.

Causes of the Decline of Global Fisheries

Flawed Policy and Poor Management

Many of the world's fisheries are effectively unmanaged. This was the case in the U.S. until the mid-1970s. Open access to fisheries allowed fishermen to catch as much as they could without regard to the overall resource as a whole. This policy approach, or lack thereof, often resulted in a "tragedy of the commons", a concept that has been discussed in previous chapters. Under this system, fishermen would maximize their catch while ultimately undermining the sustainable use of the fishery as a whole. As fish stocks declined, it became apparent that collective action, at least on some level, would be required.

In 1976, the U.S. Congress passed a Bill into law to regulate the use of fisheries. It was just the beginning. Over that last several decades that law has undergone numerous changes and is now generally referred to as the Magnuson-Stevens Fishery Conservation and Management Act, or MSA. The MSA established a 200 nautical mile Exclusive Economic Zone (EEZ) around the U.S. (preventing foreign exploitation of the resource), created regional fishery management councils, and developed ten national standards for fishery management plans. In spite of these efforts, fish stocks continued to decline and private sector economic returns suffered.[1]

Management plans typically included a variety of measures aimed at addressing problems of overfishing and diminishing economic returns. Unfortunately, many of these tools failed to solve the problem and some even exacerbated it. Among the most popular tools used include limitations on the Total Allowable Catch (TAC), which places a limit on the total amount of a particular species that can be fished over a defined period of time in a particular area. Other

---

[1]U.S. Department of Commerce National Oceanic and Atmospheric Administration, "Magnuson-Stevens Fishery Conservation and Management Act." (May 2007); available online at http://www.nmfs.noaa.gov/sfa/magact/MSA_Amended_2007%20.pdf.

measures aim at limiting the catch by imposing trip limits or by establishing narrow windows of time in which fishing can occur. Because there are often no limitations placed on individual vessels or fishing companies, they become incentivized to catch as much as possible or be forced to see other fishermen catch the limited supply. This practice, coupled with narrow time windows for fishing created a phenomenon known as the race for fish, whereby fishermen attempt to maximize their catch in the shortest amount of time by building more and larger vessels and work longer hours often under harsh conditions. These command-and-control approaches have often times resulted in technological innovations that attempt to increase the amount of fish caught within the constraints imposed by the law. An oversupply of fishing vessels is common under command-and-control policy.

Other traditional management tools included restricting the number of days at sea, closing fisheries during certain periods in an effort to guard against depleting the supply of young fish, limiting access to sensitive habitats, and limiting by-catch or species caught unintentionally while attempting to catch other fish. These management techniques, while presumably implemented in good faith, provide an incentive structure which is typically not well aligned with the overall goals of the fishermen involved and thus are met with resistance and often have poor outcomes. Many of these poor outcomes are in fact magnified through financial subsidies offered by governments.

Subsidization of Commercial Fishing

It is estimated that global fisheries subsidies are currently valued at U.S.$30–34 billion per year, representing 35–40% of the first sale value of total fisheries production. In an effort to better the economics of commercial fishing, subsidies often come in the form of subsidized construction and modernization of domestic fishing vessels, infrastructure projects such as ports construction and improvement, fuel discounts, direct income supports, fish price supports, and subsidized decommissioning of fishing vessels.[2]

While not all fishing subsidies result in negative outcomes, the vast majority create incentives for fishing beyond the point where it would otherwise be unprofitable under standard economic circumstances. This not only results in negative economic outcomes but also causes further depletion of the fishery. As with many types of subsidies, the World Trade Organization is seeking to reduce the subsidization of commercial fisheries.

Poor Governance

Recent research has confirmed the relationship between governance and illegal, unregulated and unreported (IIU) fishing. As one might suspect, countries that score low on good governance measures often higher rates of IIU fishing. Solving problems of good governance as it relates to fisheries is obviously complex. One approach that has yielded results in areas such as the Philippines and South Africa is the decentralization of decision making, incorporating members of the fisheries community into the decision making process. As those who are most affected by fisheries regulations become involved in the decision making, the fishing community has shown a greater willingness to comply with new rules and participate in data collection, monitoring, and assessment efforts.[3]

Lack of Data

As is the case with many of earth's natural resources, we are only just beginning to understand how fisheries function and how they interact with other systems. While it is easy to dismiss some decision

---

[2] U. Rashid Sumaila, Ahmed S. Khan, Andrew J. Dyck, Reg Watson, Gordon Munro, Peter Jydemers and Daniel Pauly, "A Bottom-up Re-estimation of Global Fisheries Subsidies." *Journal of Bioeconomics* 12 (2010): 201–225.

[3] David J. Agnew, John Pearce, Ganapathiraju Pramod, Tom Peatman, Reg Watson, John R. Beddington and Tony J. Pitcher (2009), "Estimating the Worldwide Extent of Illegal Fishing." *PLoS ONE*, 4(2).

makers as poor managers or being guilty of poor governance as it relates to fisheries, they are often dealing with very limited data and a great deal of uncertainty when making decisions about how best to protect the resource while optimizing output. The status of over half of the U.S. fish stocks are classified as being in uncertain status due to lack of reliable data.

In order to apply effective limitations on the allowable catch it is necessary for decision makers to understand the biology, ecology, and productivity of the fishery, and its interactions with the broader environment and other species. Given that this data is rarely, if ever, available to the extent desired, decision makers must take management and policy actions using imperfect information and maintain the flexibility to modify policy as new data becomes available.

Impacts of the Decline in Global Fisheries

Diminishing Economic Returns and Overcapacity

Open access fisheries managed without market-based incentives have provided incentives not only for over utilization of the resource but also overinvestment. As can be seen in Table 10.1, the race to catch as many fish as possible has resulted in a dramatic increase in the number of fishing vessels. In 1990, landings of fish excluding pollock (which prior to 1977 was not exclusive to U.S. fleets) was only 40% higher than in 1935 in spite of the fact that the number of fishing vessels increased 460% over the same period. While not depicted in Figure 10.1, the size of vessels and the amount of gear on board to capture fish has increased as well.[4]

In addition to the overcapitalization of fishing vessels, the fish processing industry also becomes overcapitalized in many traditionally managed fisheries. In order to handle the glut of fish that arrives

---

[4]Dietmar Grimm, Ivan Barkhorn, David Festa, Kate Bonzon, Judd Boomhower, Valerie Hovland and Jason Blau, "Assessing Catch Shares' Effects Evidence from Federal United States and Associated British Columbian Fisheries." *Marine Policy* 36 (2012).

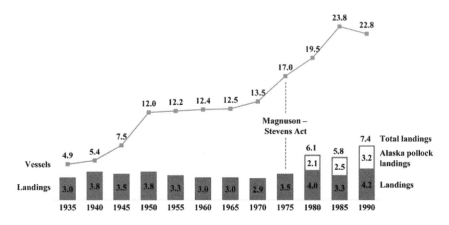

Figure 10.1. Total U.S. Commercial Domestic Vessels (Thousands) and Landings (Billions of Pounds).[5]

all at once, processors have to add capacity that would not be needed under normal circumstances.

The glut of fish generated under traditional management programs also generates poor returns for fishermen. They are selling into an oversupplied market and often will need to freeze fish thereby diminishing its value relative to fresh fish sold at a premium. Related negative impacts include poor handling practices and a decreased percentage of the fish used in the finished product.

Safety Concerns

As fish stocks have declined, safety concerns have increased. Commercial fishing is among the world's most dangerous occupations. In the U.S., fishermen have an occupational fatality rate as much as 35 times higher than the average worker. Safety concerns stem from a variety of factors (see Figure 10.2). Among the primary causes often cited are long work hours and harsh conditions such as hazardous waters far removed from medical assistance. Under traditional management, the race to fish incentivizes fishermen to operate

---

[5] *Ibid.*

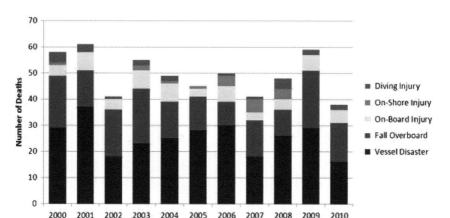

Figure 10.2. Fisheries Related Injuries in the United States.[6]

under dangerous weather conditions and push their equipment to the limit, while attempting to maximize their catch by working for days at a time without sleep.[7]

Declining Fish Stocks

While global fish consumption has steadily increased over the last half century or more, the amount of fish available to feed a growing population has been declining. With wild fish populations declining, much of the increase in fish demand has been met with supply from aquaculture (i.e., fish farms). It is estimated that 28% of the global stocks are currently overexploited, depleted, or recovering (see Figure 10.3). Since the 1970s, this figure has tripled. Of this 28%, 19% are overexploited, 8% depleted, and 1% recovering. It is estimated that 20% of the global stocks are moderately exploited or underexploited. Half of the global stocks are fully exploited,

---

[6]Center for Disease Control and Prevention, "Commercial Fishing Safety." (March 2014); available online at http://www.cdc.gov/niosh/topics/fishing/.
　[7]*Ibid.*

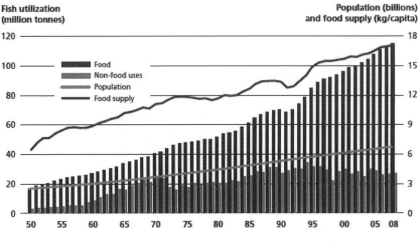

Figure 10.3. World Fish Utilization and Supply.[8]

meaning they are producing catches at, or near, their maximum sustainable yields. In the U.S., 54 stocks are classified as overfished and 45 stocks are experiencing overfishing.[9]

In recent years, declining local fish stocks result in demand being met through imports or with species which were previously viewed as unmarketable. In Europe, the Common Fisheries Policy is a highly complex and largely ineffective policy regulating fisheries throughout the EU. Despite this policy, 88% of fish stocks in European waters are overexploited and its fishing fleet is estimated to be 2–3 times larger than necessary. As a result, Europe now imports 60% of its fish.[10]

---

[8]Food and Agriculture Organization of the United Nations Fisheries and Aquaculture Department, "The State of World Fisheries and Aquaculture." (2010); available online at http://www.fao.org/docrep/013/i1820e/i1820e.pdf.

[9]*Ibid.*

[10]Marine Resources Assessment Group, "Towards Sustainable Fisheries Management: International Examples of Innovation." (2010); available online at http://www.pcfisu.org/wp-content/uploads/2010/12/MRAG-report_best-practice-examples1.pdf.

Increasing By-Catch, Discards, and Other Environmental Damages

Commercial fishing has a wide range of negative environmental impacts including the death of birds, mammals, and reptiles, the destruction of the ocean floor and catch, and potential discard of unwanted marine species. By-catch and discards are among the most harmful of these impacts. By-catch is defined as catching a species unintentionally that is not the target species or catching juveniles of the target species. By-catch may still have value in the market and be kept and sold. Discards are generally species that lack sufficient economic value or are prohibited by regulation; discards are thrown back to the water and usually die in the process. It is estimated that on a global basis, discards account for 8% (6.8 million metric tons) of the fish caught annually (see also Figure 10.4).[11]

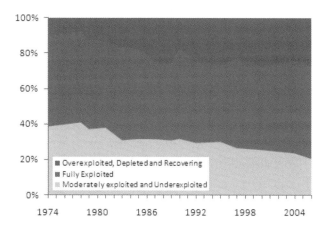

Figure 10.4. The Status of Global Fish Stocks, 1974–2006.[12]

---

[11] FAO Fisheries and Aquaculture Department, "The State of World Fisheries and Aquaculture." *op. cit.*

[12] Food and Agriculture Organization of the United Nations, *State of the World's Fisheries and Aquaculture 2008* (Rome, Italy: FAO, 2009).

Solutions to the Problem

The Theory of Market-Based Fisheries Management

Market-based approaches to fisheries management known as catch shares, Limited Access Privilege Programs (LAPP), or Individual Transfer Quotas (ITQ) began their development in the 1970s in Australia, New Zealand, and Iceland. Catch shares provide a secure share of fish to an individual fisherman. This share is for a percentage of the total catch limit for a fishery. Catch shares are allocated on an annual basis prior to the fishing season.

Many catch shares programs allow trading of shares among fishermen and occasionally, outside parties. For instance, if a fisherman decides not to fish for a season, he can sell his share of the catch to someone else who would like to catch more than his allotted share. This is similar to the cap-and-trade concepts described in other parts of this book. The sale of a fisherman's catch quota could take the form of a permanent transfer or a temporary lease. Catch shares programs lead to more efficient outcomes by allowing fishermen with lower marginal costs of productivity to purchase shares from fishermen with higher costs. In much the same way that market-based management approaches provide incentives for clean air and clean water, fishermen have incentives to protect the long-term viability of the fishery while being rewarded for new and innovative practices that increase the efficiency of their operations.

Catch shares also eliminate the need to race for fish. Fishermen can be more calculated and methodical in their approach to fishing, allowing them to use less gear and provide fish to the market during periods when they expect to yield the highest returns. Because they are no longer confined to fishing in narrow windows of time, fishermen can wait for optimal weather conditions and work at a reasonable pace. Importantly, monitoring and verification requirements to insure that fishermen are adhering to regulations are more relaxed and easier to enforce under catch shares. This is in part due to the fact that there are fewer regulations to enforce but also because fishermen are incentivized to sustain the long-term viability of the fishery since their share of the quota will decline in future years if the fishery becomes overfished. If fishermen do exceed their quota, they are required to buy additional shares on the market or pay a large fine.

Improved Economic Returns

Market-based management programs for fisheries such as catch shares have been shown to dramatically improve the economics of commercial fishing in many fisheries (see Figure 10.5). Revenues on a per vessel basis have been shown to double in many studies of catch shares fisheries. Reasons for the dramatic increase include decreased trawl time, decreased discarded fish, and longer fishing seasons which allow for fishing in better conditions. Fishermen have also experienced higher prices due to a smoother supply of fish as well as an increased ability to sell fresh fish.[13]

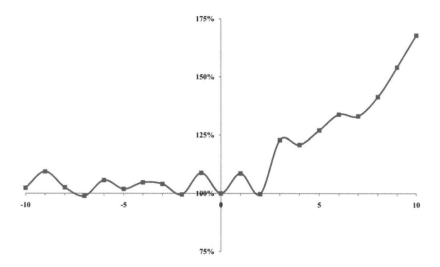

Figure 10.5. Average Revenues Across Fisheries versus The Year Before Implementation of Catch Shares Management.[14]

---

[13]Grim *et al.* (2012).
[14]*Ibid.*

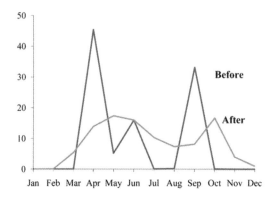

Figure 10.6. Percentage of British Columbia Halibut Catch by Month, Two-Year Average Before and After Catch Shares Implementation in 1991.[15]

The fish processing industry in catch shares managed fisheries is impacted favorably by a more smooth supply of fish relative to traditional management methods. As can be seen in Figure 10.6, the British Columbia (B.C.) halibut fishery experienced two large influxes of supply each year with 45% of the fish supplied in April and another 33% in September. Under the catch shares management approach, the April supply is only 14% of the total. A smoother supply of fish also allows for increased quality resulting from better handling.[16]

Improved Safety

Catch shares programs have proven to be effective in increasing safety of fishermen. Eliminating the "race for fish" allows fishermen to work better hours and in more optimal weather conditions. A study on the effectiveness of catch shares on safety showed that leading up to the implementation of the market-based management regime, shortened seasons and catches resulted in safety declining by an average of 20% from previous levels. In the five years following the implementation of catch shares, safety as measured by fatalities, vessels lost, search and rescue missions, and

[15–16]Grim *et al.* (2012).

safety violations improved by an average of 250%. Fisheries under traditional management regimes were on average only 26% to 38% as safe as the same fisheries operating under catch shares programs. In the U.S., the Alaskan Halibut and Sablefish Fisheries experienced a decline in search and rescue missions from 33 to less than 10 per year along with a decrease in fatalities of 15% over five years.[17]

Increasing Fish Stocks

The foundation of any catch shares program includes the implementation of the Total Allowable Catch (TAC). Although traditionally managed fisheries may also incorporate a TAC, adherence to the TAC is more common in catch shares fisheries. As can be seen in Figure 10.7, it has been shown that for the U.S. and BC fisheries, catches beyond the TAC are reduced under catch shares fisheries. This is in part due to increased monitoring and verification of the catch in catch shares fisheries. Also, there is a greater financial interest on the part of fishermen in the long-term sustainability of the fishery as they become part owners of the resource.[18]

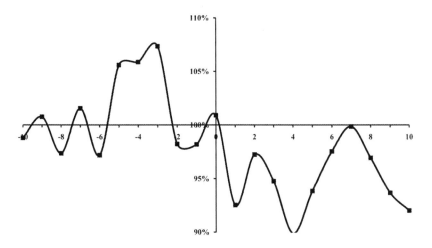

Figure 10.7. Landings per Total Allowable Catch (Average across U.S. and B.C. Fisheries).[19]

[17-19]Grim *et al.* (2012)

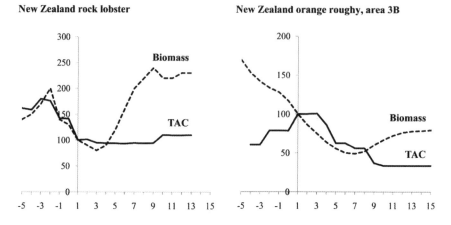

Figure 10.8. Biomass Relative to the First Year of Catch Shares Introduction.[20]

The New Zealand rock lobster and orange roughy fisheries provide a good example of the potential for increases in stocks as a result of the implementation of catch shares programs. Both fisheries have a long and well-studied history with catch shares. As can been seen in Figure 10.8, the rock lobster fishery experienced a 50% decrease in TAC relative to previous levels. Over 10 years, the amount of rock lobster doubled as a result, which allowed the fishery manager to raise the TAC. The orange roughy saw similar increases (60%) in biomass overtime although the intial TAC for the fishery was set too high.[21]

Decreasing By-Catch and Discards

Under market-based management programs such as catch shares, fisheries in the U.S. and British Columbia saw discards decline by 31% over 5 years and 66% over 10 years (see Figure 10.9).

[20–21]Grim *et al.* (2012).

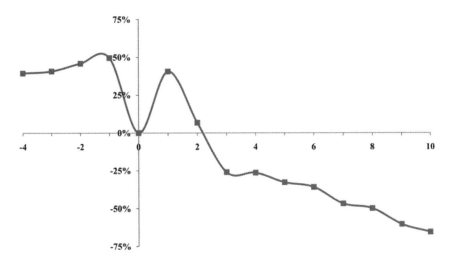

Figure 10.9. Percentage Reduction in Discards versus Baseline Year (Year Before Catch Shares).[22]

Nearly all of the fisheries studied saw lower discards rates than under traditional management. Some fisheries experienced dramatic declines in discards. The British Columbia halibut fishery saw discard decreases of over 90% and discards of Alaska Pollock, Alaska Sablefish, and Alaska Halibut Fisheries saw decreases of 50–65% by the 10th year of management under catch shares. Some fisheries in the U.S. and British Columbia that have implemented catch shares programs have also seen improvements in non-commercial and pro-hibited by-catch. The Alaska Sablefish Fishery saw non-commercial by-catch drop by nearly 50%, with crab and salmon discards drop-ping by nearly 90%.[23]

Catch shares promote decreased by-catch and discards in several ways. Firstly, there is no longer a free for all system whereby boats attempt to capture as much as possible. The race

---

[22–23]Grim *et al.* (2012).

to fish is eliminated and allows fishermen to be more strategic in their pursuit of the target species. Additionally, since each fisherman's quota is tied back to the long-term stock level of the fishery, there is an incentive to avoid juvenile fish and other fish that may be helpful to the long-term sustainability of the fishery.

While market-based management systems have proved to have a positive impact on discards and by-catch, other technical measures have also been put to use. The most often used devices are known as by-catch reduction devices, which are systems that allow fishermen to sort larger and smaller species from their trawl net. Also used are devices that allow turtles escape from the trawl net and to be separated from the target species. Bird scaring devices as well as different types of hooks and bait are also used to reduce bird and turtle deaths.

An Example of Success

Implementation of Market-Based Management Systems in the U.S.: Gulf of Mexico Red Snapper Individual Fishing Quota Program [24]

The U.S. is the world's fifth largest fishing nation with an annual harvest of over five million metric tons. The U.S. fishery is managed under the Maguson-Stevens Fishery Conservation and Management Act of 1996 and administered by the National Marine Fisheries Service. The Act established eight fisheries management councils broken down by region (see Figure 10.10).

The first U.S. Individual Fishing Quota (IFQ) systems were introduced in 1990 for the mid-Atlantic surf clam/ocean quahog. The early programs were well received and thus additional programs

---

[24] Information on the Gulf of Mexico Red Snapper Individual Fishing Quota Program is found primarily through the National Marine Fisheries Service Southeast Regional Office. Much of the material in this section is available online at http://sero.nmfs.noaa.gov/sustainable_fisheries/lapp_dm/documents/pdfs/2013/2012_rs_annualreport.pdf.

Figure 10.10. Fisheries Management Regions of the U.S.

were brought forth until the U.S. Congress declared a temporary moratorium on the implementation of additional IFQ systems in 1996, citing the need for further study on their impact. After further studies were conducted, U.S. Congress allowed additional IFQ systems to be developed. There are now 12 major ITQ fisheries in the U.S. along with three associated shared stock IFQ fisheries in British Columbia. This section will focus on the IFQ market for the Gulf of Mexico red snapper. The Red Snapper IFQ market not only provides a nice case study for the potential impacts of an IFQ on a fishery but also offers investors and analysts an opportunity to gain exposure to fisheries markets through direct participation as it is open to participation by outside investors.

After several previous attempts at implementing an IFQ program, holders of red snapper licenses were issued on 22 November 2006 (see Figure 10.11 for a detailed timeline of events) an initial share of the fishery based on their historical landings. The pre-IFQ catch was 4.19 million pounds gutted weight. Because the fishery

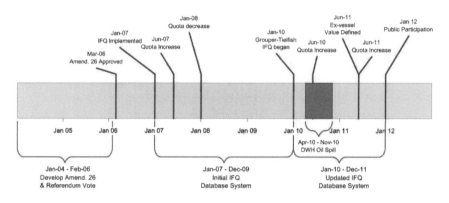

Figure 10.11. Timeline of Events: Red Snapper Individual Fishing Quota Program.[25]

was in decline, the initial catch limits of 2.98 million for the end of the year 2007 were a significant decrease from the pre-IFQ level. Overtime, as the fishery has become healthier, the catch limits have increased, and stood at 3.71 million for the end of year 2012. At an ex-vessel price of $3 per pound, this initial decrease in catch represents a loss of over $3.6 million. However, assuming that same $3 price, the end of year 2012 catch increased by nearly $2.2 million, making up much of the initial losses.

The red snapper IFQ (RS-IFQ) program is for red snappers only (i.e., single species), where participants in the program use an online account to manage transactions such as transfers of shares and allocations as well as information related to landings. In part, because of the program's online account system, the RS-IFQ has better data than most IFQ or catch-shares programs.

An allocation in the RS-IFQ refers to the actual number of pounds that is possessed, landed, or sold during a given calendar year. A share on the other hand is a percentage of the total quota

[25] National Oceanic and Atmospheric Administration, "2012 Gulf of Mexico Red Snapper Individual Fishing Quota Annual Report." (July 2013); available online at http://sero.nmfs.noaa.gov/sustainable_fisheries/lapp_dm/documents/pdfs/2013/2012_rs_annual report.pdf.

for the fishery. Each year, the allocations are distributed based on the annual quota and the share percentage held by the account owner. Allocations can be transferred to other account holders or can be used to catch red snapper. The quota for red snapper can be adjusted based on the condition of the fishery with any adjustment resulting in a proportional increase or decrease in the individual quota percentage shares. As an example, let us assume that the quota for the year is 100 pounds of red snapper. Our fisherman in this example has a 10% share of the quota. His allocation for the year will be 10 pounds. If next year's quota is raised to 200 pounds, our fisherman will have an allocation of 20 pounds. He can choose to sell this allocation to another fisherman or use it to catch red snapper himself.

The primary motivations for implementing the RS-IFQ were similar to those made in many of the other fisheries where IFQs have started. The fishery was characterized by an overcapacity of fishing vessels and equipment which resulted from a short fishing season meant to protect the health of the fishery. Unfortunately, both the health of the fish and fishermen suffered under the pre-IFQ management regime. As you will see in the paragraphs below, the early indications are that the RS-IFQ program has resulted in social, economic, and biological benefits.

Since the implementation of the RS-IFQ program, the fishery has undergone consolidation in the number of shareholders (see Table 10.1). In particular, small shareholders have decreased significantly from a pre-IFQ level of 415 account holders to a 2012 level of 273. The bulk of this reduction occurred in the first year of the IFQ program but while the number of small shareholders has decreased, they still make up the vast majority of the total number of shareholder accounts, and new shareholders have entered the program each year. In 2010, the program saw a 4.41% increase in the number of shareholders in part due to the start of the Gulf of Mexico Grouper-Tilefish IFQ program. Many red snapper fishermen also fish for grouper or tilefish

Table 10.1. Accounts by Shareholding Size.[26]

Year	Small	Medium	Large	Total
Initial	415	125	14	**554**
2007	368	112	17	**497**
2008	346	111	17	**474**
2009	313	108	18	**439**
2010	297	109	19	**425**
2011	284	116	18	**418**
2012	273	117	17	**407**

Note: Initial values were calculated on 1/1/2007, while 2007–2012 values were calculated on 12/31. Small accounts hold <0.05%; medium accounts hold 0.05%–1.4999%; and large accounts hold ≥1.5% shares.

and therefore participate in both IFQ programs. Interestingly, exchanges in shares and allocations occur between the two programs although data on these exchanges between programs is not available.

Beginning in 2012, the RS-IFQ program allowed individuals without fishing permits to purchase and trade both allocations and shares. Prior to this time, a valid Gulf reef fish permit was required in order to open an account, but once opened, an account could hold shares and allocation without maintaining a permit. This has allowed outside investors easier access to the RS-IFQ program. As of 2012, just under 30% of the RS-IFQ accounts belonged to participants without fishing permits.

The Gulf red snapper fishery, like many U.S. fisheries, was over-capitalized in terms of the number of vessels dedicated to catching red snapper and the equipment these vessels held. As the industry has undergone consolidation, the number of vessels harvesting red snapper has decreased by approximately 23% since the pre-IFQ period (see Table 10.2).

[26]National Oceanic and Atmospheric Administration (2012), *op. cit.*

Table 10.2. Vessels Harvesting Red Snapper.[27]

Year	Total	FL	AL/MS	LA	TX
2002–2006 average	485	—	—	—	—
2007	305	219	3	25	58
2008	297	216	12	24	45
2009	289	217	10	23	39
2010	384	306	12	20	46
2011	362	290	23	17	32
2012	371	304	21	19	27

Table 10.3. Share Transactions.[28]

Year	N	%	Avg. %
2007	108	10.7428	0.0995
2008	42	4.8150	0.1146
2009	75	6.0233	0.0803
2010	79	8.4748	0.1073
2011	78	5.0979	0.0654
2012	81	7.5608	0.0933

Trading activity in the RS-IFQ is better documented than in most fisheries. Although price and volume data in the early years of the program were not monitored as well as they are today, the transfer of shares and allocations has been well documented throughout the life of the RS-IFQ. As can be seen in Table 10.3, the greatest number of shares was transferred in the first year of the RS-IFQ. This is likely a reflection of the initial consolidation that occurred in the fishery. With the exception of 2008, share transactions have been relatively stable at 75–80 transfers per year.

---

[27] National Oceanic and Atmospheric Administration (2013), *op. cit.*
[28] *Ibid.*

Table 10.4. Allocation Transactions.[29]

Year	N	Lbs.	Avg. lbs.	Median lbs.	Quota (%)
2007	808	1,686,218	2,087	671	56.5
2008	683	1,371,100	2,007	600	59.7
2009	843	1,539,479	1,826	500	67.0
2010	1,719	3,065,736	1,793	500	96.1
2011	2,155	3,639,394	1,689	500	110.3
2012	2,251	3,741,966	1,467	400	100.8

Table 10.5. Share Transfer Prices.[30]

Year	N[a]	% of all trans.	Avg. price/lb	Median price/lb	Inflation-adj. avg. price/lb[b]
2007	21	19	$11.04	$12.51	$11.99
2008	22	52	$11.56	$10.50	$12.28
2009	38	51	$20.64	$20.00	$21.74
2010	33	42	$19.58	$21.50	$20.36
2011	26	33	$28.87	$27.00	$29.39
2012	35	43	$35.68	$35.00	$35.68

[a]Number of share transactions that had prices greater than $9/lb equivalent and less than $36/lb equivalent.
[b]Inflation adjustments from: http://www.bea.gov/ with 2012 as the base year using the GDP deflator.

Transfers of allocations in the Gulf red snapper fishery have also been well documented. An allocation is the number of pounds of red snapper an account can process, lend, or sell during a given calendar year. As can be seen in Tables 10.4 and 10.5, the number of allocation transactions has increased annually since the beginning of the program, amounting to over 100% of the quota in the past two years while the average number of pounds in each transaction has steadily decreased. While there has been a steady increase

29–30 *Ibid.*

in transfers of allocations and shares, there has been a decrease in the number accounts that land red snapper and also hold shares. At the start of the IFQ program, 87% of those who landed red snapper held shares; that number is now down to 57%. This suggests that simply trading red snapper instead of fishing for red snapper is becoming increasingly common. This is important because it suggests that the market forces of the catch shares program are beginning to push resource allocations to their highest and best use as less efficient fishermen sell their shares to those who are more efficient.

Many of the price patterns seen in the RS-IFQ program suggest that the market is indeed achieving its desired impacts. As fishermen are allowed to fish over a greater number of days with less capital costs dedicated to vessels and unnecessary equipment, profits have increased. Fishermen are able to deliver fresh fish all year round and avoid a glut in supply caused by the narrow time windows during which fishing was once allowed. Much of this is reflected in share and allocation transfer prices as well as ex-vessel transfer prices.

Price information for transfers of shares and allocations was not required in the early years of the program. As a result, roughly half of all share transfers had missing or erroneous price information. However, even after removing outlier reported prices, the available data still provides insight into the value of shares in the RS-IFQ. As can be seen in Table 10.6, the value of shares on a per pound basis has nearly tripled since the beginning of the IFQ program.

Allocation transfer prices have also risen steadily since the beginning of the program from an initial average price per pound of $1.97 to a 2012 price of $3.00.

The Gulf red snapper fishery has also seen increases in ex-vessel prices (see Table 10.7). The ex-vessel price is the price received by fisherman for red snapper landed at the dock. Average ex-vessel prices for 2012 were $4.44 per pound compared to a pre-IFQ program average of $2.80.

Efforts to catch red snapper were also monitored and recorded under the IFQ program. Effort was defined as the average landings

Table 10.6. Allocation Transfer Prices.[31]

Year	N[a]	% of all trans.	Avg. price/lb	Median price/lb	Inflation-adj. avg. price/lb[b]
2007	155	19	$1.97	$2.00	$2.14
2008	152	22	$2.31	$2.25	$2.45
2009	283	34	$2.69	$2.75	$2.83
2010	344	20	$2.88	$3.00	$3.00
2011	476	22	$2.96	$3.00	$3.01
2012	781	31	$3.00	$3.00	$3.00

[a]Number of allocation transactions that had price greater than $1.20/lb and less than $5.00/lb.
[b]Inflation adjustments from: http://www.bea.gov/ with 2012 as the base year using the GDP deflator.

Table 10.7. Ex-vessel Transfer Prices ($/lb).[32]

Year	N[a]	% of all trans.	Avg.	Median	Inflation-adj. avg.[b]
Pre-IFQ[c]	—	—	$2.80	$2.81	$3.32
2007	2,455	92	$3.74	$3.75	$4.06
2008	2,023	85	$4.06	$4.25	$4.31
2009	1,963	79	$4.13	$4.25	$4.35
2010	2,319	71	$4.17	$4.25	$4.34
2011	2,985	77	$4.26	$4.25	$4.34
2012	3,319	84	$4.44	$4.50	$4.44

[a]Number of allocation transactions that had price greater or equal to $2.60/lb and less than $10.00/lb.
[b]Inflation adjustments from: http://www.bea.gov/ with 2012 as the base year using the GDP deflator.
[c]Pre-IFQ averages are from 2002–2006.

per trip and the program also tracked the number of days on the water along with the number of trips and the average length of each trip. Because the IFQ program allowed for an expansion in the number of days in the fishing season, changes in the quota, as well

---

[31–32] *Ibid.*

Table 10.8. Effort Harvesting Red Snapper.[33]

Year	Trips	Days away[a]	Avg. days per trip	Avg. RS landings per trip
2002–2006 average	4,709	12,856	2.64	1,417
2007	2,632	11,165	4.33	1,075
2008	2,343	9,464	4.24	937
2009	2,451	9,444	4.05	898
2010	3,220	13,207	4.45	949
2011	3,823	14,613	4.31	847
2012	3,893	14,230	4.37	934

[a]Days away are calculated from the SEFSC Coastal Logbook records as of 3/12/2013 and therefore may not contain the complete 2012 data.

as regulations on other reef fish species, it is difficult to understand what the direct impact of the IFQ has been. As can be seen in Table 10.8, the number of trips made has decreased while the length of those trips has increased. Average landings per trip have also decreased from the pre-RS-IFQ level.

In addition to the positive economic impacts the IFQ has had on fishermen, the program has also helped move the fishery closer to achieving biological and environmental goals. In 2005, it was determined that the Gulf red snapper fishery was overfished. As a result, a plan to improve the health of the fishery was put into place in 2007 which included a reduction in fishing quotas, attempts at reducing by-catch, as well as other measures. In subsequent assessments of the fishery in 2009 and 2013, it was determined that spawning stock biomass had increased due to the measures taken in 2007. Increases in the spawning stock biomass allowed for increases in the annual catch limits in subsequent years (see Table 10.9). Although the commercial quota continues to be increased, it should be noted that it is still below the pre-RS-IFQ level of 4.19 million pounds gutted weight.

---

[33] *Ibid.*

Table 10.9. IFQ Commercial Quota (Gutted Weight).[34]

Year	Jan 1	Quota increase	Increase date	Dec 31
2007	2,297,297	689,189	June 1	2,986,486
2008	2,297,297	N/A	N/A	2,297,297
2009	2,297,297	N/A	N/A	2,297,297
2010	2,297,297	893,694	June 2	3,190,991
2011	3,190,991	109,910	May 31	3,300,901
2012	3,300,901	411,712	June 29	3,712,613

Year	Total IFQ cases	RS Cases	Pounds Seized	Seized value
2007	20	7	7,678	$33,270
2008	17	6	1,622	$6,525
2009	20	2	250	$910
2010	9	4	538	$2,170
2011	10	6	6,683	$26,619
2012	6	5	5,855	$27,482

Figure 10.12. Federal IFQ Law Enforcement Action.[35]

Verification and monitoring of the RS-IFQ is conducted by a variety of agencies and officers including the NOAA Office of Law Enforcement, the U.S. Coast Guard, as well as state wildlife officers and game wardens. It is a common myth that market-based programs such as catch shares are too difficult to monitor and verify but the reality suggests otherwise. Monitoring is conducted by waterfront patrol, meeting vessels upon landing, monitoring offloads, and random monitoring of vessels by special agents. Violations since the implementation of the program range from major violations such as false reporting of species harvested, to less significant infractions like landing at an unapproved location. In 2012, law enforcement officials spent a total of 11,836 hours monitoring the red snapper and Gulf tile fish IFQ fisheries. A total of six law enforcement actions

---

[34-35] *Ibid.*

were taken resulting in 5,855 pounds seized at a value of $27,482. A summary of law enforcement actions since the 2007 program start date is provided in Figure 10.12.

Conclusion

Catch shares programs have resulted in economic, environmental, and social gains in many of the fisheries where they have been implemented. Traditionally managed fisheries often attempt to regulate overfishing by placing limits on when fishermen can catch fish. This has resulted in an increase in the size and number of fishing vessels in an attempt to catch as many fish as possible in the short window of time available. This race to fish has put fishermen's lives at risk as they endure long hours and adverse weather conditions. It results in the overcapitalization of fisheries and fails to appropriately address the need to reduce the number of fish taken from the ocean in order to maintain healthy fish stocks.

Catch shares have remedied many of these issues by putting fishermen's incentives in line with those of the long-term health of the fishery. As fishermen become part owners of the fish stock, they have a financial interest in seeing that the stock remains healthy. Because a cap is placed on the amount of fish that can be taken from the ocean, rather than a cap on the time allowed to fish, fishermen are no longer incentivized to overcapitalize their fleets and are allowed to fish at their discretion. This results in better fishery economics and safer fishermen.

The ecological benefits to catch shares are many. Fishermen are not only no longer incentivized to overfish, but are able to reduce "ghost catches" created by stranded nets and gear that often result from the race for fish. By-catch and discards are also greatly reduced as fishermen can be more methodical in their approach and more easily avoid non-target species.

This chapter focused on the relationship between sustainability and an important component of the food cycle (fisheries). The next chapter will focus on the sustainability concerns related to the potential impact of the rise of anthropogenic emissions in the increase of catastrophic events such as hurricanes, typhoons, heavy storms, and floods. These weather events are discussed in the context of financial products to mitigate the impacts of weather events, most notably catastrophe insurance. Damage from these weather events is increasingly impacting personal property and the livelihoods of those such as fishermen who suffer damage to boats and equipment.

Chapter 11

WEATHER RISKS AND
ASSOCIATED ASSET CLASSES

On 29 October 2012 just Northeast of Atlantic City, New Jersey, Hurricane Sandy made landfall. "Superstorm Sandy" as it became known, delivered hurricane-force winds, and widespread flooding through a storm which surged across the eastern seaboard; the likes of which had not been experienced since the Great New England Hurricane of 1938. As a result, insured losses — primarily in the U.S. but stretching from Jamaica to Canada and most points in between — totaled $30 billion with uninsured losses totaling $35 billion. A total of 210 people lost their lives.[1] Unfortunately, this is not an isolated incident but rather a continuation in greater damages resulting from catastrophic events.

The short-term trend is undeniable. Natural disasters, such as hurricanes and earthquakes, have been increasing in frequency over the last several decades.[2] The dollar value of damages has been escalating as well. The latter is somewhat explained by the fact that the U.S. population has been gradually migrating toward coastal regions, where the threat of natural disasters pose much greater damage risks. These demographic trends require new and improved infrastructure, as well as, commercial buildings, factories, and expensive dwellings. As a result, the value of insured property

---

[1] Munich RE NatCatSERVICE (Download Center for Statistics on Natural Catastrophes); available online at www.munichre.com/en/reinsurance/business/non-life/natcatservice/index. html.

[2] *Ibid.*

has soared. This has created a need for more capital in the insurance and reinsurance sectors. Reinsurance is defined as the sharing of risk by insurance companies. One insurance company will often assume some of the risk of another insurance company in exchange for a portion of the premium.

This chapter covers four major attempts to address these capital needs, including fixed income instruments, and futures and options. First, it discusses the creation of new entrants into the market, the evolution of existing providers, and the establishment of Bermuda as a center for insurance and reinsurance. Second, it looks at the development of catastrophe bonds (also known as CAT bonds). Third, it discusses the growth of Industry Loss Warranties (ILWs) and index-based insurance products and swaps. Lastly, it addresses the role of weather derivatives — catastrophe futures and options, and heating/cooling degree day contracts.

This chapter will further explore the intersection of environmental and capital markets by discussing the instruments listed above and the opportunities they provide for investment and risk management. It is divided into three sections: (1) An overview of major catastrophes in the last 25 years; (2) an explanation of the four changes that have taken place to address the capital needs of the insurance and reinsurance industries; and (3) concluding remarks on the potential significance of these markets.

A Brief and Recent History of Natural Disasters and Insured and Uninsured Losses

The 1970s were a relatively quiet decade in terms of natural disasters. Most insurance and reinsurance companies covered their risk exposure internally. Insured losses up until the late 1980s typically did not exceed $1 billion. This all changed on 10 September 1989. Making landfall in the U.S. in Charleston, South Carolina Hurricane Hugo was a Category 4[3] hurricane that

---

[3]The Saffir–Simpson Hurricane Wind Scale rates hurricanes from 1–5 based on its sustained wind speed. This scale estimates potential property damage. Hurricanes that are Category 3 and higher are considered severe.

caused widespread damage including 27 fatalities in South Carolina and 34 in the Caribbean. Total economic losses were estimated at $10 billion with roughly half of those being insured. Prior to Hugo, the largest insured loss from a hurricane was Hurricane Betsy in 1965 with insured losses of $2.3 billion. It is easy to see why the insurance and reinsurance industries had been lulled into a feeling of relative calm. Unfortunately, Hugo was only the beginning. Three years later, Hurricane Andrew hit South Florida, Louisiana, and the Bahamas as a Category 4 hurricane, resulting in nearly $16 billion in insured damages. Prior to Hurricane Andrew, the cumulative insured damages from hurricanes in the U.S. from 1949 forward were approximately $16.8 billion. Needless to say, it served as a wake-up call to the insurance and reinsurance industry — increased capital and diversification would be needed.

There is an increasing body of evidence that the number and severity of natural disasters is on the rise and it is clear that the financial impacts are greater than at any other time in history. In Table 11.1, all 10 of the costliest natural catastrophes in history have occurred since 1990, with 8 of the 10 occurring within the last decade. This can in part be attributed to a rise in global population, a migration toward coastal areas where damages from catastrophes are higher, and a rise in insured property. Take for instance three of the most populated States in the U.S.: California, Texas, and Florida. As is shown in Figure 11.1, each of these states has seen a two- to three-fold increase in population since 1960. They are also coastal states with significant exposure to hurricanes, earthquakes, and drought.

Not only have catastrophes become more frequent but the level of insured and uninsured losses has risen as population has grown and property values increased (see Figure 11.2).

And although North America has accounted for over half of global insured losses since 1980, losses in Asia and South America are on the rise due to these same factors (see Figure 11.3).

Table 11.1. Ten Costliest Events Worldwide Ordered by Insured Losses (1980–2011).

Period	Event	Affected area	Overall losses	Insured losses	Fatalities
			U.S.$ m, original values		
25–30.8.2005	Hurricane Katrina, storm surge	USA: LA, New Orleans, Slidell; MS, Biloxi, Pascagoula, Waveland, Gulfport	125,000	62,200	1,322
11.3.2011	Earthquake, tsunami	Japan: Honshu, Aomori, Tohoku; Miyagi, Sendai; Fukushima, Mito; Ibaraki; Tochigi, Utsunomiya	210,000	40,000	15,840
24–31.10.2012	Hurricane Sandy, storm surge	Bahamas, Cuba, Dominican Republic, Haiti, Jamaica, Puerto Rico, USA, Canada	65,000	30,000	210
6–14.9.2008	Hurricane Ike	USA, Cuba, Haiti, Dominican Republic, Turks and Caicos Islands, Bahamas	38,000	18,500	170
23–27.3.1992	Hurricane Andrew	USA: FL, Homestead; LA; Bahamas	26,500	17,000	62
1.8–15.11.2011	Floods	Thailand: Phichit, Nakhon Sawan, Phra Nakhon Si Ayuttaya, Pathumthani, Nonthaburi, Bangkok	43,000	16,000	813

(*Continued*)

Table 11.1. (*Continued*)

Period	Event	Affected area	Overall losses	Insured losses	Fatalities
			U.S.$ m, original values		
June–Sept 2012	Drought, heat wave	USA: Midwest	20,000	15,000–17,000	100
17.1.1994	Earthquake	USA: CA, Northridge, Los Angeles, San Fernando Valley, Ventura, Orange	44,000	15,300	61
7–21.9.2004	Hurricane Ivan	USA, Caribbean, Venezuela, Colombia, Mexico	23,000	13,800	120
22.2.2011	Earthquake	New Zealand: South Island, Canterbury, Christchurch, Lyttelton	16,000	13,000	185

Source: Munich Re, Geo Risks Research, NatCatSERVICE (2014).

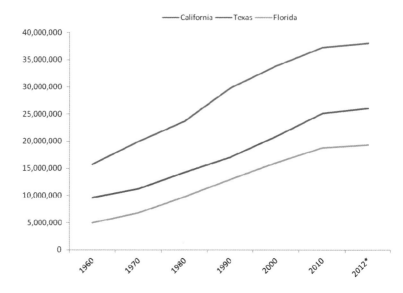

Figure 11.1. Population Growth in Select U.S. States.

Source: U.S. Census Bureau Estimate.

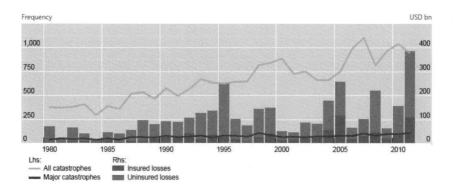

Figure 11.2. Natural Catastrophes: Frequencies and Losses.[4]

---

[4]Sebastian von Dahlen and Goetz von Peter, "Natural Catastrophes and Global Reinsurance — Exploring the Linkages." BIS Quarterly Review (December 2012). Data: Artemis, Guy Carpenter.

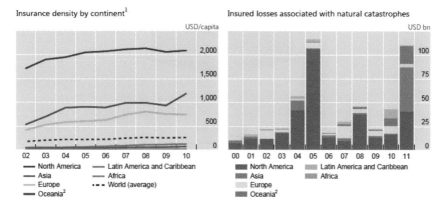

Figure 11.3. Insurance Density and Catastrophe Losses.[5]

Notes: [1]Insurance density is measured as the premium per capita that insurance companies receive for domestically insuring non-life (property and casualty) risks. [2]Australia, New Zealand Pacific islands.

Each of the concepts and products presented in the next section including insurance, reinsurance, catastrophe bonds, etc. provide a way of transferring risk. This section will attempt to address how risk is transferred (the main acts of risk transfer take place between primary insurers which then transfer risk to reinsurers), risk transfer between reinsurers (known as retrocession), and finally the role of institutions such as hedge funds and other financial institutions who are beginning to assume this risk. While much of the focus is on insurance and reinsurance companies, many losses unfortunately go uninsured as you can see in Figure 11.4. In 2011, the public and private sector spent $4,596 billion on some type of insurance protection. Of that only $215 billion was reinsured by primary insurers. Approximately $165 billion of the reinsured amount came from property and casualty coverage with $65 billion focused on protection against peak risk and $18 billion for specific natural

---

[5] *Ibid.*

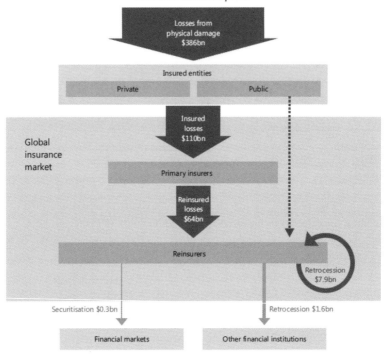

Figure 11.4. Catastrophe Risk Transfer in 2011.[6]

Note: The size of the arrows is proportional to the volume of losses caused by natural catastrophes in 2011. Reinsured losses are estimated from the average reinsurance share of insured peak losses for major natural catastrophes (0.6 * $106 billion = $64 billion). In line with this estimate, seven of the 10 largest reinsurance companies, accounting for about 40% of the market, declared a combined $26.4 billion in catastrophe-related losses in their 2011 annual reports. Losses transferred via retrocession are estimated by apportioning insured losses in proportion to the premium payments the ultimate bearers received in 2011. The loss-sharing with financial markets comes from a triggered catastrophe bond.

catastrophe contracts. Reinsurers then purchased protection from other reinsurers (a concept known as retrocession) and hedge funds

---

[6] *Ibid.*

to the tune of $25 billion. As the figure illustrates, securitization through catastrophe bonds still accounts for a small fraction of the total market.

Attempts to Address the Need for Additional Capital

The Reinsurance Market and the Establishment of Bermuda as a Market Center

The reinsurance market

The reinsurance industry's primary function is to mitigate peak risks associated with natural catastrophes held by primary insurers. Reinsurers are able to mitigate this risk by purchasing a broad portfolio or risk types across a variety of locations under the assumption that natural catastrophes are largely uncorrelated one-off events. Reinsurers also use time as a form of diversification since premiums are collected over many years while payments on claims are paid out over a period of months. This accumulation of premium payments that are not immediately used to pay claims are invested in assets and held for claims expected to occur in the future. While this allows reinsurers to create gains from their investments it also exposes them to the ups and downs of the broader financial markets. As can be seen in Figure 11.5, the 2008 global financial crises resulted in a 59% decline in the share prices of insurance companies. Compare this to years 2005 and 2011 when reinsurers recorded record high catastrophe losses and it becomes plainly evident that reinsurer's biggest risks may not be those they have written policies for.[7]

---

[7] *Ibid.*

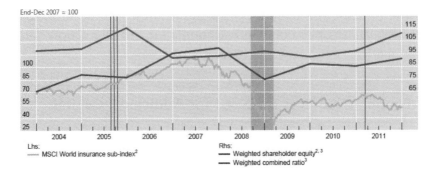

End-Dec 2007 = 100

Lhs:
----- MSCI World insurance sub-index[2]

Rhs:
—— Weighted shareholder equity[2, 3]
—— Weighted combined ratio[3]

Figure 11.5. Reinsurance Industry Financial Indicators.[8]

Notes: [1]The vertical lines indicate the dates of Hurricanes Katrina (29 August 2005), Rita (24 September 2005), and Wilma (22 October 2005), and the Great East Japan earthquake and tsunami (11 March 2011). The shaded area represents the period between the Lehman Brothers bankruptcy (15 September 2008) and the equity market trough (9 March 2009). [2]The MSCI insurance sub-index and shareholder equity are rebased; 31 December 2007 = 100. The combined ratio weighted is in percent. [3]Ten largest companies, excluding Berkshire Hathway and Reinsurance Group of America, weighted by their yearly respective market share in gross premium income. The combined ratio expresses losses plus expenses as a share premium income.

Is Typhoon Haiyan a once in a hundred years event or...

Perhaps somewhat surprisingly, failures of reinsurance companies have been fairly limited (see Figure 11.6). That said, an event like Typhoon Haiyan in November 2013 hitting a major city like New York or London could likely put many reinsurance companies in peril. Typhoon Haiyan was a Category 5 super typhoon believed to be the strongest ever recorded, which devastated parts of Southeast Asia, killing well over 5,000 people, and caused significant damage in the Philippines, China, Vietnam, Taiwan, and other nearby countries. It is estimated that 12% of the natural catastrophe-related risk accepted by the reinsurance industry is transferred to other reinsurers which implies that the majority of the risk is retained

---

[8] *Ibid.*

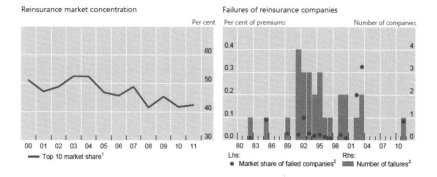

Figure 11.6. Reinsurance Market Concentration and Failures.[9]
Notes: [1] Market share of the 10 largest reinsurance companies, measured as a share of gross premiums written by reinsurance companies worldwide in the non-life (property and casualty) business. [2] In relation to total market size as measured by gross premiums written (premiums ceded by insurers to reinsurance companies). [3] Number of failures of reinsurance companies worldwide, per calendar year.

by the industry as opposed to mitigated through other financial instruments outside the industry.

The establishment of Bermuda as a market center

Bermuda is home to over half of the major global reinsurance companies and is considered to be a global hub and thought leader of the insurance industry. As of 2012, Bermuda is home to 1,400 insurance companies with total assets of $442 billion.[10] This is primarily due to Bermuda's favorable tax structure — there is no tax on corporate profits — as well as a relatively stable political and economic environment.

Reinsurance offers insurance companies a way to further spread risk, provide financing, and increase the amount of coverage they can provide. Primary insurers pass on some of the risk they incur from writing homeowners or auto policies to another insurer or reinsurer. Reinsurers sometimes then pass on or retrocede this risk to additional reinsurers in an effort to further spread risk.

---

[9] *Ibid.*

[10] ILS Flock to the BSX. Bermuda Re/insurance (Spring 2012); available online at <http://www.bermudareinsurancemagazine.com/article/ils-flock-to-the-bsx>.

In the early 1960s, "captive" insurance companies — those owned by large companies to insure their employees — began to establish themselves in Bermuda. As the number of captives grew, Bermuda began to establish infrastructure that allowed the insurance industry to grow. The Insurance Act of 1978 was passed and the Insurance Advisory Committee, a group of insurance companies who advise the government of Bermuda on matters related to the industry, was formed.

As Hurricanes Hugo and Andrew awoke the insurance and reinsurance industries from their multi-century lull, new companies were created to address the need for additional capital. This realignment of the reinsurance industry resulted in the formation of numerous Bermuda-based companies beginning with Mid Ocean Reinsurance in 1992. Prior to this, there were no reinsurance companies that specialized in property catastrophe reinsurance. But while additional capital was injected into the industry through new reinsurance companies, it was clear that the industry would need to move to non-traditional sources of financing in order to access additional risk capital. Catastrophe bonds would become one such source. As these new financing instruments evolved, so would investors with the emergence of dedicated CAT funds.

Bermuda Stock Exchange (BSX)

The BSX is the world's largest offshore, fully electronic exchange offering listings and trading opportunities for international and domestic issuers of equity, debt, depository receipts, insurance securitization, and derivative warrants. As of May 2013, the total volume of insurance-linked listings, which includes catastrophe bonds and reinsurance-linked investment funds, on the BSX exceeded $7.06 billion.[11]

---

[11] ARTEMIS, "Over $7 Billion ILS and CAT Bonds Listed on Bermuda Stock Exchange for First Time." www.artemis.com (May 2013); available online at http://www.artemis.bm/blog/2013/05/21/over-7-billion-ils-and-cat-bonds-listed-on-bermuda-stock-exchange-for-first-time/.

Catastrophe Bonds

A catastrophe bond, or a "CAT bond", is a fixed income instrument where the payment of the coupon or the return of the principal of the bond or both is linked to the occurrence of a specified catastrophic event. CAT bonds have become the primary way of spreading insured catastrophe risk to the capital markets (see Figure 11.7). The issuers, or sponsors, typically include insurance and reinsurance companies, corporations, and government agencies, and the investors are generally large institutional investors, hedge funds, pension funds, bond funds, and other insurance and reinsurance companies.

CAT bonds along with industry loss warranties, side cars,[12] and collateralized reinsurance[13] are collectively referred to as alternative

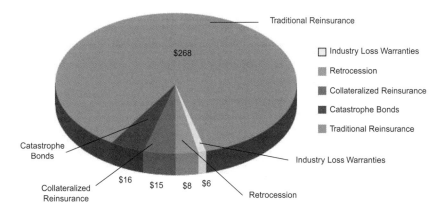

Figure 11.7. Global Property Catastrophe Reinsurance by Source (U.S.\$ Billion).[14]
Source: Guy Carpenter (2014).

---

[12]Sidecars allow investors to work alongside insurance companies by purchasing a portion of an insurance policy written by the insurer. This allows investors to share in the profits or losses from the insurance policy.

[13]Collateralized reinsurance is a privately structured security that allows investors to gain exposure to the traditional reinsurance market.

[14]Guy Carpenter, "Capital Stewardship: Charting the Course to Profitable Growth." *Marsh & McLennan Companies* (September 2013); available online at http://www.guycarp.com/content/dam/guycarp/en/documents/dynamic-content/Mid-Year-Market-Overview-Sept-2013.pdf.

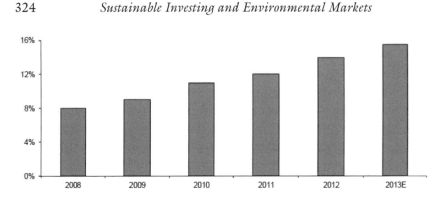

Figure 11.8. Growth In Alternative Capacity as a Percentage of Global Property Catastrophe Reinsurance Limit.

capacity. This group of instruments of which CAT bonds is the largest, has grown steadily (see Figure 11.8) and is predicted to reach $100 billion by 2018 according to broker Aon.

As opportunities in alternative capacity have grown, so too have entrants into the market. Figure 11.9 provides a timeline of entrants and developments in alternative capacity. While not all of the development has been in CAT bonds, they have certainly been the driving factor.

CAT bonds emerged in the 1990s in response to the large-scale economic impacts resulting from several U.S. hurricanes. The bonds are rated by ratings agencies and sold through investment banks much the way traditional bonds are rated and sold. CAT bonds are created as Special Purpose Vehicles (SPV) usually domiciled in Bermuda or the Cayman Islands. The SPV has a reinsurance agreement with the sponsor. Investors purchase the bonds through primary issuances. The proceeds from the bond sale are deposited into a trust account. The sponsor will deposit a premium payment to a trust account. The proceeds from the bond sale and the premium from the sponsor are typically invested in treasury money market accounts. Quarterly, the investors are paid interest from the money invested and a portion of the premium in the form of coupons. If the events characterized in the CAT bond prospectus were to occur, the SPV would release the collateral held in the trust account owned by the SPV to the sponsor.

Since capital markets have such a large capacity to absorb risk, CAT bonds have become a useful tool for insurers to diversify their capital base from other entities that may have a portfolio concentrated on catastrophe risk, such as reinsurers. Additionally, since the credit crisis, capital market participants and institutional capital have viewed CAT bonds as a diversifying asset class given its gains and losses are not directly tied with that of the financial markets. The diversification benefits of including these instruments in investment portfolios have been supported by a number of notable studies. Cummins and Weiss (2009), for example, measured the correlation between the investment performance of CAT bonds with that of various bond instruments and indices. The results for the period preceding the global financial crisis (January 2002 to June 2007) show almost no correlations between CAT bond returns and these other investments (see Figure 11.9).

CAT bonds are often viewed as inherently risky in part because of their binary nature. Their payoffs are usually tied to either an indemnity trigger, index trigger, or a parametric trigger (see ILW section). An indemnity trigger is the actual loss incurred by the insurer after an event has taken place, in a pre-specified geographic region and line of business, e.g., Illinois snowstorm with damages in excess of $20 million, between 1 January 2013 to 1 February 2014. If the catastrophe for which the bond is written occurs, then the buyer may lose their entire investment. Although the likelihood of that particular catastrophe occurring is remote, the downside is clearly substantial. If the catastrophe does not occur, then the insurance company pays the buyer a pre-specified rate of return.

The first CAT bond was issued in 1995. The market saw several CAT bond issuances in 1996 and 1997 involving sponsors and underwriters from both the U.S. and abroad that covered numerous types of perils including earthquakes, wind, hail, aviation, marine, and others, and ranged over a wide geography.

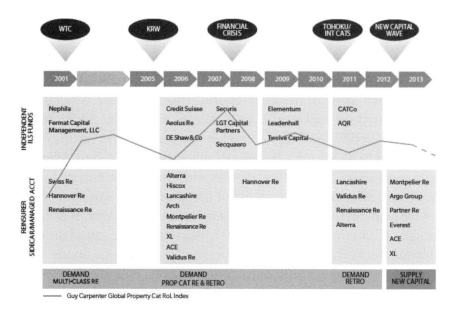

Figure 11.9. Alternative Capacity Development: 2001 to 2013.[15]

CAT bonds issuances have grown steadily since their inception 15 years ago. However, some would note that given the size of insured losses in recent years, the amount is still rather small. Figure 11.10 shows the growth in issuance over time and provides a break down by type of issuance over the last 10 years.

CAT bonds have the advantage of being able to replicate a traditional reinsurance contract. This has played a role in the popularity of CAT bonds with insurance companies. The inherent flexibility of CAT bonds also means that they can be tailored to fit the bond sponsors' specific needs. Additionally, since CAT bonds are fully collateralized from inception, unlike most traditional reinsurance agreements, the sponsors and investors can mitigate counterparty credit risk. In part as a result of increased investor demand, CAT bond spreads, or the amount the insurer pays investors to take on the risk, has decreased significantly as of the time of writing.

---

[15]Carpenter (2013), *op. cit.*

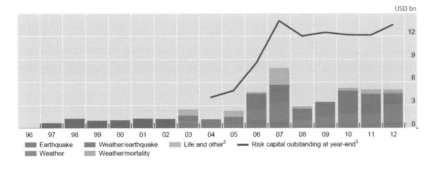

Figure 11.10. Catastrophe Bond Issuance by Type of Risk.[16]

Industry Loss Warranties, Index-Based Insurance, and Swaps (ILWs)

Unlike traditional (re)insurance policies, which are contracts of indemnification, Industry Loss Warranties (ILWs) are contracts for differences. The pay-off of a contract of indemnity is based on the damage done to a tangible asset, i.e., the insurance company pays the insured for any realized losses. On the other hand, the pay-off of a contract for differences is based on an event, such as a change in the market price of an asset. In the case of an ILW, when the market price rises, the buyer is rewarded and vice versa. For example, a reinsurance company could offer a policy that was event-based. An earthquake in the City of San Francisco with a magnitude of 7.0 on the Richter scale would trigger the policy payment. The payment would be based on the premium to be paid by the insurance company. Assuming the San Francisco scenario described above, the reinsurance policy would simply state a $200,000 premium for $10 million in coverage. The $10 million would be paid if a previously

---

[16]Three things can be noted: (1) Data before 2003 are not broken down by type. (2) Includes mortality, peril, life, and worldwide risks. (3) Values for 2012 are partial-year. *Source*: Sebastian von Dahlen and Goetz von Peter, "*Natural Catastrophes and Global Reinsurance — Exploring the Linkages*." Data: Artemis, Guy Carpenter.

approved verifier reported an earthquake in a pre-determined geographical area of 7.0 or higher magnitude. The premium would be a function the probability of the event occurring plus an additional consideration for the credit risk associated with the parties involved and a further premium necessary to attract buyers.

ILWs are another way the capital markets have assumed the catastrophe risk of the (re)insurance industry. A distinguishing feature of ILWs is the use of an industry loss index or parametric index as a trigger for the payout.[17] The industry loss index most commonly used in the United States is calculated by Property Claims Service (PCS). PCS industry loss estimates are based on a survey of industry representatives such as insurers and emergency managers. Other indexes or data sets used are Munich Re NatCatSERVICE, Carvill Hurricane Index, PERILS, and Swiss Re sigma.[18] Unlike the industry loss trigger, parametric triggers are based on the physical characteristics of a catastrophic event, such as the San Francisco example given above. However, since parametric triggers are not based on insured losses, the insured may not receive the precise loss amount resulting from a catastrophic event.[19] It should be noted that some CAT bonds are also triggered by industry losses and catastrophe parameters. The next section discusses parametric insurance in further detail.

As seen from above, ILW contracts are typically framed in terms of geographical location, type of event (windstorm, earthquake), magnitude of event, line of business, and the time period in which the event occurs. In general, the payout of an ILW is triggered when the insured losses from an event exceed a predefined level outlined in the ILW Agreement. Typically, the trigger is the insured losses reported by the insurance industry in response to a particular or a series of catastrophic events that occur in a given time period. The

---

[17] ILWs can also feature a dual trigger design that includes a protection buyer indemnity trigger.

[18] "Industry Loss Warranties: The Basics." de Burca PLLC (August 2011); available online at http://www.jdsupra.com/documents/9eae29ba-0249-46d3-86b9-711cea275007.pdf.

[19] "CAT Bonds Demystified: RMS Guide to the Asset Class." (2012); available online at https://support.rms.com/Publications/CAT_Bonds_Demystified.pdf.

seller of the ILW, typically a reinsurer, is paid a premium by the buyer with the understanding that if the triggering event occurs, the buyer will receive a payout of a pre-specified loss payment from the seller. A classic ILW takes the form of a bilateral reinsurance contract, but there are also index products that take the form of derivatives or exchange-traded instruments.

ILWs have been in existence since the 1980s and have gained traction due to their relative simplicity. Because the payout is triggered by an index tracking losses to all the insurers with exposure to a catastrophe, it allows the investor to focus on the quality of the index rather than having to conduct due diligence on the underwriting criteria of a particular insurer. This allows for ILWs to more easily be standardized. The downside to this standardization is the basis risk[20] associated with the instrument. Often the ILW does not correlate well with the potential losses of the insurer and can therefore be seen as less desirable when compared to alternatives such as catastrophe bonds.

Although there is no centralized database for pricing and volume of ILWs, some reinsurance companies and researchers publish estimates. Figure 11.11 presents estimates for ILW capacity and premiums (also known as Rate on Line (ROL)). As Figure 11.11 shows, the ILW market is nearing record highs for both price and volume in 2012.

Parametric or index-based insurance

As described above, parametric or index-based insurance products are those that use a weather or geological event or index to trigger the payment or settlement of a contract. Examples include protection of crop losses from pre-specified temperature or rainfall

---

[20]The CFTC Glossary defines basis risk as: "Basis is the difference between the spot or cash price of a commodity and the price of the nearest futures contract for the same or a related commodity (typically calculated as cash minus futures). Basis is usually computed in relation to the futures contract next to expire and may reflect different time periods, product forms, grades, or locations. Basis risk refers to the risk associated with an unexpected widening or narrowing of the basis between the time a hedge position is established and the time it is lifted."

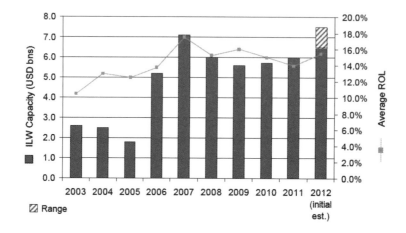

Figure 11.11. ILW Capacity and Premiums.

Source: Willis Re.

conditions and protection of property losses from earthquakes of a pre-specified intensity. In each case, the insurance payouts from a parametric or index-based insurance contract are determined by an index rather than the losses of individual policy holders. This means that the actual losses of the insured may not match with payouts made by the insurance company since the index serves as a proxy for losses and not actual losses. The difference between the indexed losses and actual losses is commonly referred to as basis risk.

The concept of index-based or parametric insurance has been around for over 60 years but was only implemented more recently in the 1990s. In recent history, Lloyds of London had policies for maritime insurance called tonners which set out the global gross tonnage loss by ships for a year. If this loss level exceeded, the policy paid out. Interestingly, these policies were banned in the early 1980s because they were viewed as a form of gambling since the premium paid could be seen as a wager on a particular event occurring.[21] Despite this early setback, index-based products have found some traction. There are several advantages to index-based

---

[21] Peter Green, " 'Tonner' Policies." *Lloyd's* (June 1981); available online at http://www. lloyds.com/~/media/Files/The%20Market/Communications/Market%20Bulletins/Market%20bulletins%20pre%2005%202010/1990_1999/2192.pdf.

or parametric insurance over traditional models. Firstly, because the indemnifications are triggered by an index such as rainfall amounts or wind speed, and not the losses of individual policy holders, there is no need for on the ground assessments of damages to crops, property, etc. This allows insurance companies to administer index insurance at a lower cost than traditional insurance products. Additionally, since the insurance is based on a third-party verifiable index, it allows insurers to share the risk with reinsurance companies. Index-based insurance also cuts down on the problems of moral hazard and adverse selection by providing all buyers of the insurance product with the same indemnity and premium per unit purchased.

Despite these positive attributes, index-insurance saw fairly slow initial uptake due to several disadvantages relative to traditional insurance models. These disadvantages often include basis risk, questions about the reliability of the index, and lastly the need to build capacity and educate potential participants on how a new insurance product will work. Index-insurance can also be more data intensive in some cases. When data regarding rainfall, wind, earthquakes, or other perils is scarce, index-insurance can be difficult to implement. Index insurance also requires significant financial resources and technical expertise to develop. In order to launch a product, insurers must first engage in research and development, build capacity at the local level, raise awareness, and market the offering, in addition to offering increased access to data.[22]

While the initial implementation of index-based insurance products was not as quick as some had hoped, the use of index-based insurance products has grown rapidly in recent years. Two areas in particular that have shown promise are index-based insurance for disaster relief and development purposes. In the context of disaster relief, index-based insurance could protect people against catastrophic losses and help to save lives by allowing the delivery of

---

[22]International Fund for Agricultural Development and World Food Programme, "The Potential for Scale and Sustainability in Weather Index Insurance for Agriculture and Rural Livelihoods." (March 2010); available online at http://www.ifad.org/ruralfinance/pub/weather.pdf.

aid via insurance payments as a quicker, more cost-effective response to a catastrophe. Index-based insurance for development purposes can help protect small scale farmers or business owners from income fluctuation caused by weather or geologic risk. Table 11.2 gives an overview of the applicability of index-based insurance for disaster relief and development purposes in small, medium, and large size participants. Following Table 11.2 is a real world example of an index-based insurance product in Mexico.

Case study: Agroasemex in Mexico[23]

In 2002, Mexico piloted a catastrophe risk insurance product for farmers based on weather indexes. Prior to the implementation of this program, poor rural farmers lacked access to agricultural insurance and would receive disaster relief in the case of a natural disaster. This disaster relief came from the Ministry of Agriculture's Programa de Atencion a Contingencias Climatologicas (PACC). Farmers traditionally lacked risk management tools for catastrophes outside of crop rotation and diversification along with borrowing funds from friends and family when disaster struck.

The PACC program was funded by state and federal tax revenues and was seen as financially unsustainable. The introduction of the index-based insurance program was an attempt to improve the use and distribution of funds to farmers. The initial pilot was implemented in Guanajuato State on 75,000 hectares of corn and sorghum. The product was based on a rainfall index and was a protection against drought for the farmers that were covered. The program was run by Agroasemex, which is a government owned rural insurer and reinsurer. A second pilot was conducted in 2003 on 107,600 hectares of corn and sorghum with data collected from six weather stations in the region. The second pilot insured a total of U.S.$3.5 million with $338,000 in gross premiums.

---

[23] *Ibid.*

Table 11.2. Index-based Insurance for Disaster Relief and Development, and the Various Beneficiaries.[24]

	Index insurance for disaster relief	Index insurance for development
Macro		
Government	Government protects itself against shocks: early liquidity/first relief outlays	Government reinsures insurers
Relief agency	Funds its operations through an index-based risk-transfer contract or provides coverage through an index trigger contingent voucher	
Meso		
Financial Service Provider (FSP)	Government could use banks, FSPs, input suppliers, farmers' associations, and NGOs to distribute vouchers for catastrophe insurance	FSP buys portfolio insurance or group insurance to retail to farmers, linked to credit
Farmer association		Farmers' association buys group insurance to retail to farmers, linked to credit
Input supplier		Input supplier buys group insurance to retail to farmers, linked to input purchases
NGO		NGO buys group insurance to retail to farmers
Micro		
Farmer	Farmer receives explicit, redeemable, predictable coverage against a well-defined shock, and the premium is paid for mostly by government	Farmer buys insurance as part of a package (e.g., credit and other financial services, technology, agricultural information)

[24] *Ibid.*

In the following years, the program continued to expand. Agroasemex extended coverage to beans and barley and included regions in Puebla State. By 2008, six years after the initial pilot, the program had expanded from 75,000 hectares to 1.9 million hectares and 800,000 low income farmers with $132.5 million insured and premiums of $22 million (see Table 11.3).

For many index-based insurance products in the developing world, demand from the poor is often low. Product participation is often subsidized by governments, multilateral institutions, or non-governmental organizations. In the case of Mexico, the insurance product is sold to the federal and state government, who decides whom to cover under their policy. They target small scale, low income rural farmers who are most likely to be impacted by drought and excess moisture. Municipalities with high numbers of poor farmers receive a 90% subsidy for their premiums and areas with low to medium levels of poor farmers receive 70% subsidization.

Payouts to farmers are triggered by pre-specified drought or excess rainfall conditions (see Table 11.4). The payouts vary depending on the type of crop grown with a maximum payment of $410 for farmers growing annual and perennial crops and $2,275 for high value crops (see Table 11.5).

Swaps

Another way of spreading catastrophe risk to the capital markets is through swaps. Broadly speaking, a swap is the exchange of cash flows. A swap allows an insurer to gain exposure to the portfolio of returns of an investor while the investor gains exposure to the revenues associated with the premiums received by the insurer. Each party provides a series of periodic payments to the other. The insurer's payments are based on a portfolio of the investor's securities while the investor's payments are based on potential catastrophe losses predicted by an industry loss index. Two insurers can also engage in a swap. For example, Swiss Re can exchange part of its North Atlantic hurricane and European windstorm risks for Mitsui

Table 11.3. Index Insurance Evolution in Mexico (2003–2008).[25]

Annual crops	2003	2004	2005	2006	2007	2008
Policy terms (amounts in U.S.$; area in ha)						
Premium rate	10%	12%	15%	12%	13%	16%
Sum insured	32.8	68.2	51.8	56.1	54.3	70.2
Portfolio						
Total number of policies sold	12	40	259	393	295	407
Total number of farmers covered	47,000	108,000	478,000	600,000	650,000	800,000
Total surface area	108,000	248,000	1,160,000	1,418,000	1,519,000	1,903,000
Weather stations	6	25	185	196	170	251
Total gross premiums	338,000	2,082,000	9,142,000	9,367,000	10,497,000	21,779,000
Total net premiums earned	338,700	1,630,000	5,602,000	7,026,000	4,380,000	13,104,000
Total sum insured	3,532,000	16,942,000	60,115,000	79,577,000	82,522,000	132,562,000
Reinsurance						
Reinsurance premiums paid	—	451,000	3,540,000	2,341,000	6,118,000	8,676,000
Total proportional reinsurance (sum insured)	—	4,210,000	23,280,000	19,886,000	47,857,000	52,805,000
Performance						
Claims (payouts)	—	—	9,553,000	1,957,000	3,675,000	7,653,000
Loss ratio (claims/gross premiums)	0%	0%	104%	21%	35%	35%
Agency costs	46,000	220,000	781,000	1,035,000	1,073,000	1,723,000

Source: AGROASEMEX.

[25] International Fund for Agricultural Development and World Food Programme (2010), *op. cit.*

Table 11.4. Minimum and Maximum Triggers for all States for Drought and Excess Rainfall (2008).[26]

	Sowing	Flowering	Harvest
Drought triggers (rainfall in mm)			
Corn	29–66	49–239	26–180
Bean	26–58	45–107	24–128
Barley	35	97–140	39–52
Sorghum	36–37	54–97	29–34
Excess rainfall triggers (rainfall in mm)			
Corn	n/a	280–1,514	189–1,095
Sorghum	n/a	351–924	272–738

Note: Rainfall amounts outside of these ranges trigger the payout.

Table 11.5. Support given to Farmers through PACC.[27]

Type of crop/type of farmer	Amount of support	Surface area subject to support
Annual: Farmers with less than 20 ha	U.S.$82/ha	Up to 5 ha per producer
Perennial: Farmers with less than 5 ha		
Fruit, coffee, nopal: Farmers with less than 5 ha	U.S.$455/ha	

Source: PACC operational guidelines.

Sumitomo Insurance Company's Japanese typhoon exposure.[28] These are high-risk events for both companies and by swapping segments of it, both insurance companies can diversify their risks.

[26] *Ibid.*
[27] *Ibid.*
[28] J. David Cummins, "CAT Bonds and Other Risk-Linked Securities: State of the Market and Recent Developments" (19 November 2007).

Weather Derivatives

The discussion will now move from instruments that are generally traded over-the-counter to those traded on transparent, regulated exchanges.

Catastrophic insurance futures and options

The first catastrophic insurance futures contracts were launched by the Chicago Board of Trade (CBOT) in 1992. The basis of these futures was an index tracking the losses of almost 25 property and casualty insurers, who reported their loss data quarterly to the Insurance Services Office, Inc., a company that provides data on property/casualty insurance risk. As the first futures contract designed to mitigate other risks besides price and interest rate risk, catastrophe futures were considered too novel at the time and were not met with enthusiasm by insurance companies. The CBOT eventually changed this futures contract to a simpler cash option, which had the advantage of resembling an insurance contract. At the height of its success, catastrophe options had an open interest of 20,000 contracts. However, the options contract eventually floundered and was delisted in 1999. Since then, other exchanges including Insurance Futures Exchange (IFEX), Chicago Mercantile Exchange (CME), and EUREX have introduced variations of the catastrophe derivatives. However, none of these has received significant traction due to a variety of factors including basis risk, the lack of continuous information flow needed to support trading, and lack of education and marketing efforts.

Weather derivatives provide another means to hedge the risks associated with natural disasters or more mundane weather events, such as erratic rain/snowfall patterns. They are especially important because more than a third of total U.S. economic growth is linked to weather conditions, according to the Commerce Department figures.

Weather derivatives began in the mid-1990s, a time when energy and utility companies in the U.S. began to deregulate. The increased competition created an incentive for these companies to hedge their risk exposure in order to stabilize their earnings. Since weather conditions had a very tangible impact on energy demand, OTC weather deals between these companies started emerging. But it was not until 1999 that the Chicago Mercantile Exchange began listing futures and options on temperature indices of 10 U.S. cities.[29] In 1998, the weather derivatives market was estimated to be a $500 million industry.[30] In 2011, this market had grown to $12 billion.[31] The following section will describe some of the most common weather derivatives today and some of their practical applications.

Heating and cooling degree days

A heating degree day (HDD) measures the amount of energy required to heat a building. Specifically, a HDD is the number of degrees that a day's average temperature is below 65° Fahrenheit — the temperature below which buildings generally need to be heated. A cooling degree day (CDD) does just the reverse, by measuring the number of degrees that a day's average temperature is above 65° Fahrenheit, when people typically start to use air conditioning to cool their buildings. Given the increased fluctuation in temperature over the years — a phenomenon commonly attributed to climate change — it is not surprising that exchanges have created weather derivatives in order to hedge these risks.

The Chicago Mercantile Exchange (CME) has two such contracts listed: The U.S. Seasonal Strip Weather Heating Degree Day (HDD) and the U.S. Seasonal Strip Weather Cooling Degree Day (CDD) futures and options. The price of the HDD and CDD futures are based on the CME Degree Days Index, which tracks the

[29] Melanie Cao, Anlong Li and Jason Zhanshun Wei, "Weather Derivatives: A New Class of Financial Instruments." Joseph L. Rotman School of Management University of Toronto. (January 2004); available online at http://www.yorku.ca/mcao/cao_wei_weather_CIR.pdf.

[30] According to a 2000 paper for the Wharton Financial Institutions Center co-authored by Francis X. Diebold, Center Co-Director.

[31] PricewaterhouseCoopers, "Resilience: Winning with risk. A Journal of Strategy and Risk." (2013); available online at http://www.pwc.com/en_GX/gx/governance-risk-compliance-consulting-services/resilience/issue3/assets/pwc-harnessing-financial-innovation.pdf.

total number of HDDs or CDDs in the month. Their settlement prices are calculated by summing up these HDD and CDD values for a month and then multiplying them by $20. These instruments can help entities with weather exposure, e.g., individual companies and utilities, better manage their risk exposure to fluctuating temperature.

Other weather derivatives

Although utilities constitute the majority of the end-users of HDD/CDD contracts, there are many other businesses whose revenues are tied to the weather such as insurance, agriculture, and even ski resorts. Weather-related risks for agriculture may include rainfall levels, hurricanes, wind, and hail while ski resorts may be concerned about a lack of snow. While weather derivative instruments for each of these risks exist, they are not all traded as standardized contracts on an exchange like HDD and CDD, but are instead executed over-the-counter.

Weather-related investable indices

In recent years, banks have introduced a growing number of products that aim to encourage a broader range of investors to bet on the effects of a changing climate, namely, the impact of carbon emissions and rising global temperatures. In 2007, UBS launched a global warming index, and in the following year it launched the world's first integrated tradable investment benchmark that tracks the greenhouse effect. The latter comprises a combination of weather (CME Heating and Cooling Day futures) and emissions asset classes (EUA and CER futures traded on Intercontinental-Exchange and Nordpool, respectively) and allows market players to gain exposure to greenhouse gas emissions and their impact on the weather. The level of the index will rise as the price of carbon emissions credits and global temperatures rise. Both retail and institutional investors will be able to go long or short the UBS Greenhouse

Index in the same way they would the Dow Jones stock market indices.[32]

Weather funds

There are currently a number of specific weather funds investing in the derivatives market. An example is the Cumulus Energy Fund. By concentrating on specific weather events important to energy trading, such as temperature, snowfall, rainfall, and wind, the hedge fund is able to provide investors with exposure to weather risks they may not find in more traditional funds.[33] Another example is the Nimbus fund, which is a $2.5 billion-plus fund based in Bermuda and run by Nephila[34] that invests in weather derivatives along with catastrophic-risk insurance.

Conclusion

In 2011, the United Nations estimates natural disasters to cost the world a record figure of more than $380 billion. According to a report by Swiss Re, total economic damage from disasters — naturally occurring or otherwise — is estimated to be at least $140 billion in 2012. Hurricane Sandy alone was estimated to have inflicted between $30–$50 billion worth of damages, the second-most expensive storm in U.S. history after Hurricane Katrina ($125 billion). In 2011, the size of policy holder surplus for the U.S. insurance and reinsurance industries were $550.3 billion and $108 billion, respectively, to insure all of the property and casualty risk of a $15.6 trillion economy. A single catastrophic event

[32]"UBS Investment Bank Launches UBS Greenhouse Index." Media Releases EMEA. (10 January 2008); available online at http://www.ubs.com/global/en/about_ubs/media/global/releases/news_display_media_global.html/en/2008/01/10/ubs_investment_bank_launches_ubs_greenhouse_index.html.

[33]ARTEMIS, "Cumulus Weather & Energy Funds Transferred to City Financial Energy Fund Profits in 2012." www.artemis.bm (January 2013); available online at http://www.artemis.bm/blog/2013/01/11/cumulus-weather-energy-funds-transferred-to-city-financial-energy-fund-profits=in-2012/.

[34]Nephilia; available online at http://www.nephila.com/.

striking major wealth centers, such as California, Florida, Texas, or New York, could have wiped out the entire capital of the U.S. insurance and reinsurance sectors. Had Hurricane Katrina hit New Orleans more directly, the consequences would have been unthinkable. It should be clear then, there are tremendous opportunities for weather-related and insurance-linked securities to help shift some of these risks to the wider capital markets.

Most of the trends discussed so far can be summarized in the growth of sustainable investing in recent years. Companies and investors have to pay closer attention to how environmental and sustainability issues in air, water, and food affect stock performance. The penultimate chapter will provide an assessment of the trends and developments in sustainability as it relates to capital markets, mostly equities.

Chapter 12

SUSTAINABILITY AND ASSOCIATED ASSET CLASSES

The focus of previous chapters has been on emissions markets, user rights, and other environmental derivatives as asset classes. We then discussed investment opportunities associated with these individual asset classes. We took a bottom-up view of environmental finance. The primary focus of this chapter is a top-down view of portfolio investments that are termed "sustainable."

Sustainability investing (SI), or socially responsible investing (SRI) as it is often referred to in the United States, denotes any investment strategy that seeks to consider environmental and social considerations as well as financial return. Sustainability, viewed as an investment philosophy, has led to the development of an asset class of portfolio investments (typically, stocks and bonds) that are consistent with this philosophy. We focus specifically on portfolios of equities that reflect environmental criteria. We do not provide an exhaustive view but, rather, an overview of this important and growing investment strategy.

Since 1996, assets managed under the banner of SI have grown from $166 billion to more than $3 trillion in the United States alone — a 19% compound annual growth rate.[1] Externalities, particularly environmental externalities, are gradually being reflected in equity investments. This trend is complemented

---

[1]U.S. SIF, "2012 Report on Sustainable and Responsible Investing Trends in the United States." (2012); available online at http://www.ussif.org/trends.

by a management emphasis on sustainability and by increased transparency in corporate environmental disclosures. The undeveloped "social stock exchanges," which connect social projects and businesses with investors, that now exist could evolve to provide a marketplace for sustainable investment financial asset classes. In addition, a breed of investment popularly called "impact investment" is emerging, that ties investment returns to actual social and environmental performance criteria. Investors must learn to navigate this new investment landscape and adapt accordingly.

Overview of Sustainability Investing

Prior to the mid-1990s, the use of environmental and social criteria in investment decision making consisted almost entirely of SRI screens. These screens identify sectors in which investors choose not to invest — that is, companies or industries that are engaged in activities the investor deems harmful to society. Ethical investing was popularized during the Vietnam War with the establishment of the Pax World Fund, the first socially-screened mutual fund. It offered an alternative investment option to those opposed to weapons production. This movement became globalized in the 1970s through the Sullivan Principles, which underpinned an international effort to end apartheid in South Africa.[2]

As SI evolved, it began to use not only values-driven negative screens but also positive investment choices designed to encourage environmentally friendly business practices and maximize financial return in a socially responsible framework. Another significant development between early and modern forms of SI was the growth of shareholder activism. In the 2000s, academics and investors began to place increasing emphasis on the importance of good corporate

---

[2]The Sullivan Principles were formed by the African-American preacher Rev. Leon Sullivan. They later grew in popularity among U.S. corporations. New global Sullivan Principles were established by Rev. Sullivan and United Nations Secretary General Kofi Annan in 1999. They advocated the expansion of corporate social responsibility in all that concerns human rights and social justice regardless of national boundaries.

governance in a company's risk-and-return profile, a trend partially driven by the Sarbanes–Oxley Act of 2002.

As SI evolved, so did analysts' ability to screen companies on the basis of environmental and social criteria. Early practitioners operated primarily as niche players, but many of today's largest institutional investors use sustainability principles.

Just as corporations are adopting sustainable business practices to increase their "triple bottom line" (or positive impact on shareholders, other human stakeholders, and the natural environment), investors are pushing for greater integration of sustainability principles in their investment analyses.[3] The object is to *increase* their financial returns, not sacrifice financial return to pursue other goals. The result has been the promulgation of numerous environmental, social, and governance (ESG) measures in the mainstream investment market.[4]

Specifically, prescient investors have started to incorporate climate change and other environmental risks into their investment analyses to maximize financial return and reduce financial risks. Climate change is among the most important issues in today's sustainability universe. The physical risks of climate change — be they hurricanes, earthquakes, rising sea levels, or changes in the amount and location of arable land — together with political and regulatory shifts make it crucial for investors to factor climate change into their investment strategies.

Risks are not the only reason for SI. Exciting new opportunities await investors as sustainability becomes increasingly important. In particular, sustainability is emerging as a key driver of innovation

---

[3]The phrase "triple bottom line" was first coined in 1994 by John Elkington, who founded a British consultancy called SustainAbility. He argued that companies should be preparing three bottom lines: profit, people (a measure of how socially responsible the corporation is), and planet (a measure of how environmentally friendly it is).

[4]ESG denotes the three central factors used in measuring the sustainability and ethical impact of an investment in a company or business. Within these three areas are a broad set of concerns that are increasingly being included in the non-financial factors that figure in the valuation of equity, real estate, corporations, and fixed-income investments of all types. ESG is the catch-all term for the criteria used in SRI.

among existing corporations and startups. Rich investment opportunities are possible in the industries where innovations flourish, such as the clean technology sector.

Size and Key Drivers of the SI Market

In 2012, the U.S. SIF Foundation identified $3.74 trillion worth of assets that are either managed under ESG guidelines or held by investors who filed or co-filed shareholder resolutions on ESG issues at publicly traded companies.[5] The U.S. SIF Foundation started measuring the size of the U.S. sustainable investing market in 1995. By 2012, the assets in this space had increased by 486%. Table 12.1 shows the growth in this period.

According to the U.S. SIF Foundation 2012 report, the recent growth of SI has been driven by several factors:[6]

- The growing realization in the investment community that climate change and resource scarcity have tangible impacts on financial returns.
- Increasing demand from institutional and individual investors, together with the mission and values of their management firms. These factors are putting pressure on investment managers to incorporate ESG factors into their investment analysis and portfolio construction. According to the U.S. SIF 2012 survey, client demand and values were motivations cited by 72% of managers.
- The emergence of sustainability accounting standards. According to Trucost, an independent environmental research agency, annual "external" environmental costs (i.e., costs that do not appear on corporate financial statements) for 800 companies in

---

[5] U.S. SIF — formerly the Social Investment Forum — is the U.S. membership association for professionals, firms, institutions, and organizations engaged in sustainable and responsible investing; available online at http://ussif.org/.

[6] More information in "2012 Report on Sustainable and Responsible Investing Trends in the United States," *op. cit.*

Table 12.1. Sustainable and Responsible Investing in the United States, 1995–2012 ($ billions).

	1995	1997	1999	2001	2003	2005	2007	2010	2012
ESG	166	533	1,502	2,018	2,157	1,704	2,123	2,554	3,314
Shareholder resolutions	473	736	922	897	448	703	739	1,497	1,536
Overlapping assets	—	−84	−265	−592	−441	−117	−151	−981	−1,106
Total	639	1,185	2,159	2,323	2,164	2,290	2,711	3,069	3,744

Notes: "Overlapping assets" involved in some combination of ESG incorporation (including community investing) and shareholder advocacy are subtracted to avoid potential double-counting. Separate tracking of the overlapping strategies began only in 1997, so no data are available for 1995. Prior to 2010, assets subject to ESG incorporation were limited to socially and environmentally screened assets.
Source: U.S. SIF Foundation.

11 industry sectors rose from $566 billion to $846 billion from 2002 to 2010.[7] Accordingly, the Sustainability Accounting Standards Board (SASB) was launched in 2012. This board established industry-specific sustainability accounting standards for use in 10-K and 20-F forms. These actions caused sustainability to become an issue for chief financial officers. It complements the Financial Accounting Standards Board, which developed the accounting principles currently used in U.S. financial reporting.

- Sustainability's increasing adoption by corporate top managers as a means to grow profits and gain competitive advantage. Walmart's chief executive officer, for example, hosts biannual meetings on sustainable practices for his leadership team. At one of the recent meetings, a report noted that Walmart now earns $230 million annually through its waste-management program.
- From 2010 to 2012, increased support by voters of corporate proxies on environmental and social resolutions. In that period, 30% of environmental and social issues resolutions won support, whereas the rate was 15–18% in 2007–2009.

Building a Sustainability Portfolio

Investors have many ways to invest in a portfolio of equities with a sustainability approach. Examples include portfolios that have been screened for ESG and independently tailored to investors, green mutual funds, and investable indices for corporate sustainability.

Following the 2008 financial crisis and the establishment of the SASB in 2011, focus on integrated reporting that combines financial and sustainability information has sharpened. Sustainability reporting involves measuring, disclosing, and being accountable to internal and external stakeholders for organizational performance in progress toward sustainable business practices. "Sustainability

---

[7]These data should be taken as indicative rather than absolute.

reporting" is a broad term considered synonymous with triple bottom line, corporate responsibility reporting, and other terms that are used to describe reporting on economic, environmental, and social impacts.

The most common way to assess a company's environmental risks and sustainability measures is to evaluate the company's corporate social responsibility (CSR) report. CSR reports provide information (primarily on an annual basis) on a company's performance as it relates to environmental, social, and governance criteria. A typical CSR report includes information on a company's human resources, management, and corporate governance (diversity, career training, health and safety, etc.); environmental impact (emissions, water use, waste processing and reuse, plant safety, etc.); and social awareness (community programs, sensitivity training and awareness, etc.). Companies may also set internal targets for these measures and report that performance. Although CSR scoring and internal goals may reveal ESG profiles, analysts are encouraged to look at other aspects of a company's actions to evaluate its social and environmental performance.

In the past, corporations set and followed their own standards and reporting formats in publishing CSR information. In recent years, however, efforts have begun to standardize the reporting criteria and the measurement and reporting formats. The Global Reporting Initiative (GRI) has developed standardized reporting and measurement criteria that make corporate sustainability reporting much like financial reporting. With a framework for sustainability reporting and the benefit of standardization, the GRI allows the creation of comparable and credible reports among organizations.[8] The SASB, an independent body outside the financial regulatory system, also aims to create new standards for companies in the system.

---

[8] The standardization process for sustainable criteria is in its initial stage. The number of social and environmental screening criteria and industry-specific criteria makes this process complex. Standards cannot be assumed to be scientific or statistically valid.

In addition to individual corporate reporting and disclosures, several organizations have taken the lead in the analysis and ranking of corporate performance with respect to sustainability and environmental accountability. Notable examples are the Carbon Disclosure Project and CERES. Although each organization has its own unique method, the general approach is similar — a survey questionnaire to gauge companies' sustainability attributes and rank them accordingly.

These organizations exemplify the clear trend toward an increased appetite for standardized measurement and increased transparency. In addition to evaluating general environmental risks, a growing number of customized analytical tools have been designed to evaluate specific environmental risks, such as those associated with water and energy sources.

Sustainability-Focused Mutual Funds

Sustainability approaches are making growing inroads into the management of mutual funds. One of the earliest mutual funds in this field was the Calvert Social Investment Fund (CSIF), established in 1982, which divested (refused to invest in) certain stocks to protest apartheid in South Africa. In 1986, CSIF became the first fund to sponsor a socially responsible shareholder resolution.

Sustainability-driven funds can focus on large-, medium-, or small-cap companies. Like other mutual funds, sustainability-focused mutual funds serve both individual and institutional investors, may involve several investment strategies, and usually invest in fixed-income or equity securities. Table 12.2 provides a sampling of sustainability-focused mutual funds.

Commonly, these funds have a special ESG focus. For example, the CRA Qualified Investment Fund invests in fixed-income securities that support community development activities, such as affordable housing, environmental initiatives, and small-business development. A different approach is taken by the Neuberger Berman Socially Responsive Fund, which screens

Table 12.2. A Sampling of Sustainability-Focused Mutual Funds.

Fund category/Name	Ticker
Large-cap equity	
Vanguard FTSE Social Index Fund	VFTSX
Neuberger Berman Socially Responsive Fund	NBSRX
Parnassus Equity Income Fund	PRBLX
Small- to mid-cap equity	
Parnassus Small-Cap Fund	PARSX
Equity specialty	
TIAA-CREF Social Choice Equity Premier	TRPSX
International equity	
Gabelli SRI Green Fund	SRIAX
Praxis International Index Fund	MPLAX
Balanced equity and fixed income	
PAX World Balanced Fund	PAXWX
Fixed income	
CRA Qualified Investment Fund	CRAIX

for companies that demonstrate leadership in the environment, workplace practices, community relations, supply chain sustainability, and product integrity. Some mutual funds also screen for companies' records in public health and the nature of their products; for example, they might actively avoid investing in companies that produce alcohol, tobacco, and military weapons, which are goods and services perceived to have especially undesired externalities.

The largest sustainability-focused mutual fund today, by assets under management, is the Parnassus Equity Income Fund. With close to $6 billion in assets, while it is still significantly smaller than the top mutual funds, it is one of the best-performing funds based on average 10-year return.

Other examples of sustainability-focused mutual funds today are Guinness Atkinson Alternative Energy and Firsthand Alternative Energy, both of which invest primarily in equity securities of companies that are involved in alternative energy or the energy technology sectors.

As of 2012, some 333 mutual fund products in the United States considered environmental, social, or corporate governance in their holdings. They had total assets of $640.5 billion. In contrast, only 55 SRI funds were available in 1995, with $12 billion in assets. The Forum for Sustainable and Responsible Investment regularly updates a comprehensive database of all U.S.-based green mutual funds and makes this information available to the public.[9]

Sustainability Equity Indices

In addition to sustainability-focused mutual funds, sustainability-focused equity indexing has emerged. Sustainability indices measure the financial performance of companies that meet various ESG criteria. These indices can be a proxy for the impact that sustainable practices have on shareholder value and, therefore, serve as key reference points for company managers and investors. In this respect, sustainable indices perform a function similar to that of such equity indices as the S&P 500 or the Dow Jones Industrial Average.

Two drivers led to the conception of indices for sustainability investment in the mid-1990s. First, investors recognized that corporate sustainability has a positive impact on long-term shareholder value. Second, investors became increasingly comfortable with the idea that environmental risks and the impact of sustainable practices can be measured and quantified.

Recently, the concept of sustainability indices has evolved to include other areas in environmental finance. Not only are there indices for specific environmental sectors, such as solar energy, but there are also indices for newly commoditized environmental assets, such as carbon allowances.[10]

---

[9]More information about U.S. SIF is available online at http://www.ussif.org/about.
[10]The World Federation of Exchanges provides an exhaustive list of sustainability indices; available online at http://www.world-exchanges.org/sustainability/WFE-ESG.pdf.

Generally, sustainability indices are constructed from the stock prices of companies that satisfy certain sustainability criteria. Such an index is the earliest form of sustainability index and probably the most common. Notable indices in this category are the Dow Jones Sustainability Indices (DJSI).

The first sustainability index was the Dow Jones Sustainability World Index (DJSI World), designed by Sustainable Asset Management and Dow Jones in 1999. Today, the DJSI family is used by investors around the world to manage sustainability-driven portfolios and used by companies to evaluate their sustainability performance. In fact, a growing number of companies have defined inclusion in a sustainability index as one of their corporate goals. Not only is this trend a robust indicator of the growing importance of corporate sustainability in the business community, it demonstrates the business community's heightened awareness that companies' environmental and social strategies are linked to their market and financial strategies.

The methodology for calculating, reviewing, and publishing the DJSI mirrors that of the Dow Jones Global Indices. Using the 2,500 largest companies in the Dow Jones Global Total Stock Market Index as the starting universe, the DJSI World selects the top 10% of companies in terms of sustainability in each sector — that is, the companies considered the "best in class." This selection is based on a systematic corporate sustainability assessment.

As for public companies, their sustainability strategies are becoming more integrated with the companies' core businesses, as evidenced by a surge of companies that are publishing sustainability reports together with their usual financial reports. In addition, external verification and internal assurance systems are becoming more prevalent.

Recently, a number of equity indices has been created with exposure to specific environmental risks in mind, such as those associated with air pollutants or water scarcity. For example, FTSE has developed an index that provides carbon-risk-adjusted versions of the general FTSE index. The constituent companies are the same as those in the FTSE, but their weights have been changed on the basis of their exposure to carbon risk relative to their sector peers. This adjustment helps investors incorporate specific environmental risks into their overall investment strategies. Similarly, the S&P Global Water Index provides liquid and tradable exposure to 50 companies from around the world that are involved in water-related businesses.

Some indices focus on a specific sector, such as the WilderHill New Energy Global Innovation Index, which comprises companies worldwide that specialize in development technologies and services that focus on the generation and use of clean energy. Another example is the Deutsche Börse DAXglobal Alternative Energy Index (Bloomberg: DXAEP), which consists of companies that generate more than 50% of their revenues from alternative energy, such as natural gas, solar, wind, and hydro. Subcategories may also include geographical subindices, such as the DJSI North America.

Conclusion

Clearly, from this discussion of customized portfolios, sustainability-focused mutual funds and indices, and sustainability as an investment philosophy, the asset class of sustainability-focused investments is a growing field. Sustainability-focused investing has even percolated into emerging economies, such as China and India, which are now leaning toward transparent and standardized disclosures of companies' environmental activities. Given this continuing trend in the United States and abroad, sustainability promises to be an important asset class in the future.

Markets can be a powerful tool to promote and achieve sustainable outcomes in areas such as air, water, and food. The design and application of markets to environmental issues has now a track record with various instances of successes. They also hold great promise for new areas and geographies. It has also provided us with lessons and insights that could be useful to investors, practioners, and policymakers as they consider investments or starting these markets. We will share these with the reader in the final chapter.

Conclusion

YOU *CAN* PUT
A PRICE ON NATURE

Wealth creation in the United States has changed dramatically since 1970. After World War II, from 1945 to 1970, wealth creation in the United States was largely driven by manufacturing. U.S. manufacturing strength helped the country lead the world in value creation, as indicated by gross domestic product growth during that period: In terms of real (inflation-adjusted) chained 2005 dollars, GDP went from $2.22 trillion in 1945 to $4.70 trillion in 1970.[1]

The decade of the 1970s was different. Inflation was high, and commodity prices rose sharply. Furthermore, the 1973 Arab oil embargo, a bad wheat crop in the Soviet Union, and crop failure in the United States caused wheat and oil prices to explode upward. The combination of these factors meant that wealth creation in the 1970s was driven by commodities and other sectors that benefited from inflation. Agricultural concerns, energy companies, and storied commodity traders were the major wealth creators of the decade.

This situation changed again in the 1980s with the arrival of financial reforms in the banking and savings-and-loan community and a multitude of financial innovations. In that decade came the full development of the financial futures markets, where

---

[1] U.S. Bureau of Economic Analysis, "U.S. Real GDP by Year." (2014); available online at http://www.multpl.com/us-gdp-inflation-adjusted/table.

355

interest rates and money became commoditized. This phenomenon was punctuated with the creation of interest rate swaps. The commoditization of corporate debt via high-yield bonds led to further wealth creation. These so-called junk bonds enabled entrepreneurs who could not access the traditional capital markets to finance their ventures. Junk bonds financed, to name only a few, the first cable company and the cell phone. Such bonds also made leveraged buyouts possible, enabling inefficient companies to be taken over and reformed by new owners.

The drivers of wealth creation changed again in the 1990s. This decade was driven by innovations in technology. Great fortunes were made in personal computers, telecommunications, and software. The birth of the internet was heralded by the rise of Cisco Systems, Netscape, Yahoo, and somewhat later, Google. This trend continued with such social networks as Facebook and such communication media as Twitter. All of these developments are enabling the commoditization of data, communications, and information. What is next?

The past shows that wealth creation is guided by fundamental structural and technological changes in the economy. This lesson from history leads us to believe that the next macro trend will be the commoditization of air and water. Environmental and economic shifts, policy changes, technology improvements, and other innovations will trigger this transformation. Population growth, the rise of China and India combined with their rising incomes and energy demand, resource scarcity, and a warming planet will fundamentally affect the economic fabric of tomorrow's world.

The world population is expected to reach 10 billion by 2050, which will increase stress on the environment. Demands for food and energy are all expected to increase manifold, driving demand for water. Water is the oil of the 21st century. Consider this: China's per capita water resources are a quarter of the global average and 8 of its 28 provinces are as dry as the Middle East. Water shortages cost China 2.3% of its GDP.[2] India is not far behind. As the world continues to warm, extreme weather events appear to be on the rise.

An economic shift is also taking place in the world. China and India, where most of the world's population reside, are rapidly lifting their populations out of poverty. Within a generation, the middle class in China has the potential to be roughly four times the size of the U.S. middle class population. By 2030, China should have approximately 1.4 billion middle class consumers. India's middle class should number 1 billion in fewer than 20 years.[3] With higher incomes and standards of living comes higher demand for better-quality products, and an increasing standard of living includes a demand for better environmental quality. Governments and corporations around the world will be compelled to tackle this issue. As we have shown throughout this book, stewardship of the environment is moving out of the realm of philanthropic activity and is becoming an important business and public policy issue.

Technological advances will also provide a stimulus for this transition. The transformation is already being shaped by disruptive technology innovations in clean energy systems, environmental applications with "big data" (data sets so large and complex that they are hard to process with traditional data-processing applications), clean transportation, and building construction innovations.[4] Wind

---

[2]According to a 2009 World Bank report, "Addressing China's Water Scarcity," of 2.3%, 1.3 percentage points are attributable to the scarcity of water and 1 percentage point to the direct impact of water pollution. This estimate is likely to be below the true total cost, however, because it does not include the cost of effects for which estimates are unavailable. These effects may include the ecological impacts associated with the drying up of lakes and rivers and the amenity loss from the extensive pollution in most of China's water bodies. The report is available online at http://www-wds.worldbank.org/external/default/WDSContentServer/WDSP/IB/2009/01/14/000333037_20090114011126/Rendered/PDF/471110PUB0CHA0101OFFICIAL0USE0ONLY1.pdf.

[3]Kenneth Rapoza, "Within A Generation, China Middle Class Four Times Larger Than America's." *Forbes* (5 September 2011); available online at www.forbes.com/sites/kenrapoza/2011/09/05/within-a-generation-china-middle-class-four-times-larger-than-americas/.

[4]A "disruptive innovation" is an innovation that helps create a new market and value network and, eventually, disrupts an existing market and value network (over a few years or decades), displacing earlier technology.

power is already reaching cost parity with conventional electric power generation in some regions, and solar energy is trending in the same direction. Some 70% of the new global power generation capacity added between 2012 and 2030 is projected to be from renewable technologies. We are also witnessing improvements in energy-efficiency in a variety of applications. Such technological innovations as smart grids, batteries, and storage devices — all provide efficiencies on the demand side of electricity.

Past successful experiences with using market mechanisms to tackle environmental issues are spurring greater experimentation with these economic tools. For instance, markets are playing a greater role as a tool to sustainably manage fish stocks in the form of permits or quotas instruments. Regional markets already exist in the United States. Every major sea coastal area of the U.S. has experimented with sustainable fishing. This is a little known fact, which indicates that the prospects for further market development are bullish. The experience of local markets to date, even if limited to a few species, can provide valuable information on future design and technical issues. The authors believe the expansion of sustainable fisheries management throughout the fishing, processing, and distribution chain has the potential to be a significant new value proposition for coastal areas such as the one ranging from Alaska to Mexico.

We are also witnessing policy shifts. Closely supporting these efforts are financial and banking sector reforms, particularly in previously closed economies. For example, national exchanges have opened and trading in commodity derivative instruments has begun up in many parts of the world, including India and China. Although still in their infancy, these changes will assist in defining property rights, standardizing and commoditizing new environmental products, and most importantly, providing price discovery and transparency. All of these factors will combine to provide the structural change required for the transition to a greener economic pathway for global growth.

This book has introduced the reader to the birth of a new asset class — the environment. The commoditization of environmental assets has the potential to be the principal driver of wealth creation in the near future, and this shift has already begun. In fact, as discussed, the environment is not the commodity of the future but *today's* commodity.

The commoditization of sulfur dioxide helped in the effective management of acid rain in the United States. Similarly, carbon dioxide allowances are helping the world cope with climate change. Weather has been commoditized in an effort to deal with catastrophic events, and weather-related futures and options markets and fixed-income securities have come into being. The Metropolitan Transportation Authority (MTA) of New York announced in 2013 that it would start to use catastrophe bonds worth $200 million to insure against damages caused by a storm similar to Hurricane Sandy. The authors played a role in the education of this local government agency, and the concept seems to be attracting the interest of other municipalities which are in equally affected areas.

The increased concern for the environment has also affected the equity markets. Sustainable indices and portfolios have been created. They capitalize on investors' and portfolio managers' needs to deal with environmental, social, and governance challenges.

Our emphasis throughout this book has been on pricing various negative externalities and establishing rights of use. If property rights in public goods are established and transaction costs are minimized, prices can guide the private and public sectors toward achieving environmental and social objectives at the lowest cost to society. The cap-and-trade model and emissions trading were used to illustrate the benefits of using market-based mechanisms and economic tools for managing environmental problems.

Successful cap-and-trade programs in combating air pollution all followed 12 simple steps — the "clean dozen."

The Clean Dozen

(1) Define the commodity — the right to emit a unit of a pollutant, called an "allowance."
(2) Define clear and unambiguous property rights. Provide a legal infrastructure to ensure that the owner of a commodity has a clear title to it.
(3) Determine the covered emitters in air pollution programs.
(4) Establish a baseline — the level from which to reduce the pollution level.
(5) Establish a reduction schedule for the pollutant.
(6) Establish a registry that initializes ownership of allowances and facilitates their transfer.
(7) Using the registry, allocate those rights to the covered emitters in accordance with the reduction schedule.
(8) Monitor and verify the pollutants produced by the covered emitters.
(9) Define compliance so that if emissions by the emitters are equal to the emissions rights in the account, the covered emitters are in compliance. This step allows emitters to purchase or sell emissions rights to be in compliance.
(10) Create periodic auctions to facilitate price discovery and transparency.
(11) Facilitate over-the-counter spot and forward markets in addition to organized exchanges.
(12) Enable futures and options to be issued and traded so that covered emitters can cost-effectively minimize current and future risk.

Examples of successful markets that used the clean dozen are SO_2 allowances to combat acid rain in the United States, renewable energy certificates in New Jersey to stimulate the development of solar power, CO_2 allowances in the European Union Emissions Trading Scheme (EU ETS) to combat global warming, water rights in Australia to combat drought, and fishing rights in Alaska to prevent overfishing.

Lessons Learned

In addition to the clean dozen, a number of lessons are to be learned by policymakers and investors from the successful programs.

1. *Keep It Simple*

The message from past programs is that the perfect should not be the enemy of the good. Keep it simple. The programs provided private incentives to reach specific environmental objectives. Importantly, their goal was captured in legislation and a regulatory framework that was clear and unambiguous. More regulation did not necessarily mean better regulation. The goal was to reduce pollution, not punish the polluter. The program participants knew what the regulation entailed, who the regulator was, and the consequences of not reaching the target. These objectives were all captured in legislation and regulation that enabled the growth of the market. Collectively, the results of the programs demonstrate that the paradigm could be changed from profiting from polluting to profiting from *not* polluting.

2. *Simple Does Not Mean Easy*

Simply stating the goal is only the first step. Past successful programs facilitated building institutions that led to minimization of transaction costs in achieving the objectives. They also created the technological infrastructure needed to operate the programs successfully. Infrastructure included stack emissions monitoring to monitor SO_2 emissions in the Acid Rain Program and electronic registry systems in that program, the EU ETS, and other programs. Building these programs involved the training and use of huge numbers of human resources in the form of emissions verifiers, accountants, lawyers, traders, and so forth. History teaches us that a combination of software (in the form of human and governance structures) and hardware (in the form of technological and legal enforcement infrastructure) are required for successful execution.

3. *It Is All About Price*

Price can teach us three important lessons: It can change behavior; a low price does not imply failure; and policymakers should focus on the program's design and results, not on its price.

Price changes behavior

Once a resource is priced fairly, its use is optimized. Optimization helps the program reach the environmental objective in the most cost-effective way. In the past, forecasters underestimated the role of price in changing behavior and promoting innovation. As the Acid Rain, EU ETS, and other programs have proved, forecasters use the cost of pollution control of existing or known technology as the basis for emissions-rights pricing. They are consistently wrong. Price forces individuals and corporations to optimize and use resources judiciously. Thus, this mechanism triggered shifts to lower-pollution fuels and efficiency improvements. It also triggered better accounting for energy use and environmental impact. Price signals also spur innovation in technologies and free up resources. History has taught us that it is generally a bad idea to sell short humanity's ability to invent and adapt. Policymakers and investors are wise to be guided by the experience that these emissions trading programs provide.

Low price does not mean failure

The price of an emissions allowance is not an indicator of the success or failure of the program. Achieving the environmental goal is. Price formation is merely a function of the reduction target: If high prices in rice and wheat result in an abundance of food, we cheer. With regard to pollution rights, however, we recognize that this commodity is different from food because the scarcity of such rights is created by government regulation. Shrill voices of criticism from people of varying political persuasions were heard when prices to emit fell below the marginal costs of abatement. In the Acid Rain Program, the criticism abounded for more than a decade yet significant reductions occurred, precisely because of the flexibility of cap-and-trade. Fuel switching was responsible, and it demonstrates the power of the price signal. The same was true in the EU ETS.

Leave the price alone

The price is merely an output of the program design and drivers. Attempts to "fix" the program must not focus on making the price rise but on modifying the underlying fundamental design. For example, the low prices in the EU ETS right now can be remedied by making the environmental goals more ambitious instead of artificially manipulating the price. When changing reduction targets is not politically feasible, other policy tools, such as price floors, have emerged (as happened in California)

4. *Policy Can Make or Break a Program*

Many of the markets described in this book function on a stage built by government policy. Legislation creates these markets and drives environmental outcomes. Similarly, uncertainties in environmental policy and regulation often spell the demise of the program. Both the Acid Rain Program and the EU ETS were threatened by this phenomenon. Although command-and-control as policy is out of favor (and its application has provided ample evidence of creating economic, environmental, and even safety distortions[5]), the temptation for policymakers to conveniently resort to them for political expediency still exists.

5. *Flawed Market Architecture Hinders Success*

Faulty design can result in damages to the program and losses for investors. Renewable identification numbers in the market for

---

[5]As discussed in Chapter 10, in the case of fisheries management, command-and-control policies are recognized as contributing to lower safety levels and increased deaths.

transportation fuels are the perfect example. The lack of a registry, violating a basic principle (Rule 6) of the clean dozen, resulted in the creation of counterfeit certificates. Policymakers and investors should always be wary of these design flaws. They are often caused by a lack of institutional memory as a result of changes in elected officials. Alternatively, they may arise when the design of a new program is assigned to branches of government that lack experience in creating markets.

Food for Thought and Major Trends

The history of environmental markets, lessons learned, and structural shifts shaping tomorrow's world present us with many opportunities.

The shale revolution is already transforming the U.S. energy landscape. New technology in the form of hydraulic fracking and horizontal drilling have made it cost-effective to unearth natural gas and oil assets in shale that could make the United States the largest producer of energy in the world. Cheap natural gas is affecting all aspects of the economy, from manufacturing to power generation to transportation. What would be the implications if cheap natural gas were made available, either through domestic production or imports, to the rest of the world, particularly Asia and Europe? Shale can fundamentally change energy and, therefore, the environmental equation in the world.

What does cheaper natural gas mean for renewable energy and its competitiveness in the energy mix? Many environmentalists argue that the shale revolution could spell doom for the renewable energy industry. History has taught us that technology and innovation can be major economy shifters. Can advances in renewable energy technology enable it to be a competitive alternative to cheap fossil fuel? At the micro level, solar power continues to be a promising form of renewable energy. Developments in energy storage may drive further opportunities in wind and transportation. Biofuels may offer additional opportunities in renewable energy. Smart electrical grids may also provide investment opportunities. Price has the potential to spur energy-efficiency, but because of the current structure of how we pay for electricity (after the fact, not as we consume it), electricity prices do not have the impact on conservation that they could have.

Transportation is the elephant in the room when you consider emissions, energy-efficiency, and other topics we have discussed in this book. Transportation currently requires a highly concentrated, lightweight energy source that can be safely used in a vehicle. Hydrocarbon fuels fit the Bill. To date, externalities from transportation have not been addressed by any program in a coherent fashion. Imagine what price signals and incentives could achieve in the transportation sector — electric cars, aviation (although this sector is currently being addressed by the EU), and biofuels!

The major trends that we see are as follows:

(1) *Water is the world's most important natural resource and once it is commoditized it will be the biggest commodity of the 21st century.* Perhaps the biggest problem and, therefore, the biggest opportunities lie in water. Desertification is possibly a more immediate problem than climate change. Only three continents have a better-than-adequate supply of water — North America, South America, and Europe. As of the writing of this book 2014, this problem has only become more exacerbated, with serious droughts ocurring in places like California and Brazil. It can hence be seen, water is a critical component as an input into energy and industrial production. The economic impacts are clear, and with them, a growing call for measures that can more effectively tackle the lack of water. Water trading exists by dint of the grain trade, but it is insufficient to meet the demands in Africa, India, and China or, for that matter, to avert regional shortages in the United States and Canada. The quantity of freshwater is only one part of the equation. Water quality is the second part. The success of water markets in Australia and Pennsylvania suggests that markets can address shortages of

water quantity and quality. Pricing should create incentives to develop infrastructure, generate conservation (the equivalent of energy-efficiency in carbon markets), and foster innovation. In related developments, investors should be watching for opportunities in transporting water efficiently and economically and in setting standards for water use in the hydraulic fracturing (fracking) process. Such standardization is the first step in facilitating the limitation of pollution caused by fracking.

(2) *Environmental markets will continue to grow.* The environmental marketplace is vibrant with activity around the world. Contrary to the notion that the world will have a unified environmental market, we are witnessing a "plurilateral" system that includes regional, state, and national markets.[6] In the United States, California is leading the way. California has been an agent of change for more than a century — in film, high tech, social media, and the environment. California is already forging alliances with other carbon markets that are developing nationally and internationally. And, given the latest serious droughts affecting the state and its economy, California may start to lead in water markets as well. Policymakers and investors should follow the trends in California closely. In the United States, environmental solutions tend to begin at the state level and then percolate to the federal level.

While the developed world shies away from market solutions to environmental problems, emerging economies do not. China, with seven separate cap-and-trade markets, is leading the way. An eighth program in the city of Qingdao has been announced as of the writing of this book. Others may follow, as the expectation is that these pilots will serve as the blueprint for a national mandate in the coming years.

---

[6] *Plurilateral* refers to the development of a framework for GHG emissions trading involving a medium-sized set of countries (e.g., 5–20). The concept of a plurilateral regime was coined by Richard L. Sandor in the mid-1990s. Although it was first published in 1999, it was not fully defined until 2001 in the following publication: Richard Sandor, "The Case for Plurilateral Environmental Markets." *Environmental Finance* (September 2001).

They could also provide the motivation to foster regional markets in SO_2, NO_x, and other particulate matter pollution in major Chinese metropolitan areas. China's policies started by focusing on promoting energy-efficiency (as defined in Chapter 5), and the programs are morphing into cap-and-trade markets. India also has an energy-efficiency trading program. Cap-and-trade markets are under consideration in Brazil, South Korea, Mexico, Vietnam, and Kazakhstan. A recent survey of 66 countries shows that 61 have passed climate and clean energy laws, and the trend is starting to influence other countries to do the same.[7] Even at the national level, in the United States we might be witnessing the re-emergence of "cap-and-trade" as a policy tool. As new greenhouse gas legislation is being debated, a report by the Clean Air Task Force advocates for trading as the most cost-effective approach to reducing greenhouse gas emissions from the utility sector.[8]

In assessing the future of cap-and-trade, investors may be better served by closely watching Sacramento, California, and Beijing than by watching Washington, DC or Brussels. Emerging markets that begin developing environmental policies by setting energy-efficiency goals are on the right track, and investors should look at countries that adopt such goals as indicators that cap-and-trade markets are likely to develop.

The expected growth in market-based programs can also be measured by the number of lesser known programs in sustainable fisheries management and water. For example, the existence of 21 separate water quality programs in the United States

---

[7] Michal Nachmany, Sam Fankhauser, Terry Townshend, Murray Collins, Tucker Landesman, Adam Matthews, Carolina Pavese, Katharina Riefig, Philip Schleifer and Joana Setzer, "The GLOBE Climate Legislation Study: A Review of Climate Change Legislation in 66 Countries. Fourth Edition." (London: GLOBE International and the Grantham Research Institute, London School of Economics, 2014).

[8] Clean Air Task Force, "Power Switch: An Effective, Affordable Approach to Reducing Carbon Pollution from Existing Fossil-Fueled Power Plants." (February 2014); available online at http://catf.us/resources/publications/files/Power_Switch.pdf.

shows a fertile ground for further institutional development. These practical demonstrations are providing valuable lessons in administration, monitoring, and verification. They can also help show that the initial perception that these are unsurmountable challenges is a myth.

(3) ***The costs of catastrophic events will rise.*** Eight of the top ten most expensive weather events have occurred since 2003, and those that affected the United States cost the U.S. economy billions of dollars in losses. We expect this trend to continue and intensify, with further increases in insured and uninsured losses. Hurricane Sandy did not touch down in New York City but it caused severe impact in an area of the United States which is a major financial, transportation, and residential hub. Another event of similar or greater magnitude could have tremendous financial and physical impact. This trend has huge implications for the financial industry as a whole. Management of such catastrophes can change the nature of the private insurance industry as well as government emergency assistance and self-insurance. Does the insurance industry or government have sufficient capital to cover the extent of future catastrophic losses? In addition, the impact of major earthquakes on nuclear power generation is all too clear. The Fukushima nuclear disaster triggered shutdowns in nuclear power plants around the world. What is the effect of such shutdowns on building new nuclear capacity, particularly in India and China, where power demand is growing fastest?

On a related point, there is also a nascent role for professionals interested in the use of catastrophe-based and other alternative risk-management products in areas of the world that are also affected by natural disasters but lack developed capital markets, such as Central America and Southeast Asia. Again, the possibilities for innovation are vast.

As demonstrated throughout this book, markets in emissions and user rights have solved environmental problems and created enormous investment opportunities. They achieved these ends by commoditizing the externality and then pricing it. The same concept has been applied to weather-driven events and catastrophes. Financial innovation and markets have a significant role to play in other situations and fields where there are good and bad externalities, such as medicine, education, and biodiversity.

The convergence of the environment and finance is here to stay, and the market mechanisms described in this book are only the beginning. The new asset class of environmental goods is just in its infancy and holds enormous promise.

INDEX

ABOUT THE AUTHORS

Richard Sandor (Ph.D., Dr. Sc. h. c.) is Chairman and CEO of Chicago-based Environmental Financial Products (EFP), LLC, which specializes in inventing, designing, and developing new financial markets. EFP was established in 1998 and was the predecessor company and incubator to the Chicago Climate Exchange (CCX), the European Climate Exchange (ECX), the Chicago Climate Futures Exchange (CCFE), and the Tianjin Climate Exchange (TCX). Dr. Sandor is the Aaron Director Lecturer in Law and Economics at the University of Chicago Law School and a Visiting Fellow with the Smith School of Enterprise and the Environment at Oxford University. He was honored by the City of Chicago for his universal recognition as the "father of financial futures" and named one of TIME magazine's "Heroes of the Environment" for his work as the "Father of Carbon Trading." In October 2013, Dr. Sandor was awarded the title of *Chevalier dans l' Ordre de la Légion d'Honneur* (Knight in the French National Order of the Legion of Honor), for his accomplishments in the field of environmental finance and carbon trading. Dr. Sandor taught at the University of California, Berkeley; Stanford University; Columbia University Graduate School of Business; and the Kellogg Graduate School of Management at Northwestern

University. He served as Distinguished Professor of Environmental Finance at Guanghua School of Management at Peking University and as a member of its International Advisory Board. He holds an honorary degree of Doctor of Science, *honoris causa*, from the Swiss Federal Institute of Technology (ETHZ). Dr. Sandor is a Board Member of the Clean Energy Trust; a Member of the Advisory Board of the Center for Financial Stability and the Smithsonian Tropical Research Institute; and a Senior Fellow of the Milken Institute. He served on the Board of Directors of American Electric Power and of leading commodity and futures exchange in the United States and Europe. Dr. Sandor is the author of *Good Derivatives: A Story of Financial and Environmental Innovation*, also published in Chinese by People's Oriental Press. He received his Bachelor of Arts degree from Brooklyn College and holds a Ph.D. in Economics from the University of Minnesota.

Murali Kanakasabai (Ph.D.) is a Managing Director of Environmental Financial Products (EFP), LLC. His career has focused on designing market-based risk management and financial instruments for capital, commodity, and environmental markets. He has over a decade's experience working on climate change issues and helping build and launch environmental markets. At EFP, Dr. Kanakasabai leads design and implementation efforts for environmental markets, new environmental finance products, and guides strategy and analysis for investments in clean energy projects. Dr. Kanakasabai was among the founding team members at the Chicago Climate Exchange (CCX), where he served as Senior Vice President with primary responsibilities in research and new product innovation. Dr. Kanakasabai was part of the core team that helped establish first markets for greenhouse gas emissions in six countries across four continents, including exchanges in Europe, North America, and China. In these ventures, Dr. Kanakasabai was extensively involved in building market readiness, market architecture, and new product innovation. As the principal lead for CCX business development efforts in South Asia, he led the development and expansion of CCX membership in India. He was a senior contributor to the development of several of the world's first derivative instruments for hedging environmental risks and promoting sustainable development. Dr. Kanakasabai has led the effort for integration of agriculture, forestry, and rural environmental credits into the global environmental markets. He was a senior team member of the CCX carbon offsets team which managed a significant carbon offset portfolio and pioneered the development of several offset protocols and standards. Dr. Kanakasabai has contributed extensively to the literature on environmental markets. He is the author of *Farm Adaptation to Climate Change: Approaches to Modeling Farm Decision Environment under Uncertainty.* Dr. Kanakasabai was selected as an Emerging Leader by the Chicago Council of Global Affairs in 2011. Dr. Kanakasabai holds degrees from the Tamil Nadu Agricultural University and the Indian Agricultural Research Institute, and a Ph.D. in Agricultural Economics from the University of Kentucky.

Rafael Marques is a Managing Director of Environmental Financial Products (EFP), LLC. Prior to this position, Mr. Marques served as Senior Vice President of the Chicago Climate Exchange (CCX) where he was actively involved in all phases of the feasibility and design phases of the Chicago Climate Exchange and worked on the program's membership outreach and expansion into Latin America. He also worked in research relating to business opportunities in carbon sequestration and sustainable forestry management. He was also actively involved in the development and implementation of CCX international activities and joint ventures. Mr. Marques previously worked as a researcher at the Brazilian Embassy in Washington, where his responsibilities included research and analysis of trade-related issues.

Nathan Clark is Vice President of Wabashco, LLC, a clean fuels, carbon offset, and renewable energy development company and formerly a Managing Director of Environmental Financial Products (EFP), LLC. Prior to his work at EFP, Mr. Clark was Senior Vice President and Managing Director of Offset Programs for Chicago Climate Exchange (CCX). In that capacity, Mr. Clark managed the process of defining and implementing project-based emission reduction initiatives. Mr. Clark provided strategic leadership on research related to the CCX offsets markets and was the chief liaison for grant related activities on offsets. Mr. Clark also participated in product innovation, design, and maintenance for futures and options contracts on offsets. Mr. Clark served as Chair of the Subcommittee on Permanence for the Novecta Soil Carbon Sequestration Standards Committee and was a member of the Greenhouse Gas Evaluation Task Group of the American National Standards Institute.